Garfield
takes the cake

BY JIM DAVIS

Ballantine Books • New York

A Ballantine Book
Published by The Random House Ballantine Publishing Group
Copyright © 1982, 2003 by PAWS, Inc. All Rights Reserved.

All rights reserved under International and Pan-American Copyright Conventions. Published in the United States by The Random House Ballantine Publishing Group, a division of Random House, Inc., New York, and simultaneously in Canada by Random House of Canada Limited, Toronto. Originally published in slightly different form by The Random House Ballantine Publishing Group, a division of Random House, Inc., in 1982.

Ballantine and the Ballantine colophon are registered trademarks of Random House, Inc.

"GARFIELD" and the GARFIELD characters are registered and unregistered trademarks of PAWS, Inc.

www.ballantinebooks.com

Library of Congress Control Number: 2002091880

ISBN 0-345-44978-9

Manufactured in the United States of America

First Colorized Edition: June 2003

10 9 8 7 6 5 4 3 2 1

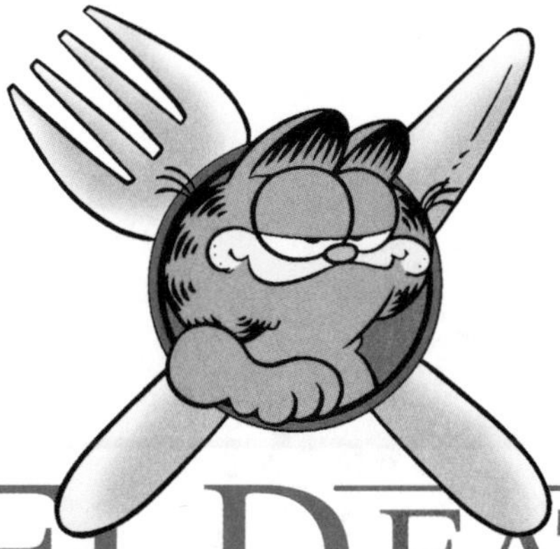

GARFIELD EATING TIPS

1. Never eat anything that's on fire.
2. Never leave your food dish under a bird cage.
3. Only play in your food if you've already eaten your toys.
4. Eat every meal as though it were your last.
5. Only snack between meals.
6. Chew your food at least once.
7. Avoid fruits and nuts: after all, you are what you eat.
8. Always dress up your leftovers: one clever way is with top hats and canes.
9. A handy breakfast tip: always check your Grape-Nuts for squirrels.
10. Don't save your dessert for last. Eat it first.

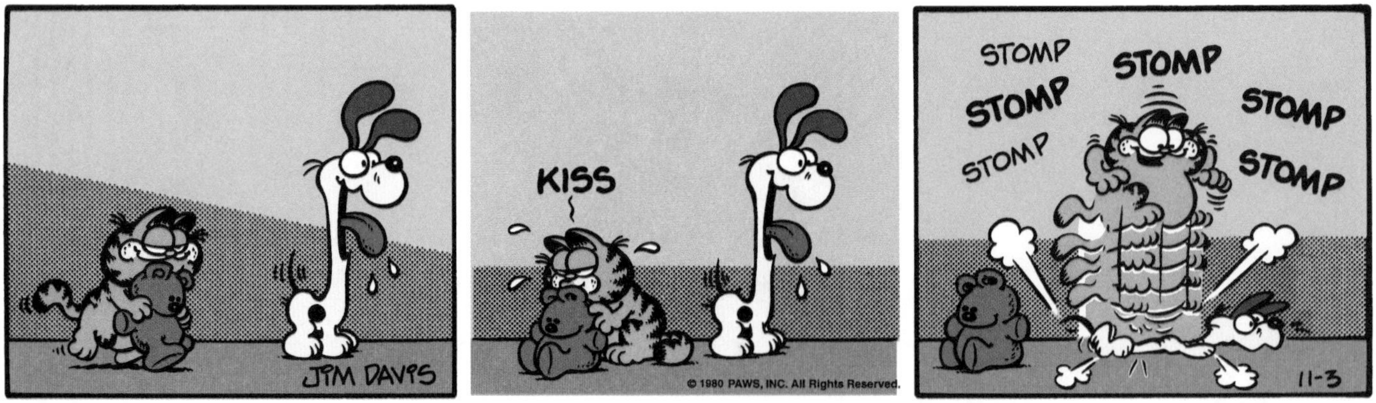
JIM DAVIS
KISS
© 1980 PAWS, INC. All Rights Reserved.
STOMP
STOMP
STOMP
STOMP
STOMP
STOMP
11-3

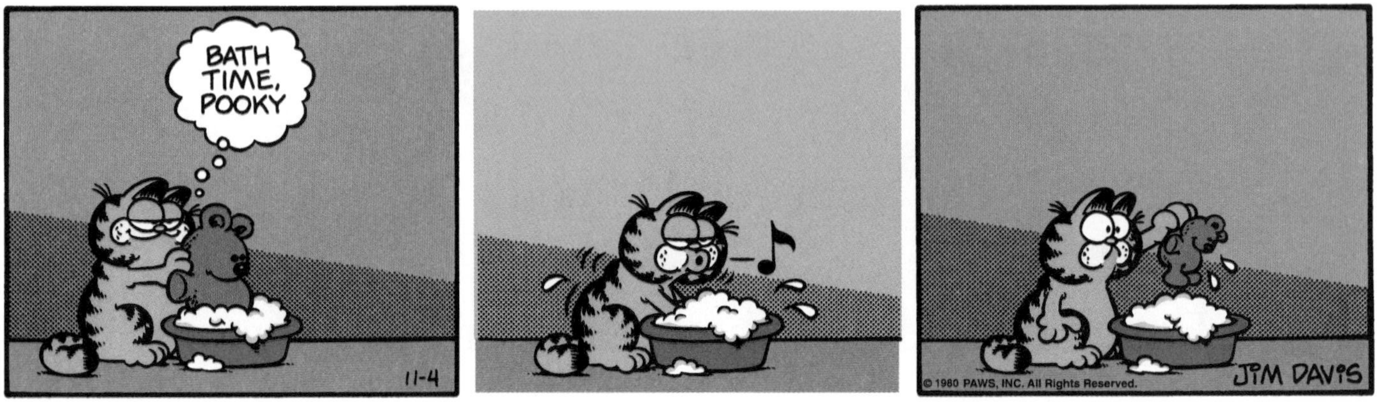
BATH TIME, POOKY
11-4
© 1980 PAWS, INC. All Rights Reserved.
JIM DAVIS

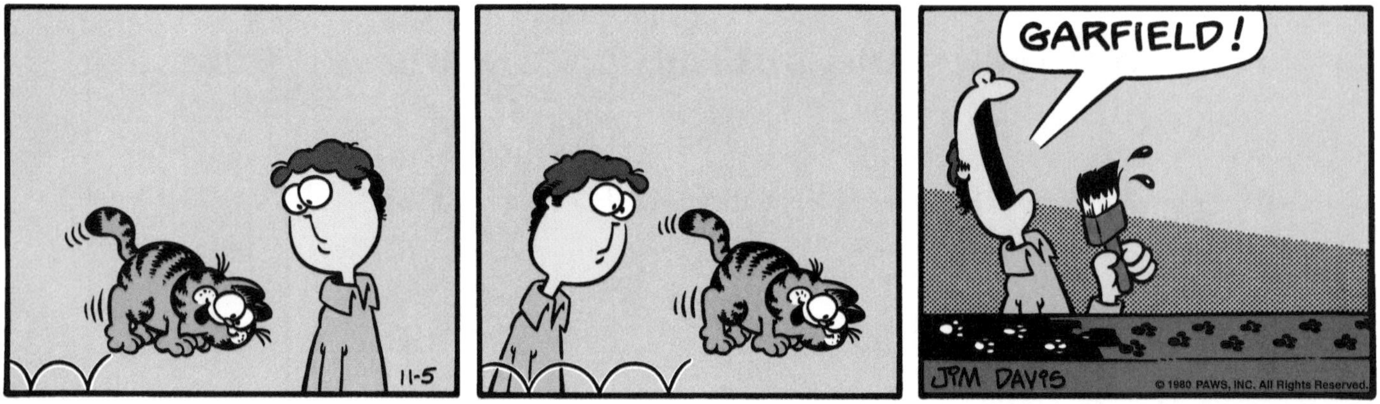
11-5
GARFIELD!
JIM DAVIS
© 1980 PAWS, INC. All Rights Reserved.

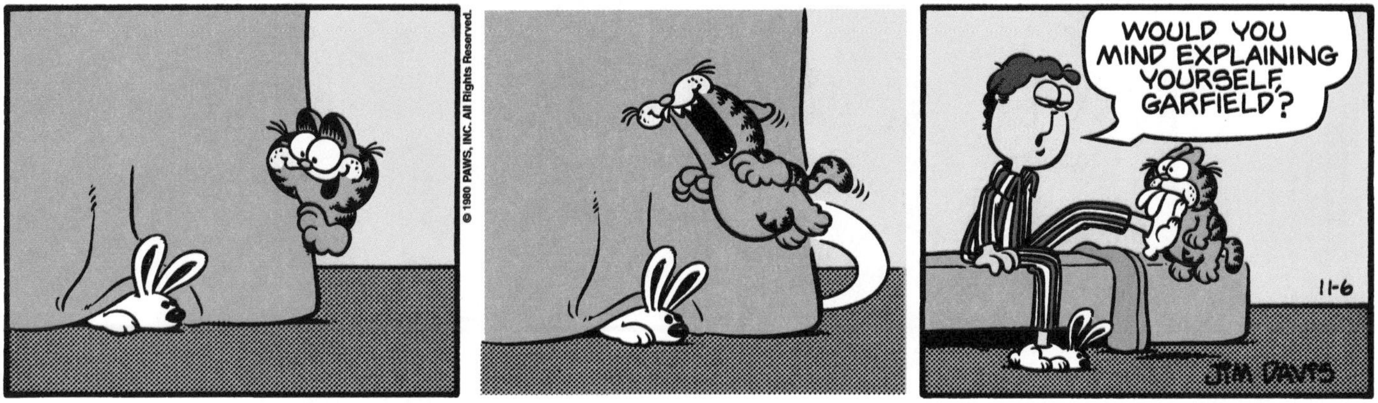
© 1980 PAWS, INC. All Rights Reserved.
WOULD YOU MIND EXPLAINING YOURSELF, GARFIELD?
11-6
JIM DAVIS

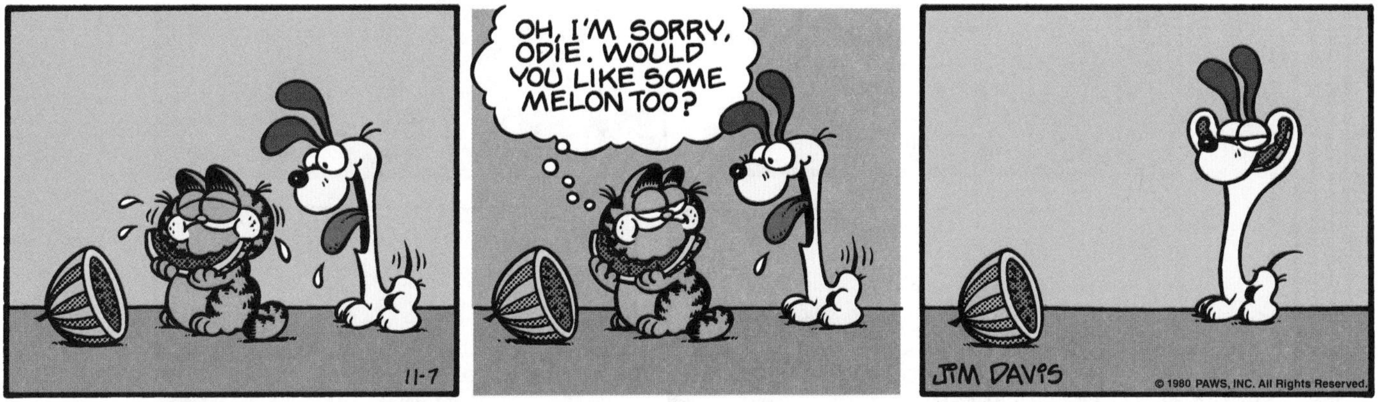
11-7
OH, I'M SORRY, ODIE. WOULD YOU LIKE SOME MELON TOO?
JIM DAVIS
© 1980 PAWS, INC. All Rights Reserved.

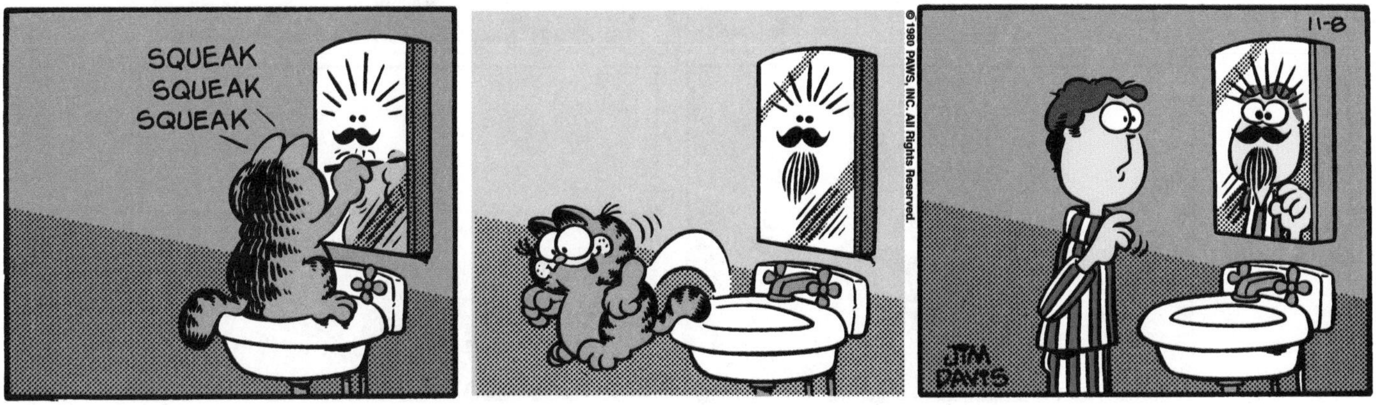
SQUEAK SQUEAK SQUEAK SQUEAK
© 1980 PAWS, INC. All Rights Reserved.
11-8
JIM DAVIS

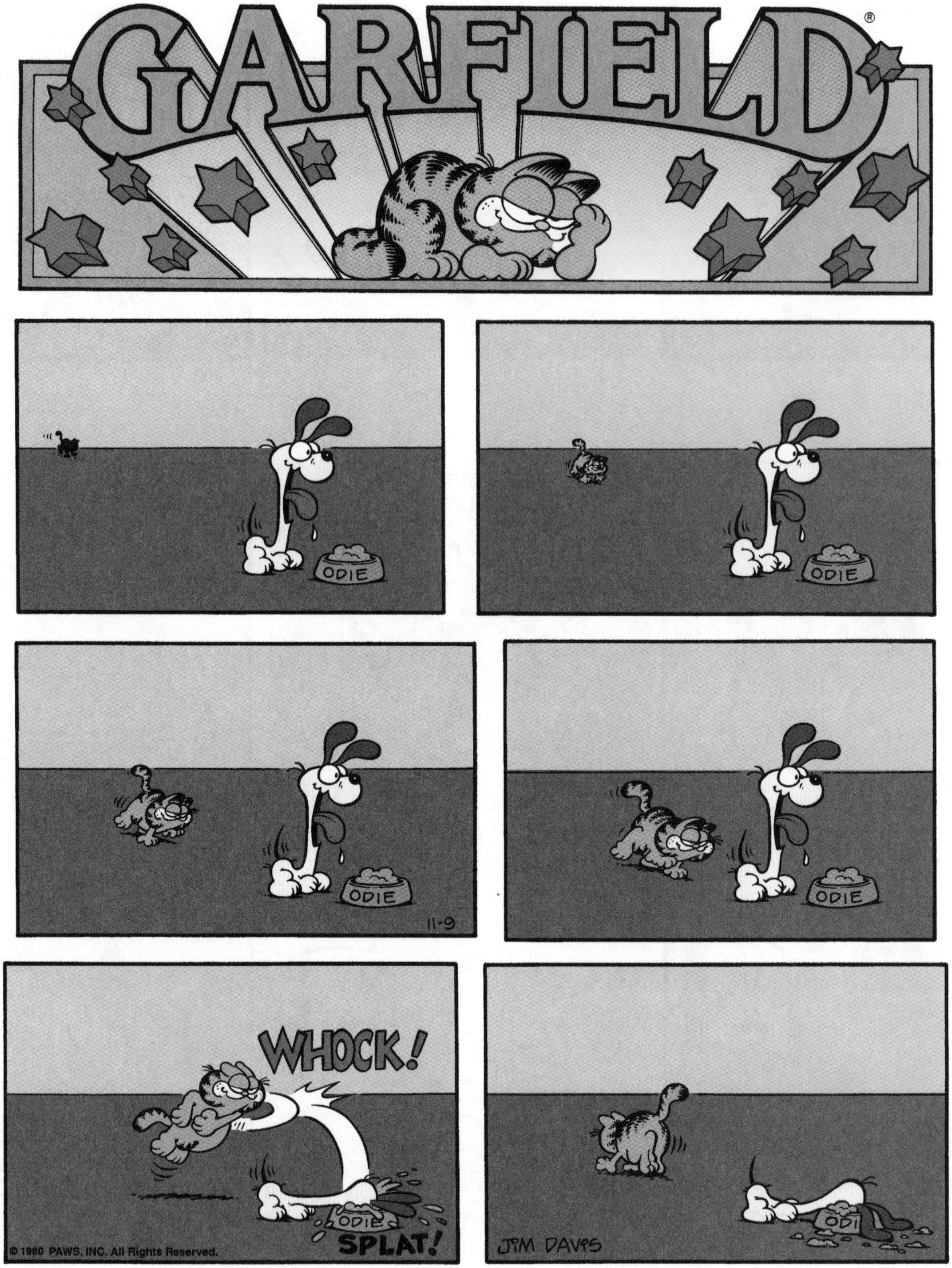
GARFIELD®
ODIE
ODIE
ODIE
11-9
ODIE
WHOCK!
ODIE
SPLAT!
© 1980 PAWS, INC. All Rights Reserved.
ODI
JIM DAVIS

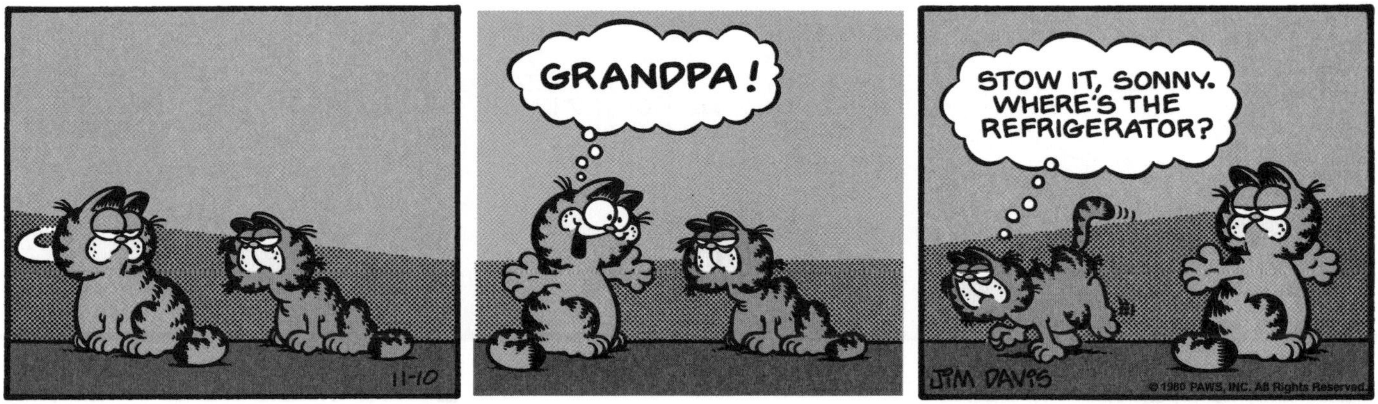
GRANDPA!
STOW IT, SONNY. WHERE'S THE REFRIGERATOR?
11-10
JIM DAVIS
© 1980 PAWS, INC. All Rights Reserved.

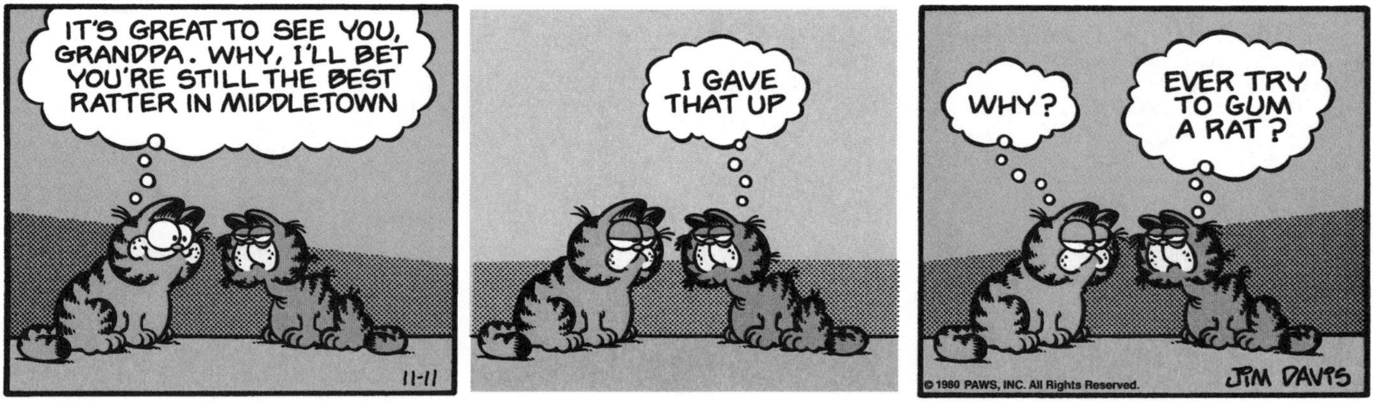
IT'S GREAT TO SEE YOU, GRANDPA. WHY, I'LL BET YOU'RE STILL THE BEST RATTER IN MIDDLETOWN
11-11
I GAVE THAT UP
WHY?
EVER TRY TO GUM A RAT?
© 1980 PAWS, INC. All Rights Reserved.
JIM DAVIS

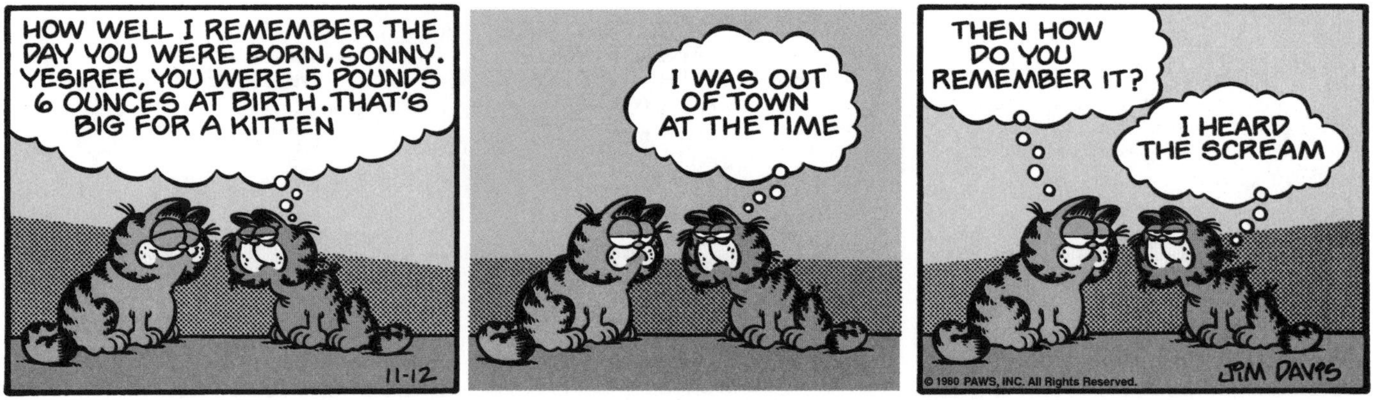
HOW WELL I REMEMBER THE DAY YOU WERE BORN, SONNY. YESIREE, YOU WERE 5 POUNDS 6 OUNCES AT BIRTH. THAT'S BIG FOR A KITTEN
11-12
I WAS OUT OF TOWN AT THE TIME
THEN HOW DO YOU REMEMBER IT?
I HEARD THE SCREAM
© 1980 PAWS, INC. All Rights Reserved.
JIM DAVIS

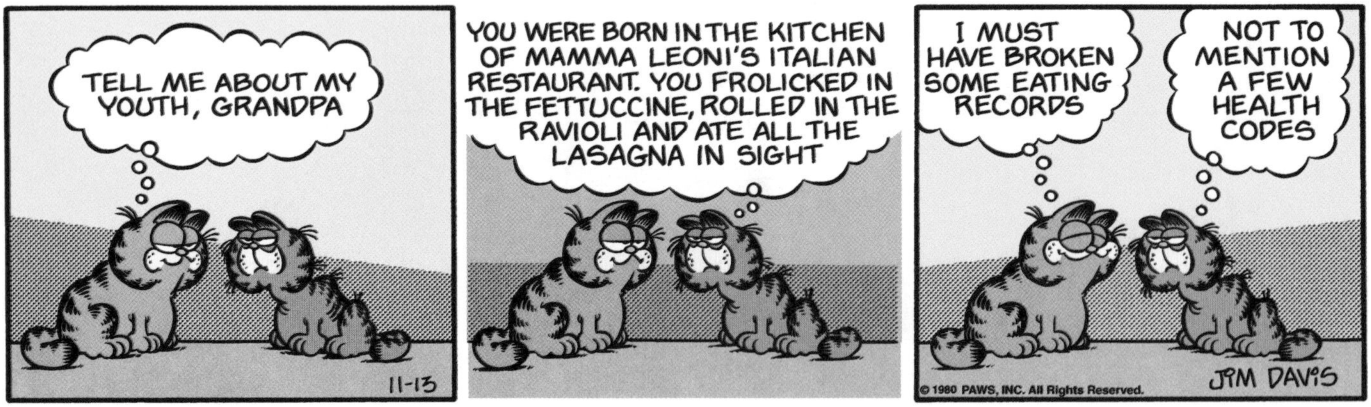
TELL ME ABOUT MY YOUTH, GRANDPA
11-13
YOU WERE BORN IN THE KITCHEN OF MAMMA LEONI'S ITALIAN RESTAURANT. YOU FROLICKED IN THE FETTUCCINE, ROLLED IN THE RAVIOLI AND ATE ALL THE LASAGNA IN SIGHT
I MUST HAVE BROKEN SOME EATING RECORDS
NOT TO MENTION A FEW HEALTH CODES
© 1980 PAWS, INC. All Rights Reserved.
JIM DAVIS

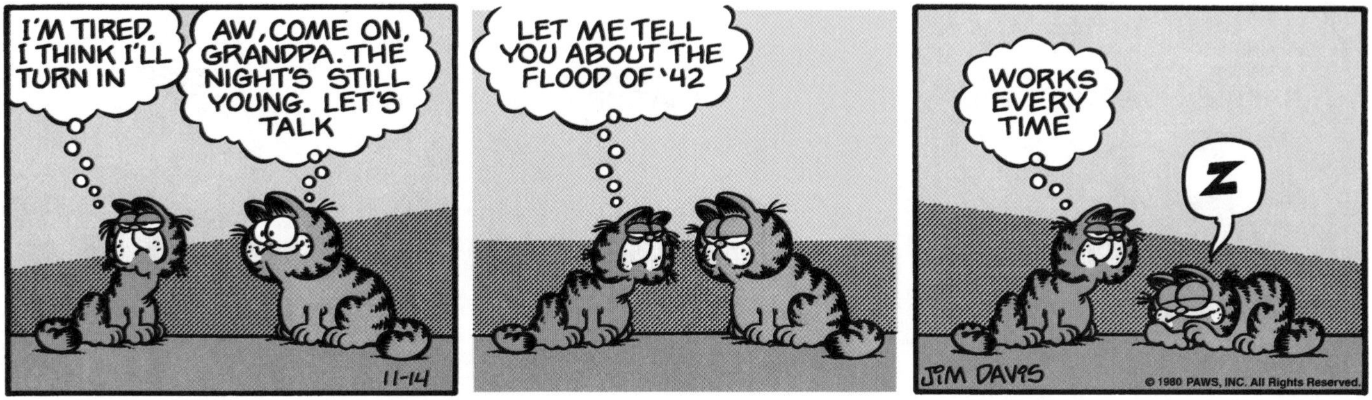
I'M TIRED. I THINK I'LL TURN IN
AW, COME ON, GRANDPA. THE NIGHT'S STILL YOUNG. LET'S TALK
11-14
LET ME TELL YOU ABOUT THE FLOOD OF '42
WORKS EVERY TIME
Z
JIM DAVIS
© 1980 PAWS, INC. All Rights Reserved.

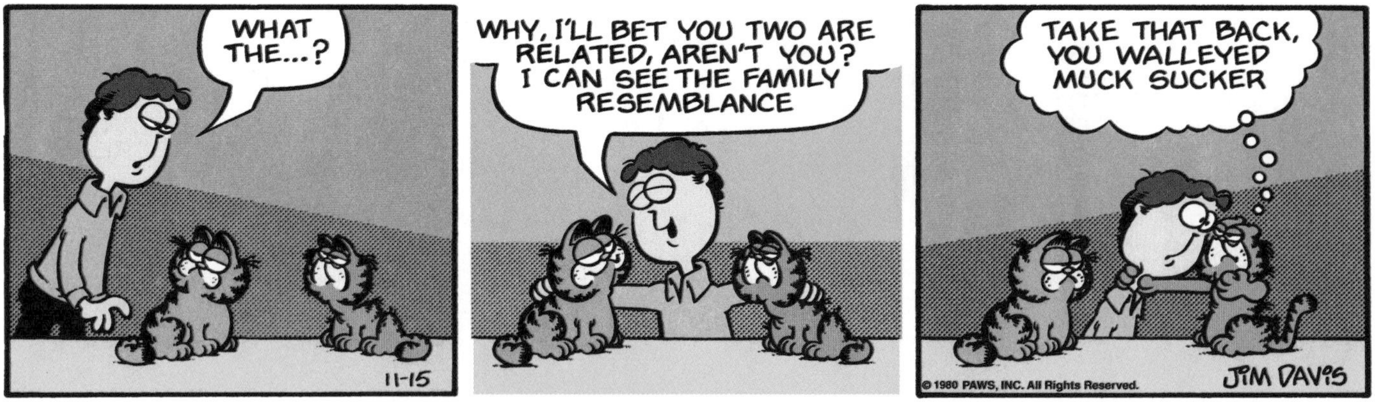
WHAT THE...?
11-15
WHY, I'LL BET YOU TWO ARE RELATED, AREN'T YOU? I CAN SEE THE FAMILY RESEMBLANCE
TAKE THAT BACK, YOU WALLEYED MUCK SUCKER
© 1980 PAWS, INC. All Rights Reserved.
JIM DAVIS

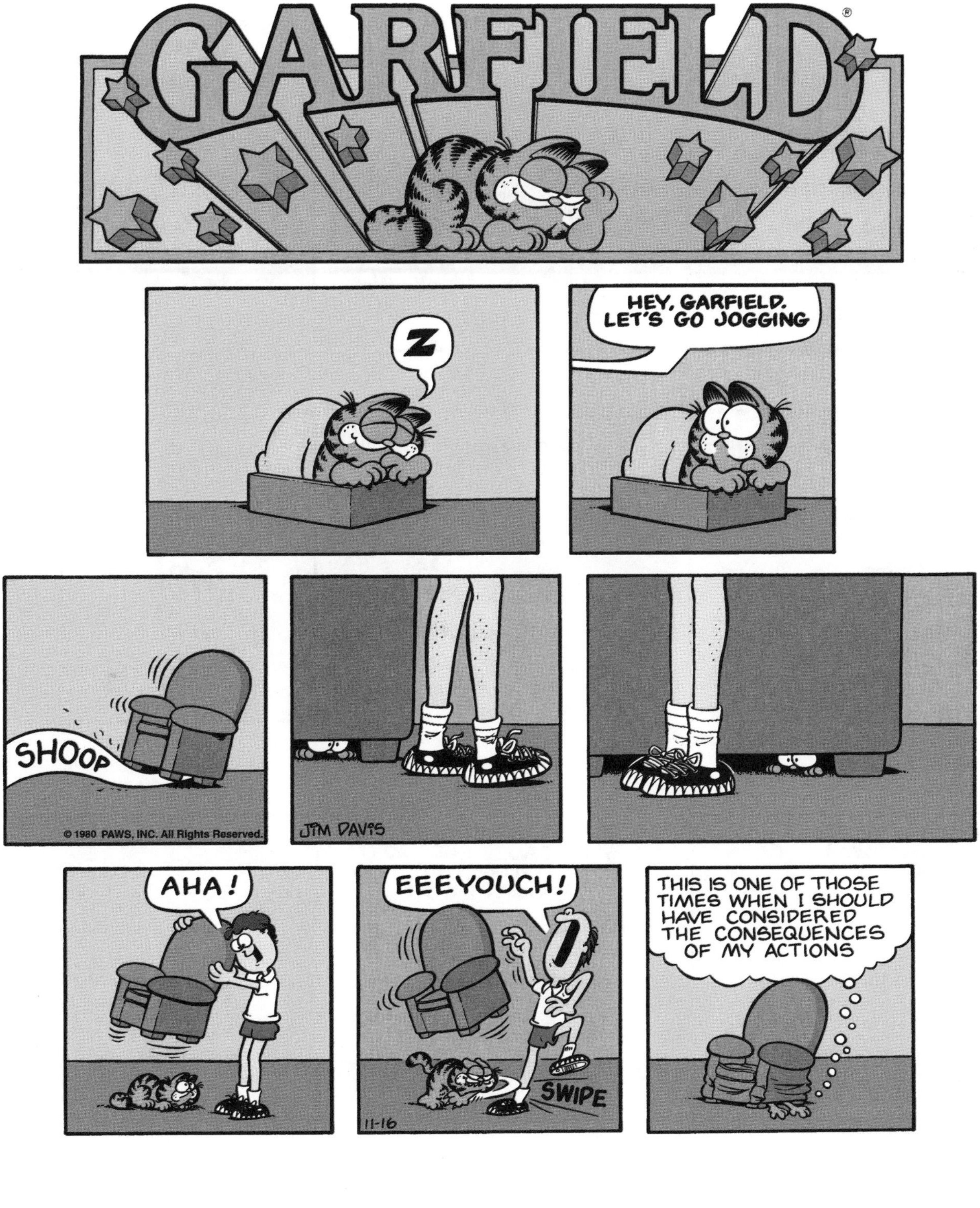
GARFIELD
Z
HEY, GARFIELD. LET'S GO JOGGING
SHOOP
© 1980 PAWS, INC. All Rights Reserved.
JIM DAVIS
AHA!
EEEYOUCH!
SWIPE
11-16
THIS IS ONE OF THOSE TIMES WHEN I SHOULD HAVE CONSIDERED THE CONSEQUENCES OF MY ACTIONS

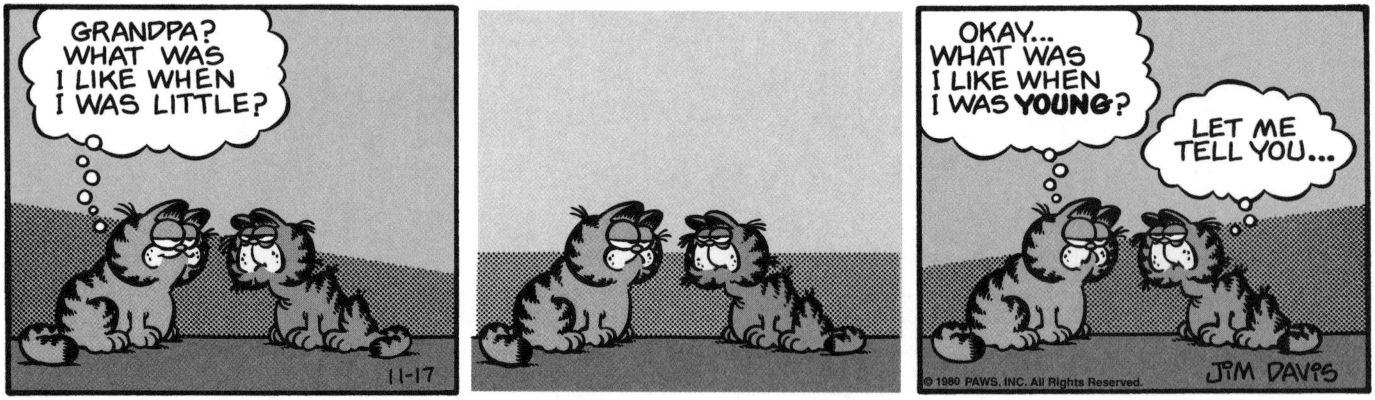
GRANDPA? WHAT WAS I LIKE WHEN I WAS LITTLE?
11-17
OKAY... WHAT WAS I LIKE WHEN I WAS **YOUNG**?
LET ME TELL YOU...
© 1980 PAWS, INC. All Rights Reserved.
JIM DAVIS

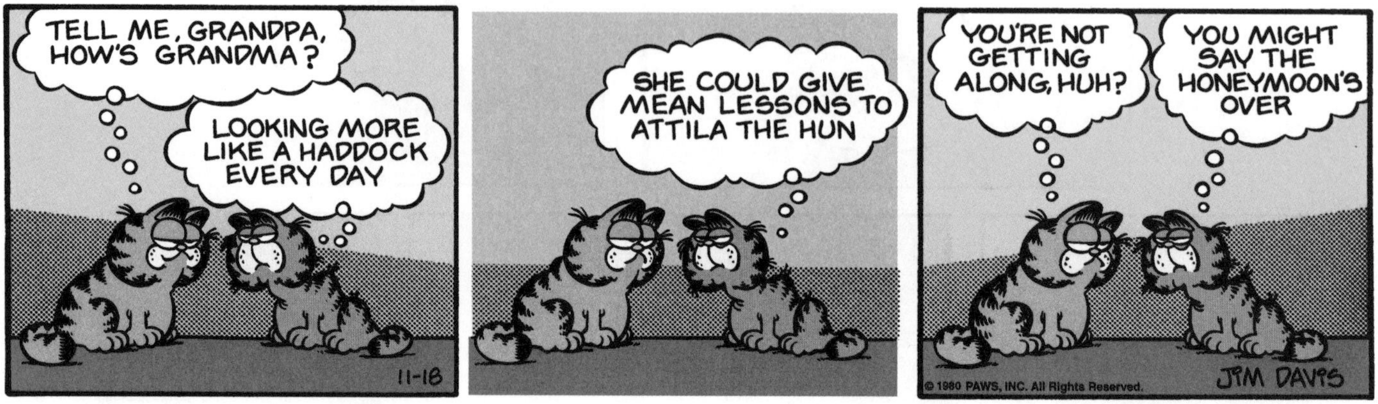
TELL ME, GRANDPA, HOW'S GRANDMA?
LOOKING MORE LIKE A HADDOCK EVERY DAY
11-18
SHE COULD GIVE MEAN LESSONS TO ATTILA THE HUN
YOU'RE NOT GETTING ALONG, HUH?
YOU MIGHT SAY THE HONEYMOON'S OVER
© 1980 PAWS, INC. All Rights Reserved.
JIM DAVIS

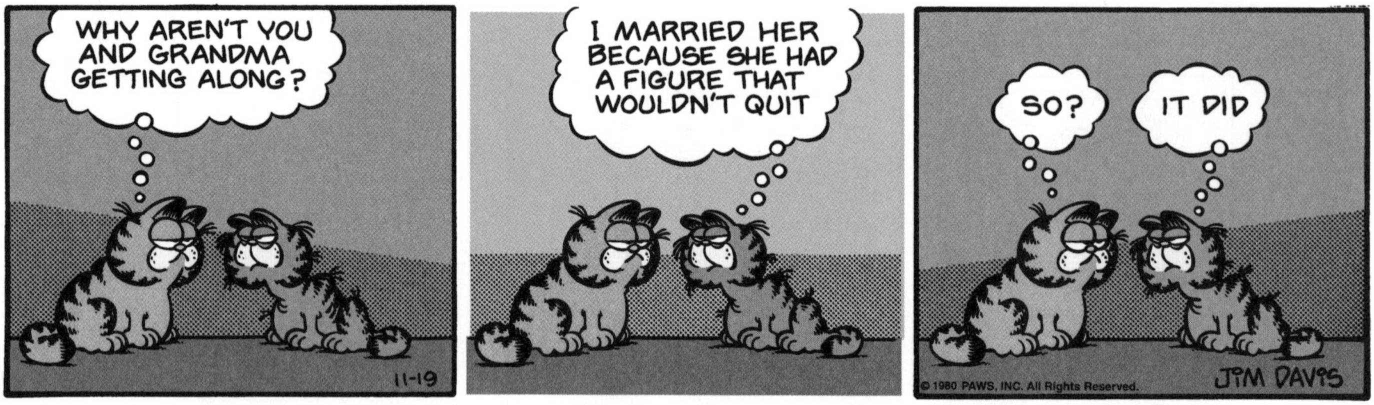
WHY AREN'T YOU AND GRANDMA GETTING ALONG?
11-19
I MARRIED HER BECAUSE SHE HAD A FIGURE THAT WOULDN'T QUIT
SO?
IT DID
© 1980 PAWS, INC. All Rights Reserved.
JIM DAVIS

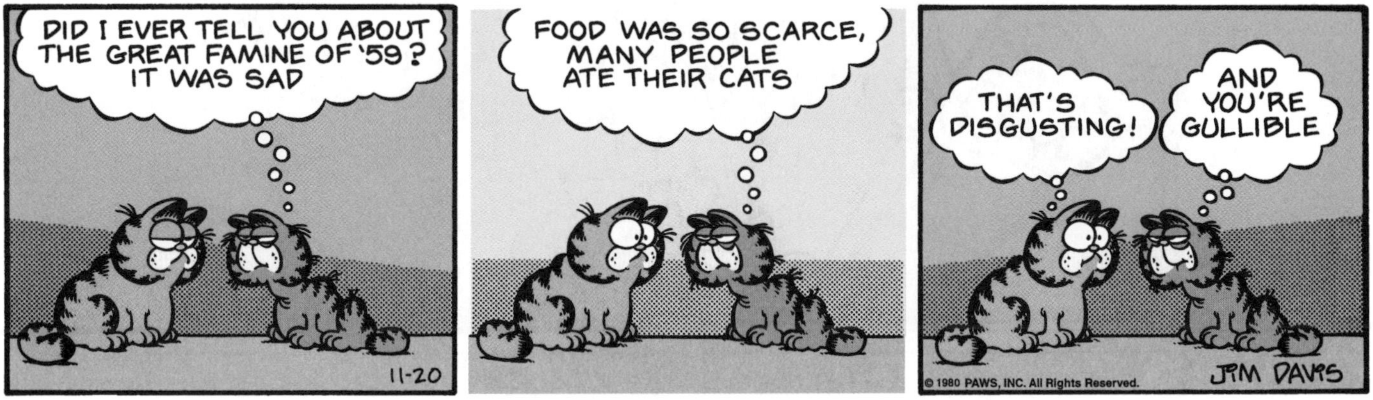
DID I EVER TELL YOU ABOUT THE GREAT FAMINE OF '59? IT WAS SAD
11-20
FOOD WAS SO SCARCE, MANY PEOPLE ATE THEIR CATS
THAT'S DISGUSTING!
AND YOU'RE GULLIBLE
© 1980 PAWS, INC. All Rights Reserved.
JIM DAVIS

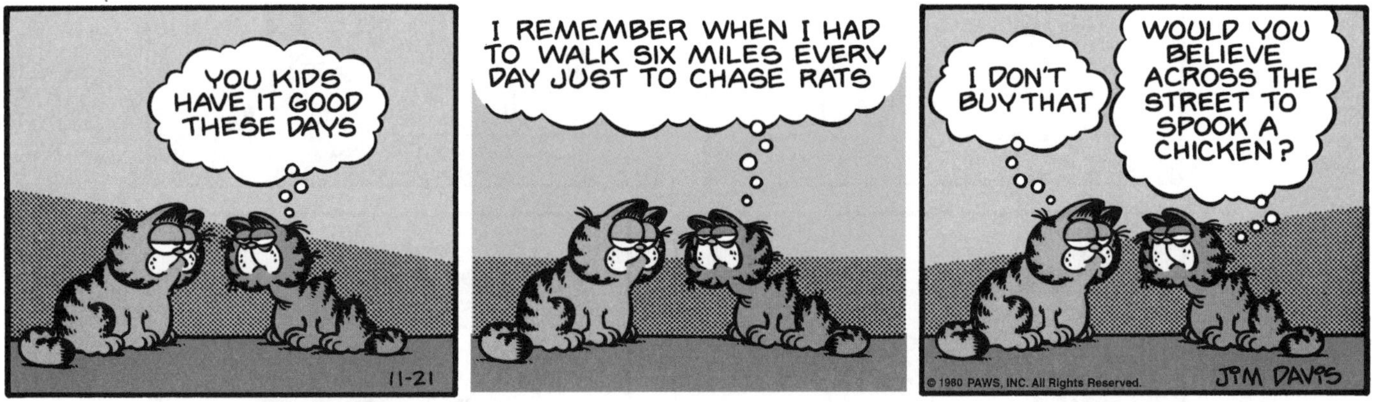
YOU KIDS HAVE IT GOOD THESE DAYS
11-21
I REMEMBER WHEN I HAD TO WALK SIX MILES EVERY DAY JUST TO CHASE RATS
I DON'T BUY THAT
WOULD YOU BELIEVE ACROSS THE STREET TO SPOOK A CHICKEN?
© 1980 PAWS, INC. All Rights Reserved.
JIM DAVIS

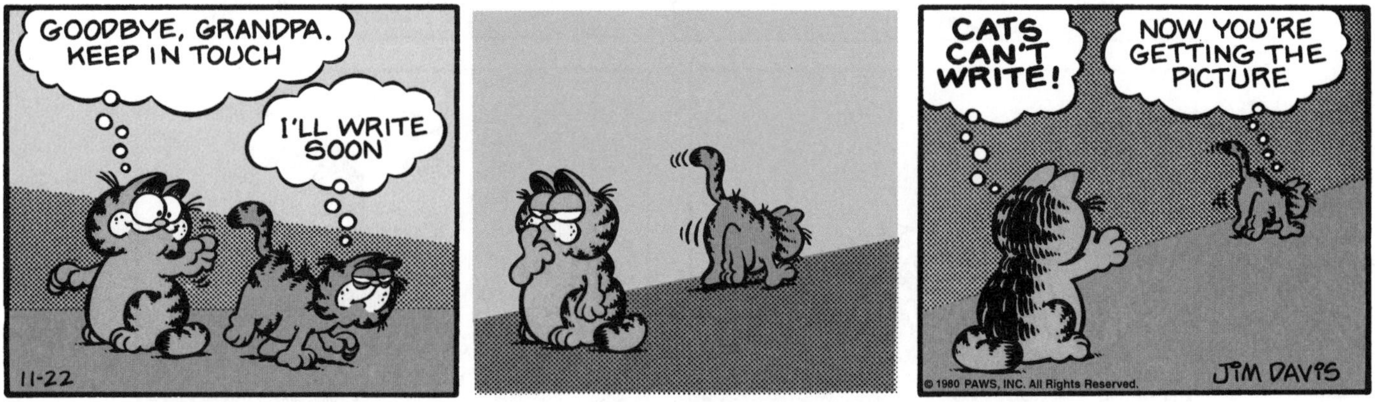
GOODBYE, GRANDPA. KEEP IN TOUCH
I'LL WRITE SOON
11-22
CATS CAN'T WRITE!
NOW YOU'RE GETTING THE PICTURE
© 1980 PAWS, INC. All Rights Reserved.
JIM DAVIS

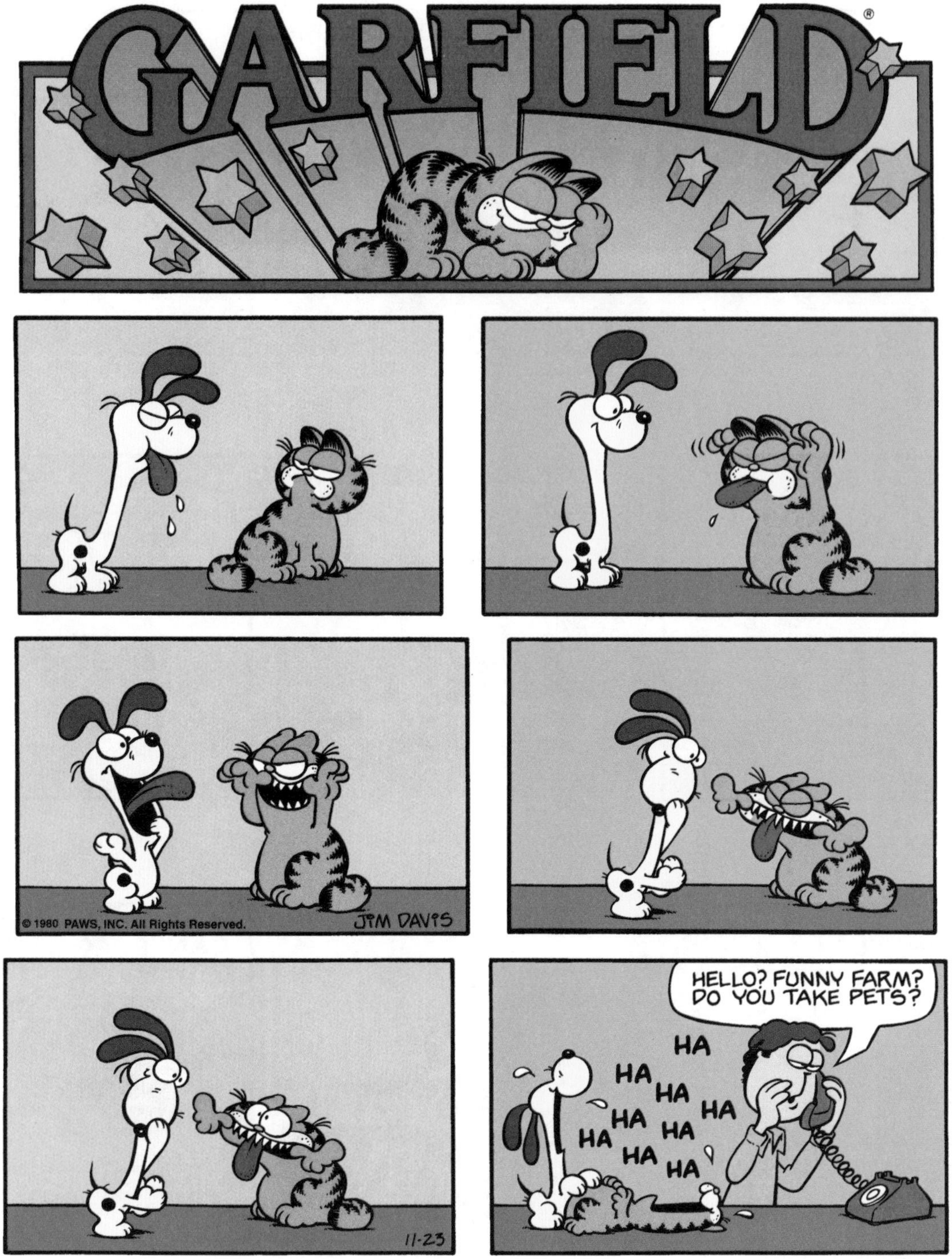
GARFIELD®
© 1980 PAWS, INC. All Rights Reserved.
JIM DAVIS
11-23
HELLO? FUNNY FARM? DO YOU TAKE PETS?
HA HA HA HA HA HA HA HA HA HA

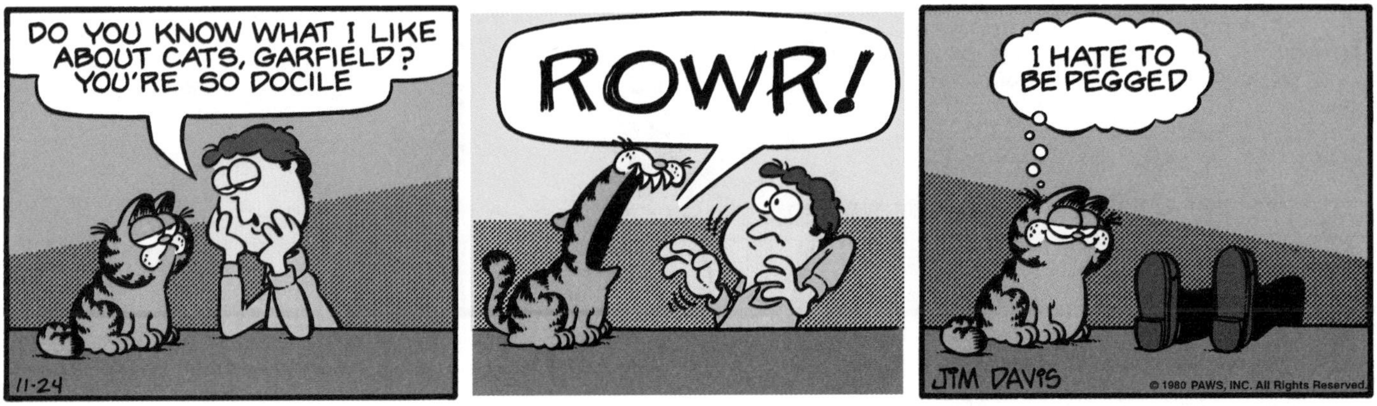
DO YOU KNOW WHAT I LIKE ABOUT CATS, GARFIELD? YOU'RE SO DOCILE
ROWR!
I HATE TO BE PEGGED
11-24
JIM DAVIS
© 1980 PAWS, INC. All Rights Reserved.

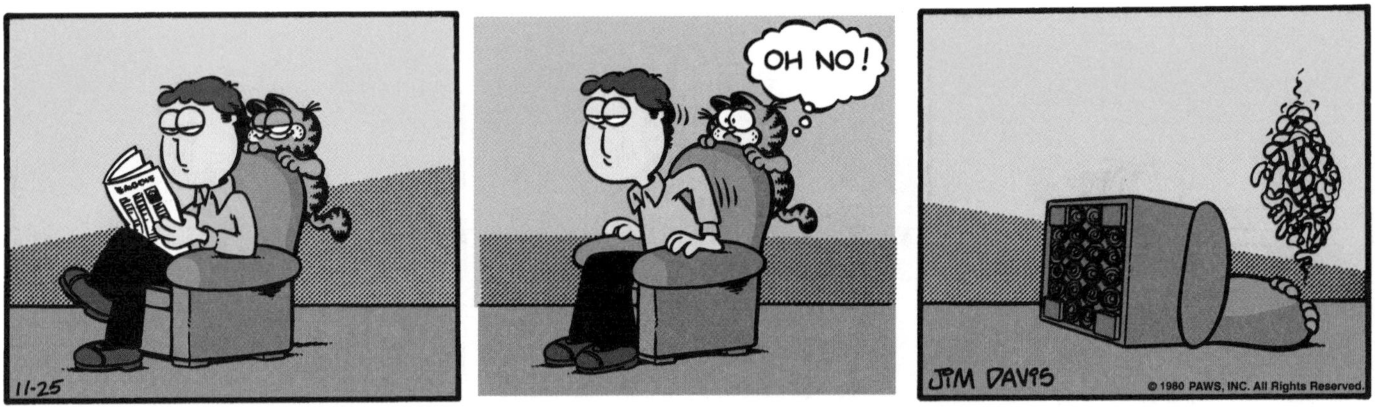
OH NO!
11-25
JIM DAVIS
© 1980 PAWS, INC. All Rights Reserved.

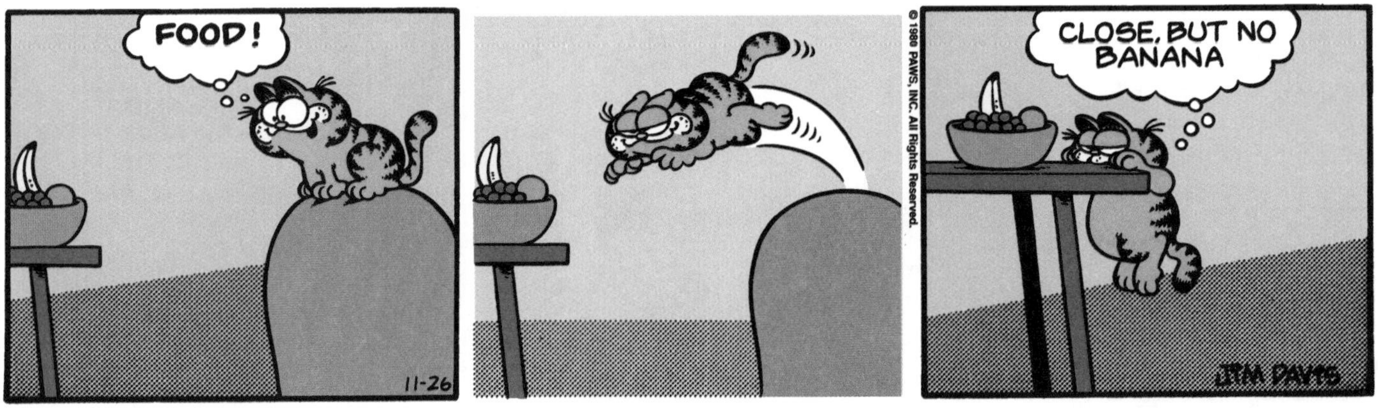
FOOD!
11-26
© 1980 PAWS, INC. All Rights Reserved.
CLOSE, BUT NO BANANA
JIM DAVIS

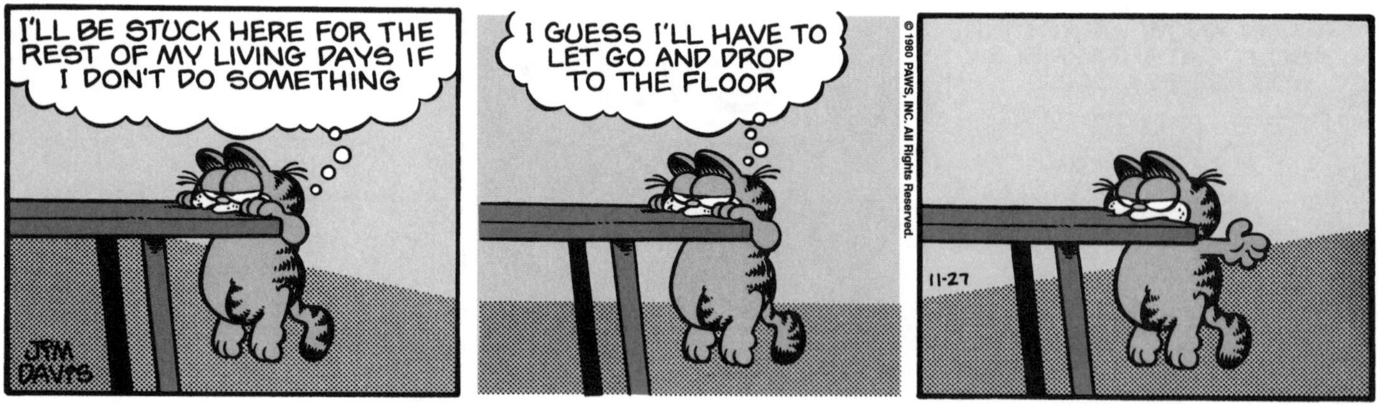
I'LL BE STUCK HERE FOR THE REST OF MY LIVING DAYS IF I DON'T DO SOMETHING
JIM DAVIS
I GUESS I'LL HAVE TO LET GO AND DROP TO THE FLOOR
© 1980 PAWS, INC. All Rights Reserved.
11-27

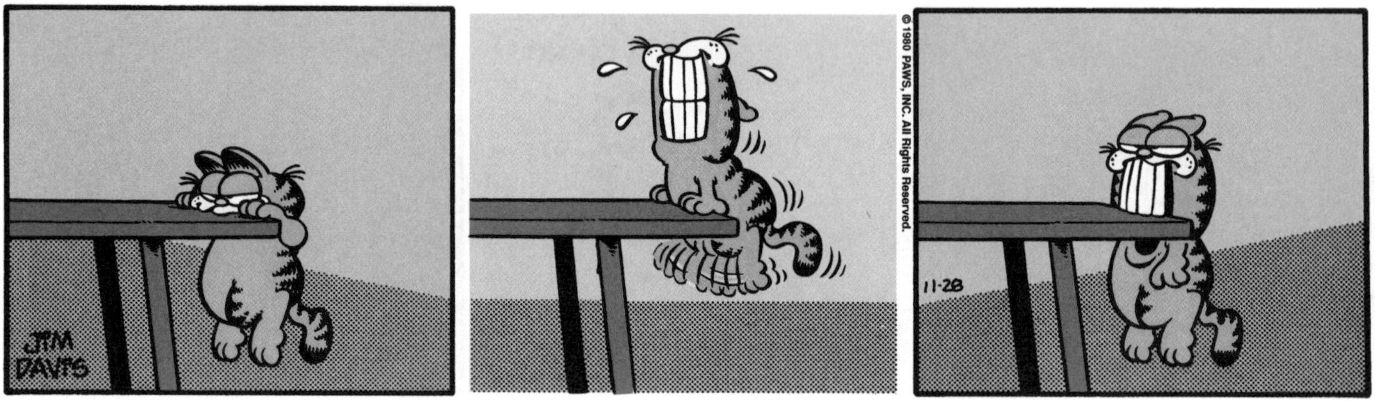
JIM DAVIS
© 1980 PAWS, INC. All Rights Reserved.
11-28

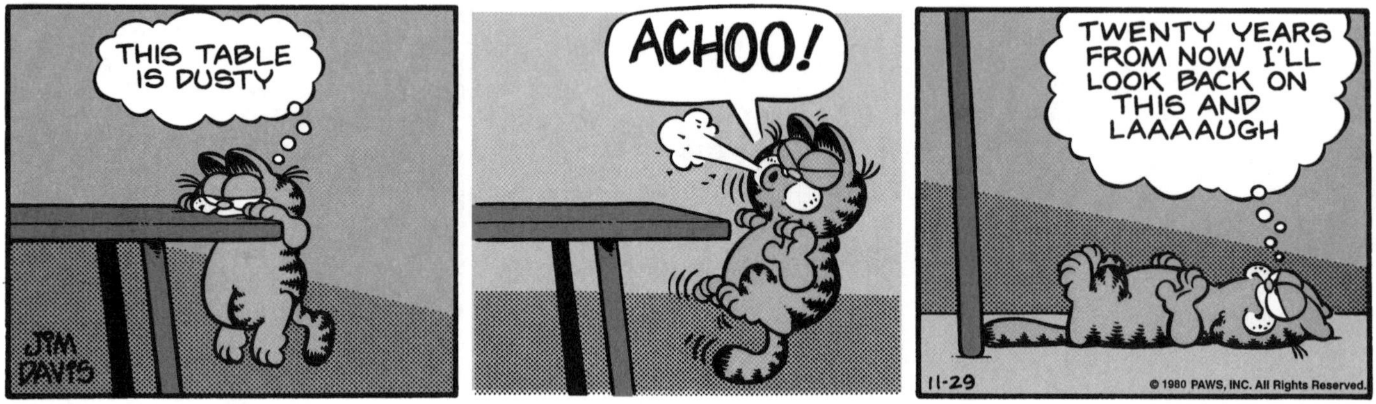
THIS TABLE IS DUSTY
JIM DAVIS
ACHOO!
TWENTY YEARS FROM NOW I'LL LOOK BACK ON THIS AND LAAAAUGH
11-29
© 1980 PAWS, INC. All Rights Reserved.

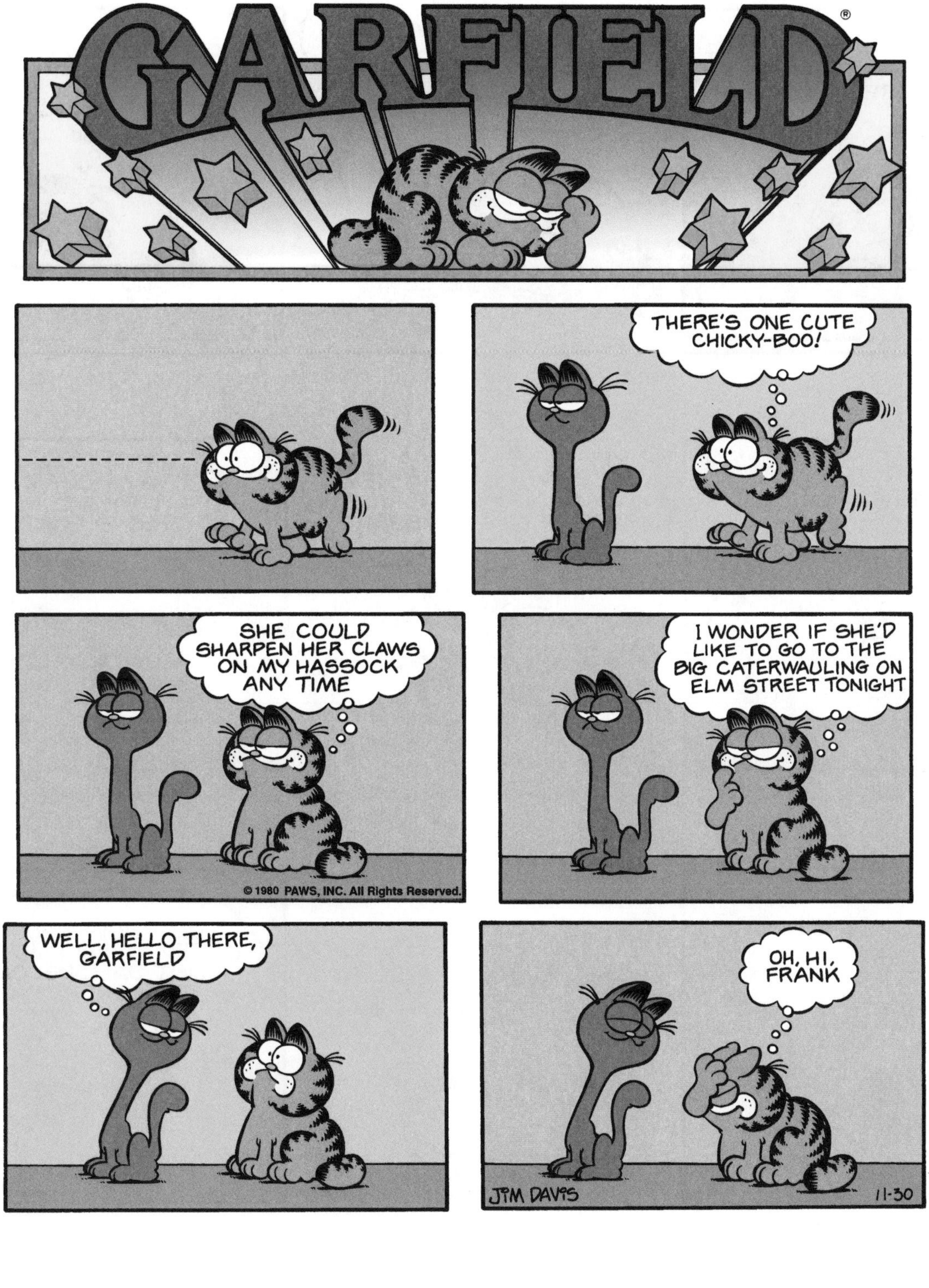
GARFIELD
THERE'S ONE CUTE CHICKY-BOO!
SHE COULD SHARPEN HER CLAWS ON MY HASSOCK ANY TIME
© 1980 PAWS, INC. All Rights Reserved.
I WONDER IF SHE'D LIKE TO GO TO THE BIG CATERWAULING ON ELM STREET TONIGHT
WELL, HELLO THERE, GARFIELD
OH, HI, FRANK
JIM DAVIS
11-30

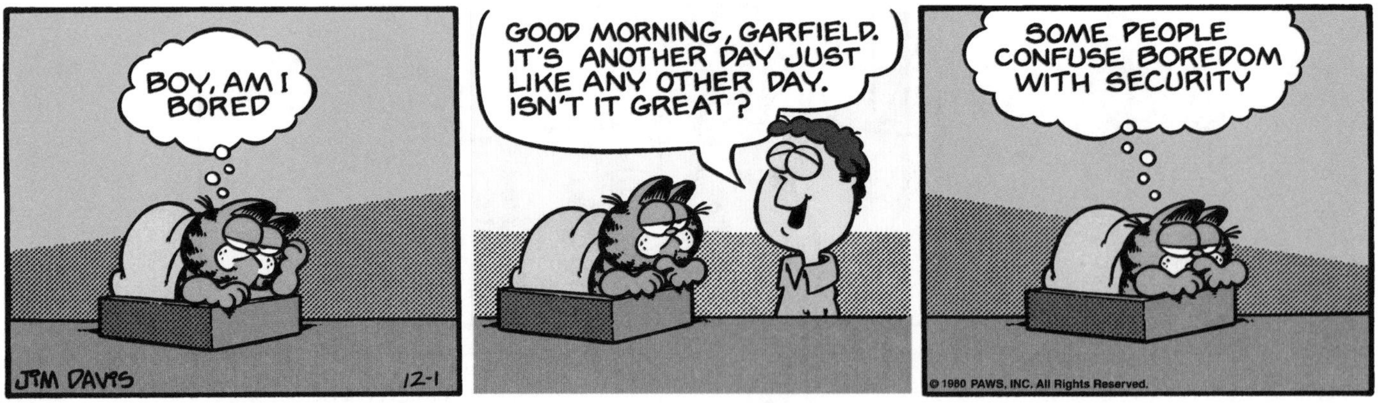
BOY, AM I BORED
JIM DAVIS
12-1
GOOD MORNING, GARFIELD. IT'S ANOTHER DAY JUST LIKE ANY OTHER DAY. ISN'T IT GREAT?
SOME PEOPLE CONFUSE BOREDOM WITH SECURITY
© 1980 PAWS, INC. All Rights Reserved.

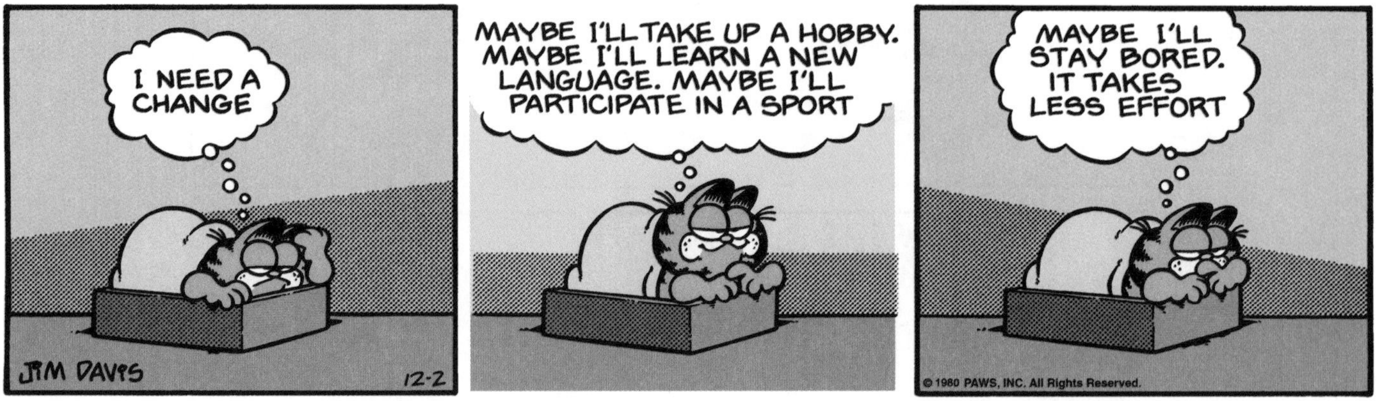
I NEED A CHANGE
JIM DAVIS
12-2
MAYBE I'LL TAKE UP A HOBBY. MAYBE I'LL LEARN A NEW LANGUAGE. MAYBE I'LL PARTICIPATE IN A SPORT
MAYBE I'LL STAY BORED. IT TAKES LESS EFFORT
© 1980 PAWS, INC. All Rights Reserved.

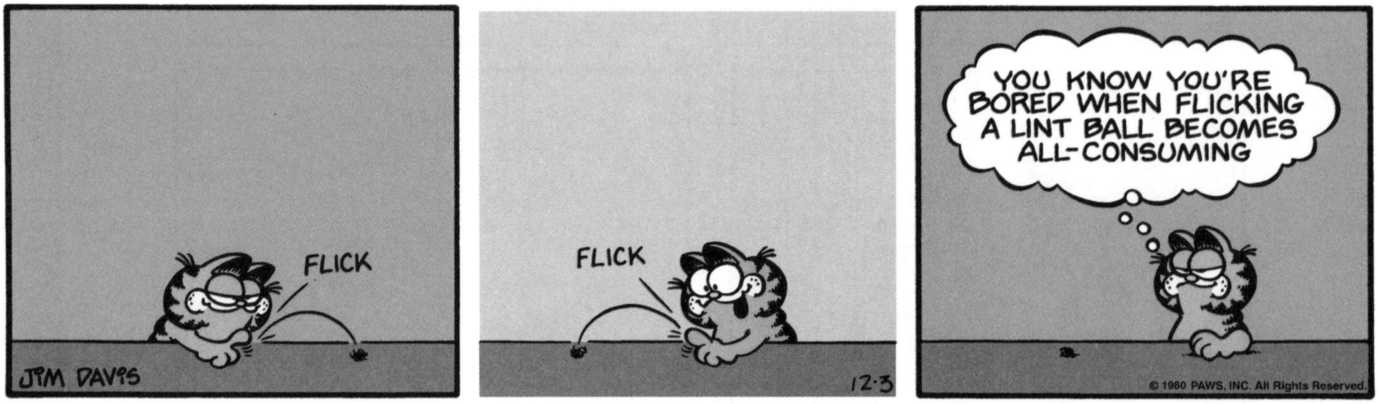
FLICK
JIM DAVIS
FLICK
12-3
YOU KNOW YOU'RE BORED WHEN FLICKING A LINT BALL BECOMES ALL-CONSUMING
© 1980 PAWS, INC. All Rights Reserved.

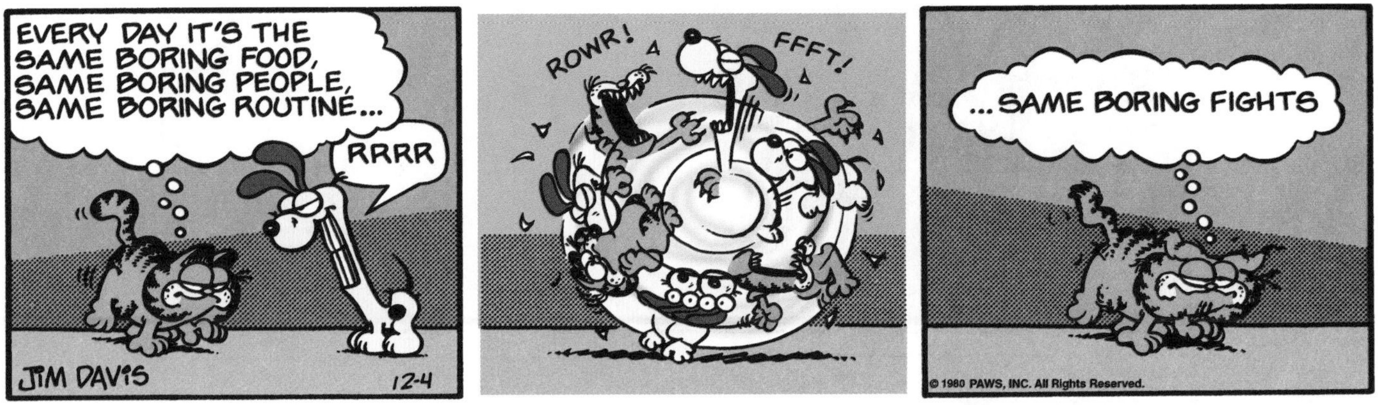
EVERY DAY IT'S THE SAME BORING FOOD, SAME BORING PEOPLE, SAME BORING ROUTINE...
RRRR
JIM DAVIS
12-4
ROWR!
FFFT!
...SAME BORING FIGHTS
© 1980 PAWS, INC. All Rights Reserved.

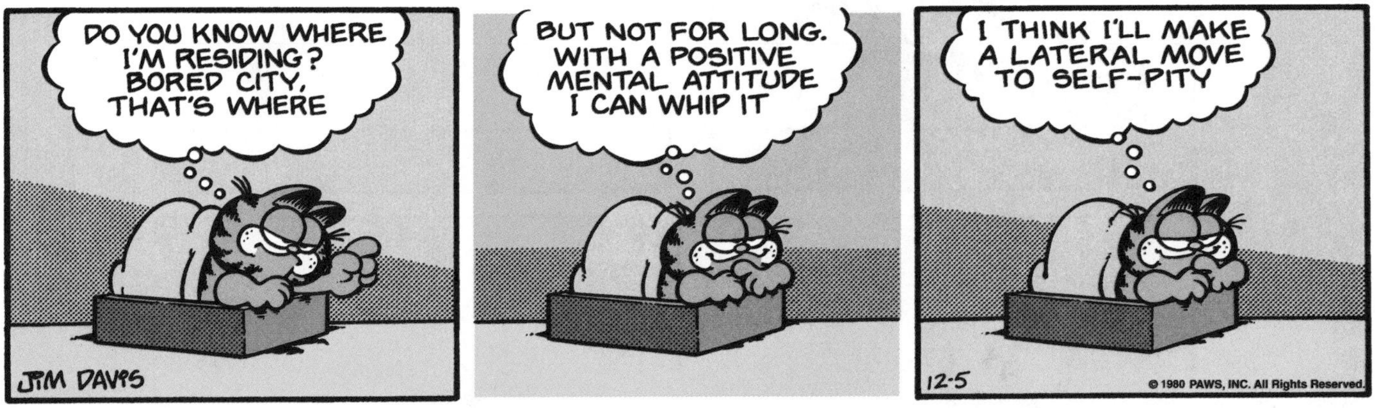
DO YOU KNOW WHERE I'M RESIDING? BORED CITY, THAT'S WHERE
JIM DAVIS
BUT NOT FOR LONG. WITH A POSITIVE MENTAL ATTITUDE I CAN WHIP IT
I THINK I'LL MAKE A LATERAL MOVE TO SELF-PITY
12-5
© 1980 PAWS, INC. All Rights Reserved.

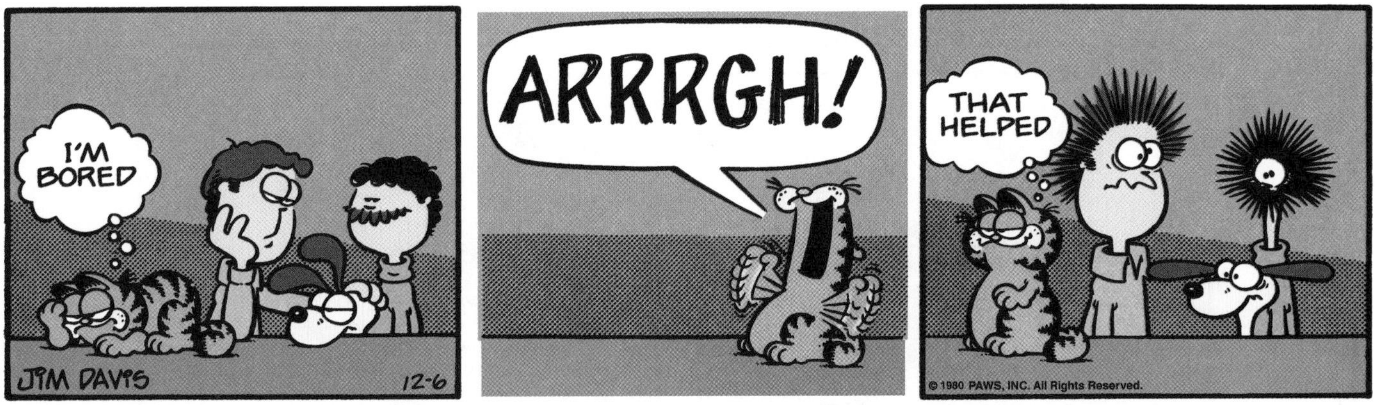
I'M BORED
JIM DAVIS
12-6
ARRRGH!
THAT HELPED
© 1980 PAWS, INC. All Rights Reserved.

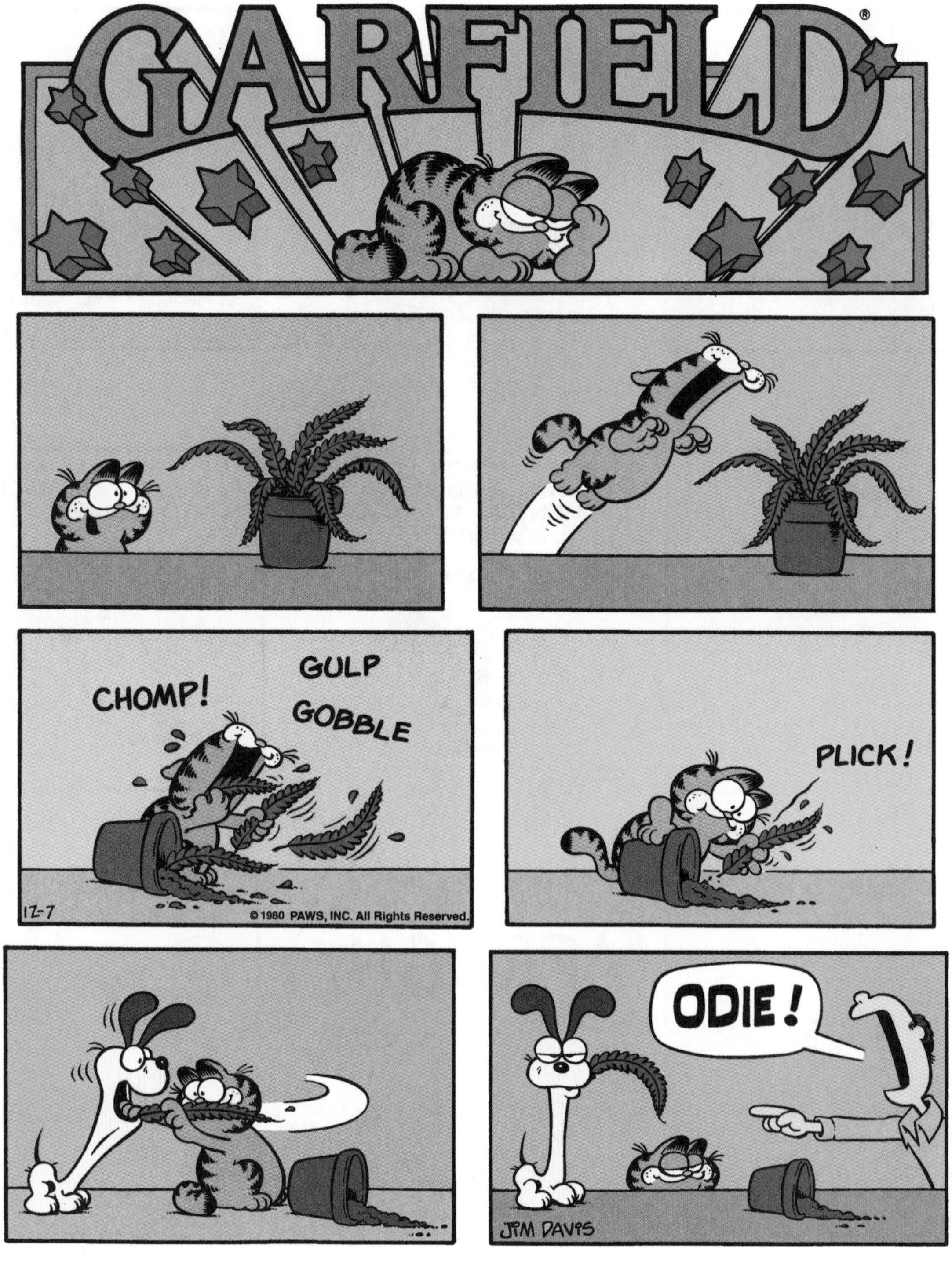
GARFIELD®
CHOMP!
GULP
GOBBLE
12-7
PLICK!
ODIE!
JIM DAVIS

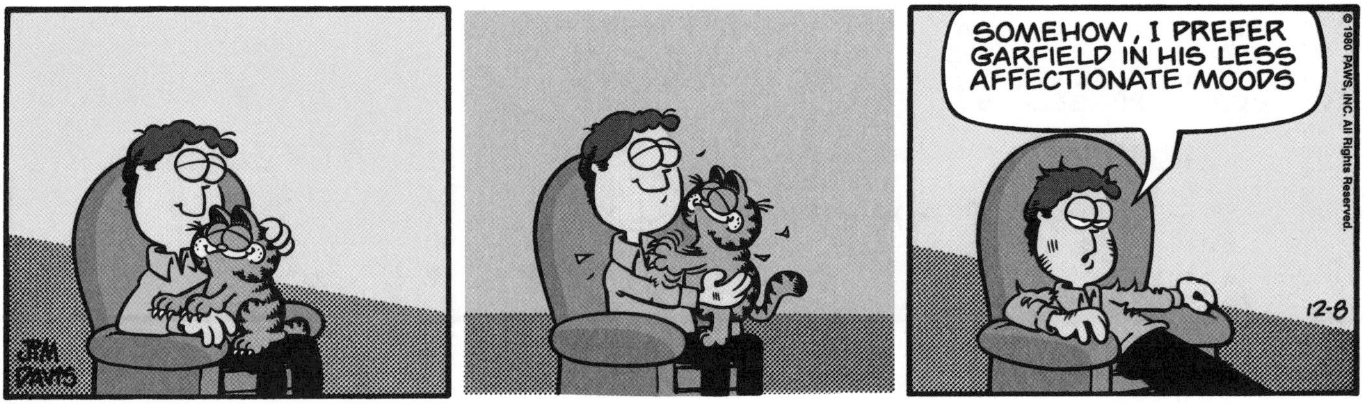
JIM DAVIS
SOMEHOW, I PREFER GARFIELD IN HIS LESS AFFECTIONATE MOODS
© 1980 PAWS, INC. All Rights Reserved.
12-8

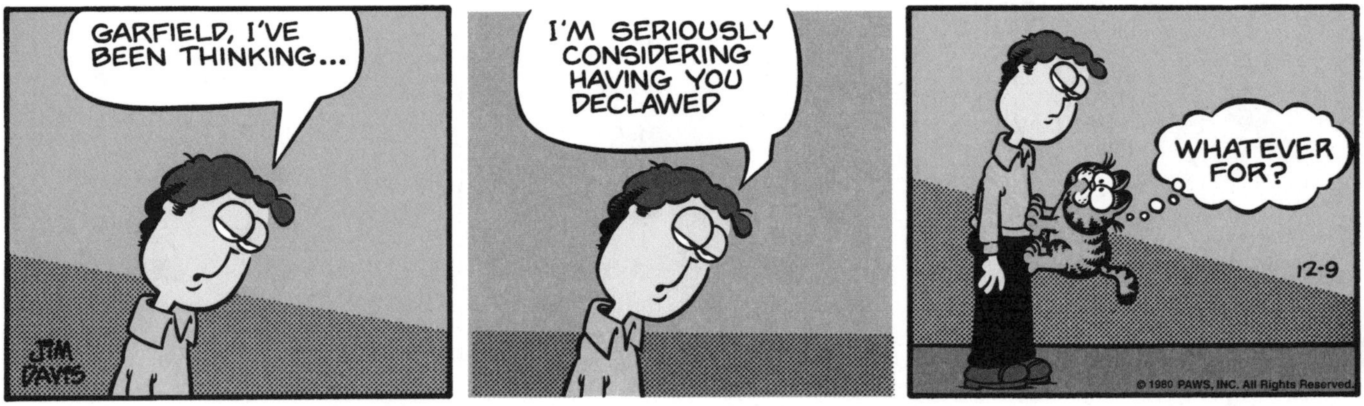
GARFIELD, I'VE BEEN THINKING...
JIM DAVIS
I'M SERIOUSLY CONSIDERING HAVING YOU DECLAWED
WHATEVER FOR?
12-9
© 1980 PAWS, INC. All Rights Reserved.

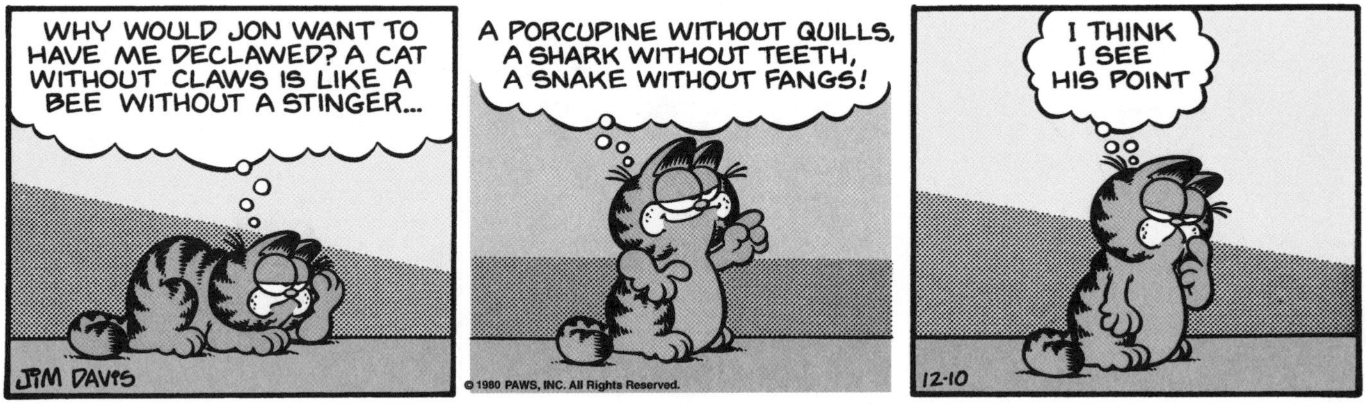
WHY WOULD JON WANT TO HAVE ME DECLAWED? A CAT WITHOUT CLAWS IS LIKE A BEE WITHOUT A STINGER...
JIM DAVIS
A PORCUPINE WITHOUT QUILLS, A SHARK WITHOUT TEETH, A SNAKE WITHOUT FANGS!
© 1980 PAWS, INC. All Rights Reserved.
I THINK I SEE HIS POINT
12-10

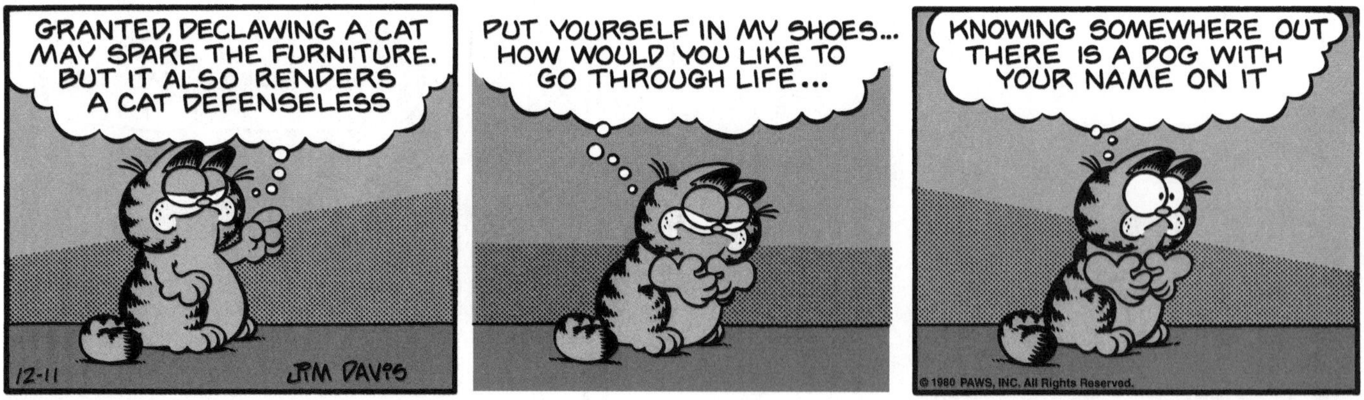
GRANTED, DECLAWING A CAT MAY SPARE THE FURNITURE. BUT IT ALSO RENDERS A CAT DEFENSELESS
12-11
JIM DAVIS
PUT YOURSELF IN MY SHOES... HOW WOULD YOU LIKE TO GO THROUGH LIFE...
KNOWING SOMEWHERE OUT THERE IS A DOG WITH YOUR NAME ON IT
© 1980 PAWS, INC. All Rights Reserved.

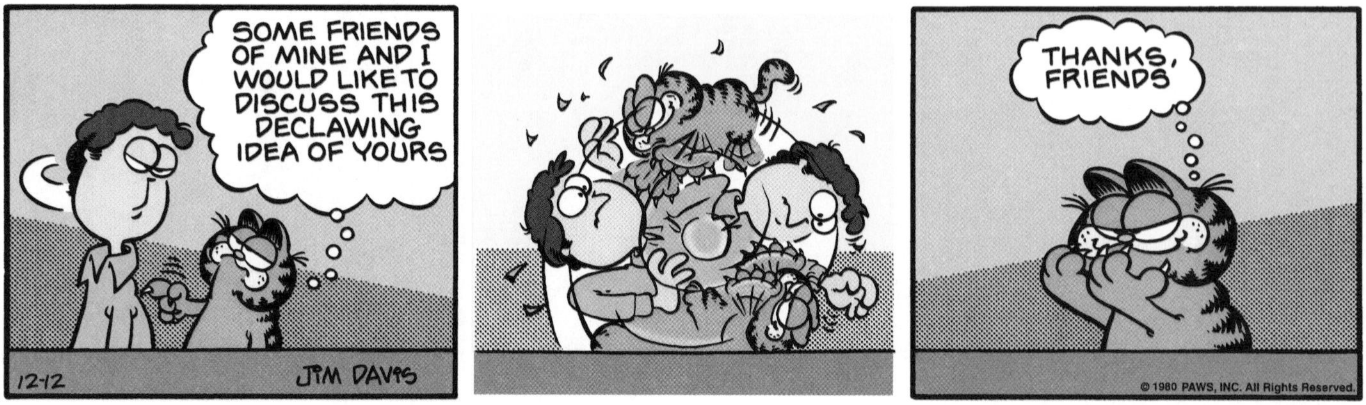
SOME FRIENDS OF MINE AND I WOULD LIKE TO DISCUSS THIS DECLAWING IDEA OF YOURS
12-12
JIM DAVIS
THANKS, FRIENDS
© 1980 PAWS, INC. All Rights Reserved.

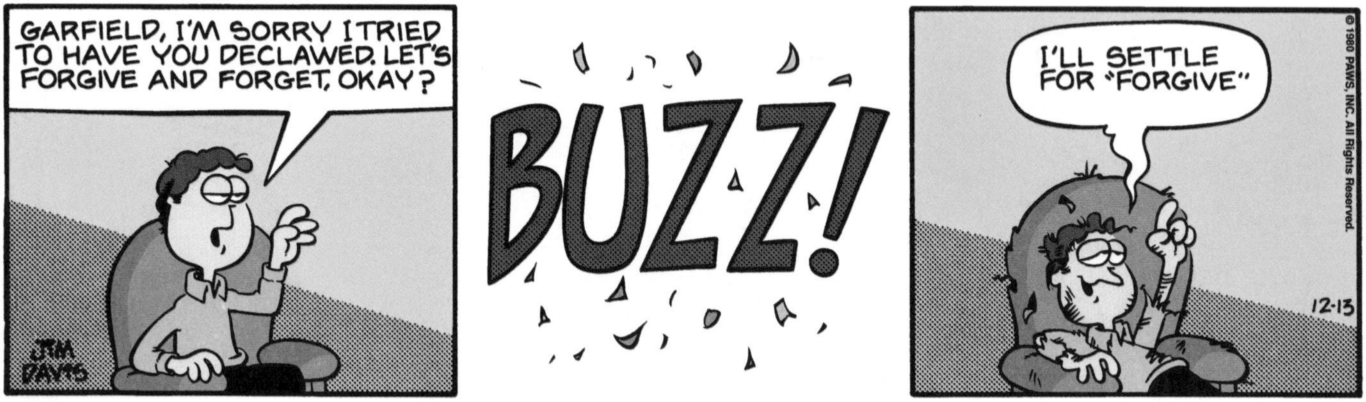
GARFIELD, I'M SORRY I TRIED TO HAVE YOU DECLAWED. LET'S FORGIVE AND FORGET, OKAY?
JIM DAVIS
BUZZ!
I'LL SETTLE FOR "FORGIVE"
© 1980 PAWS, INC. All Rights Reserved.
12-13

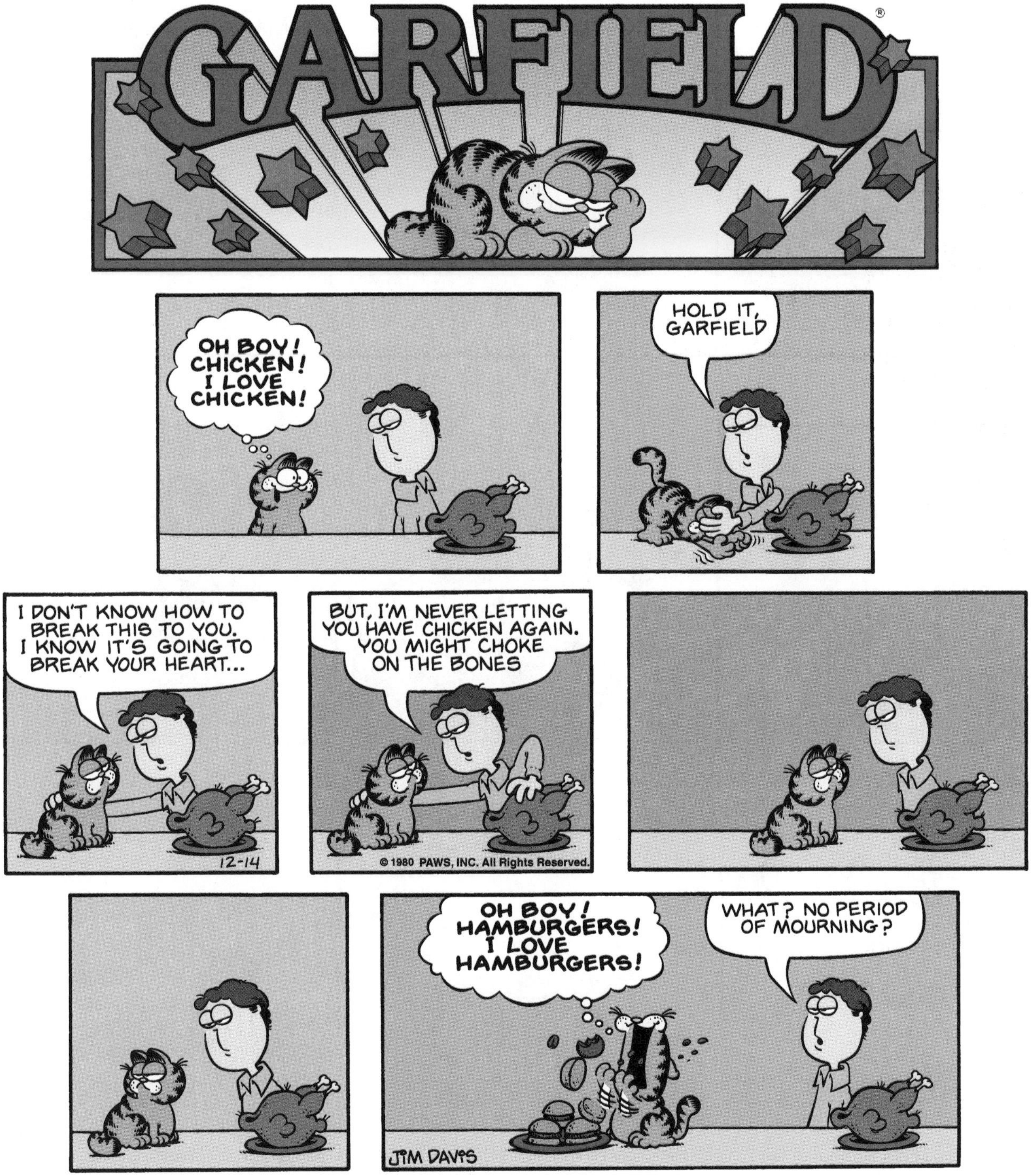
GARFIELD®
OH BOY! CHICKEN! I LOVE CHICKEN!
HOLD IT, GARFIELD
I DON'T KNOW HOW TO BREAK THIS TO YOU. I KNOW IT'S GOING TO BREAK YOUR HEART...
12-14
BUT, I'M NEVER LETTING YOU HAVE CHICKEN AGAIN. YOU MIGHT CHOKE ON THE BONES
© 1980 PAWS, INC. All Rights Reserved.
OH BOY! HAMBURGERS! I LOVE HAMBURGERS!
WHAT? NO PERIOD OF MOURNING?
JIM DAVIS

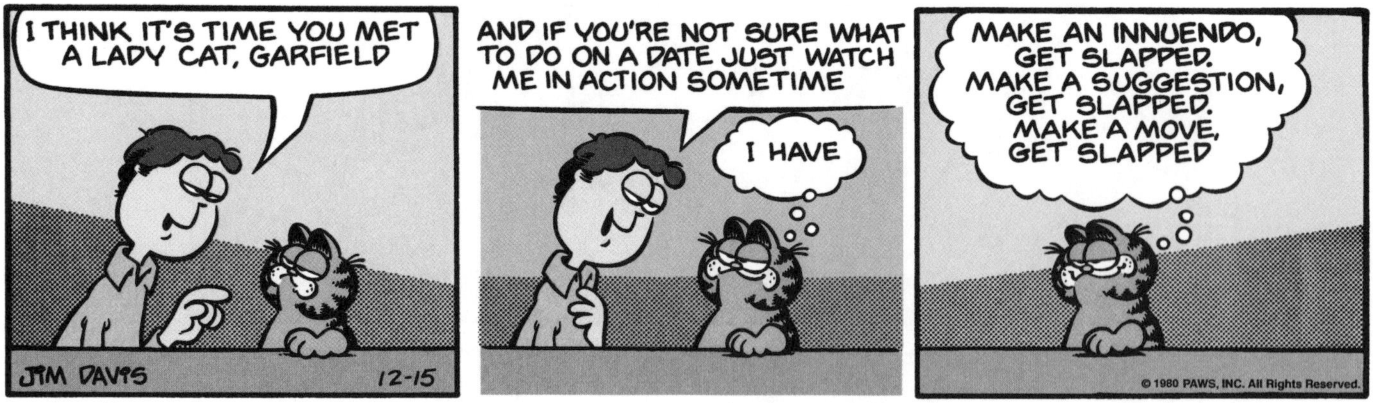
I THINK IT'S TIME YOU MET A LADY CAT, GARFIELD
JIM DAVIS
12-15
AND IF YOU'RE NOT SURE WHAT TO DO ON A DATE JUST WATCH ME IN ACTION SOMETIME
I HAVE
MAKE AN INNUENDO, GET SLAPPED. MAKE A SUGGESTION, GET SLAPPED. MAKE A MOVE, GET SLAPPED
© 1980 PAWS, INC. All Rights Reserved.

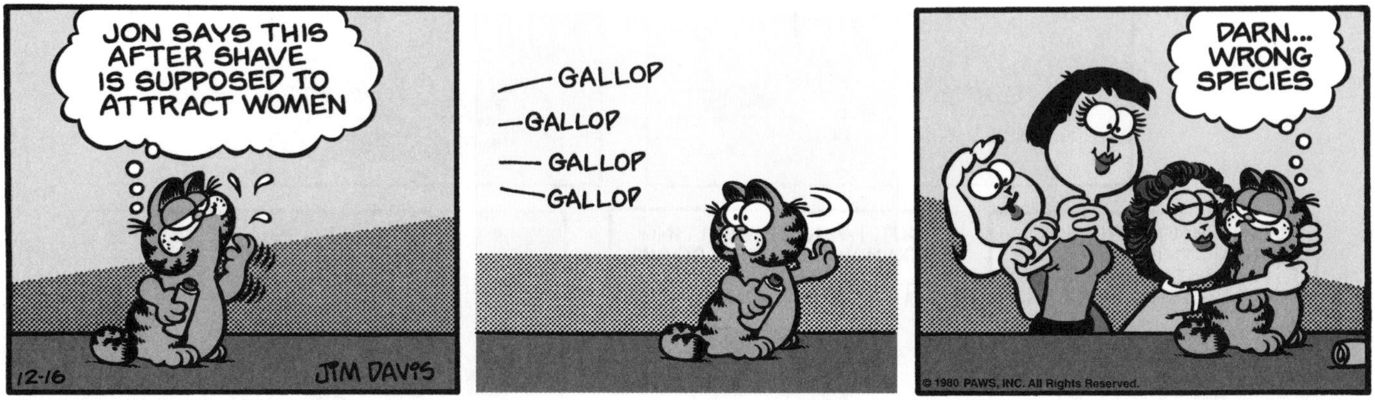
JON SAYS THIS AFTER SHAVE IS SUPPOSED TO ATTRACT WOMEN
12-16
JIM DAVIS
GALLOP
GALLOP
GALLOP
GALLOP
DARN... WRONG SPECIES
© 1980 PAWS, INC. All Rights Reserved.

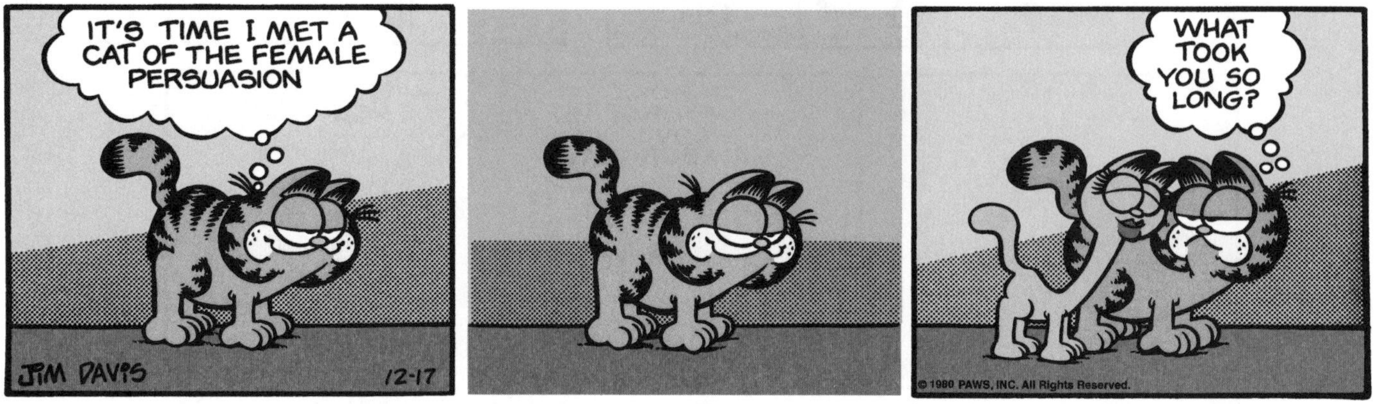
IT'S TIME I MET A CAT OF THE FEMALE PERSUASION
JIM DAVIS
12-17
WHAT TOOK YOU SO LONG?
© 1980 PAWS, INC. All Rights Reserved.

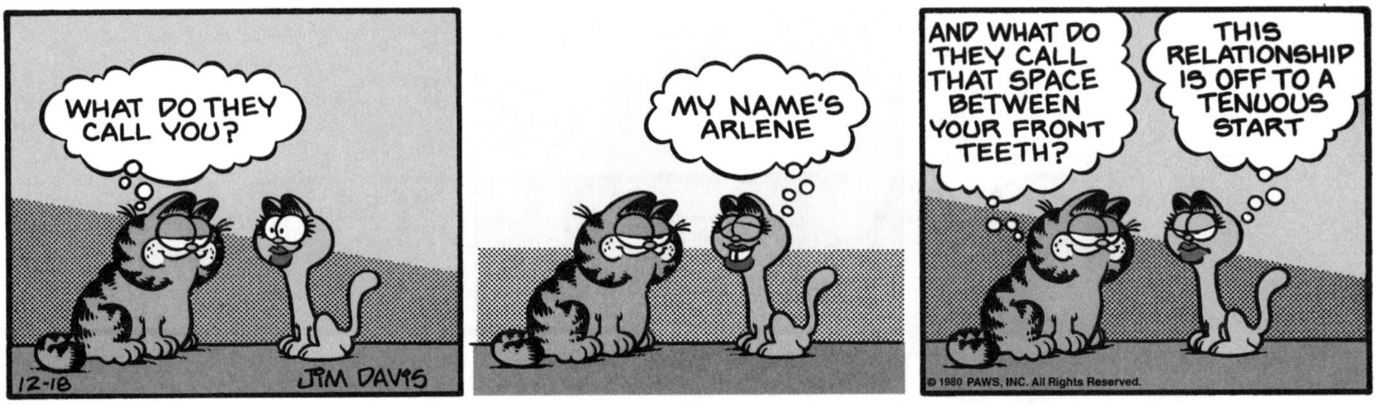
WHAT DO THEY CALL YOU?
12-18
JIM DAVIS
MY NAME'S ARLENE
AND WHAT DO THEY CALL THAT SPACE BETWEEN YOUR FRONT TEETH?
THIS RELATIONSHIP IS OFF TO A TENUOUS START
© 1980 PAWS, INC. All Rights Reserved.

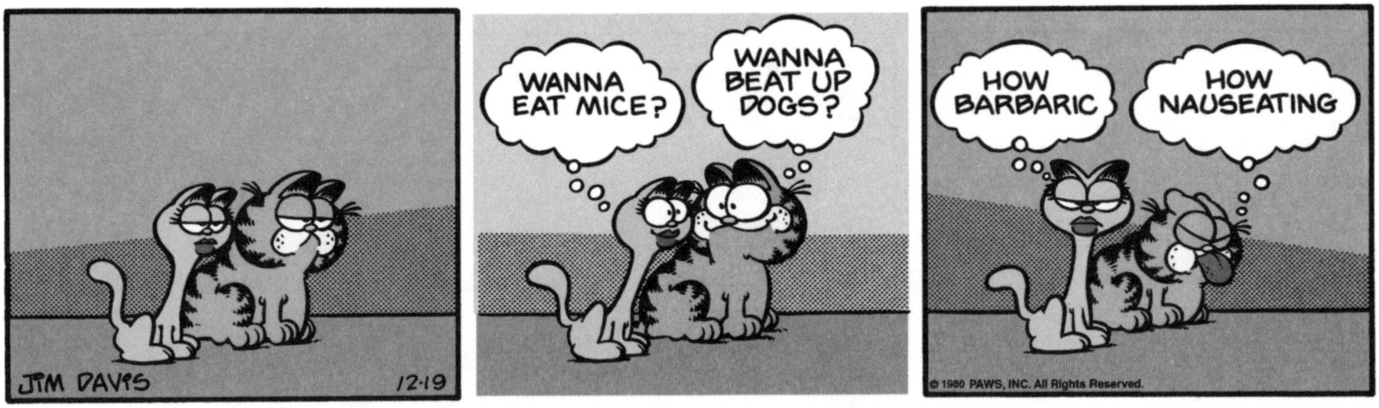
JIM DAVIS
12-19
WANNA EAT MICE?
WANNA BEAT UP DOGS?
HOW BARBARIC
HOW NAUSEATING
© 1980 PAWS, INC. All Rights Reserved.

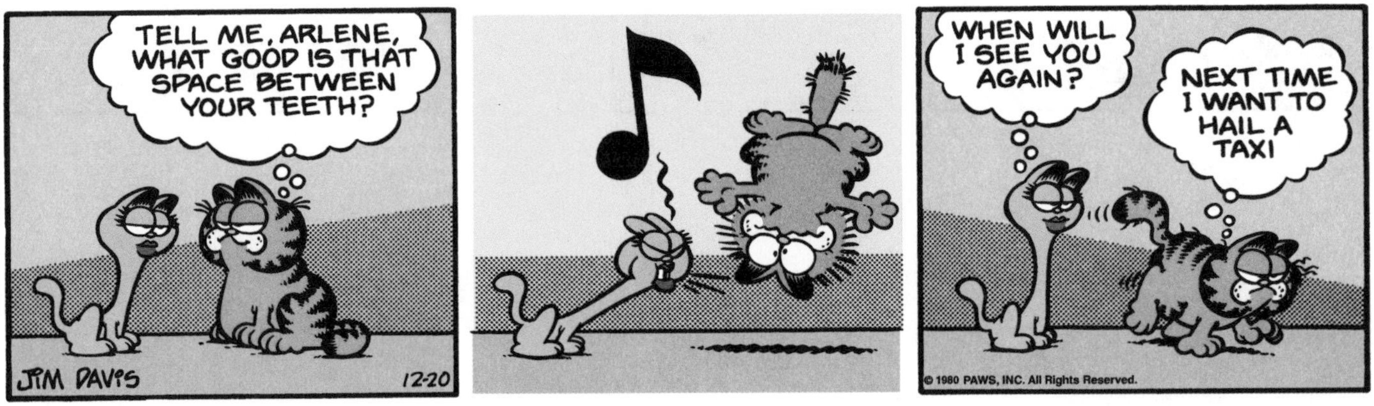
TELL ME, ARLENE, WHAT GOOD IS THAT SPACE BETWEEN YOUR TEETH?
JIM DAVIS
12-20
WHEN WILL I SEE YOU AGAIN?
NEXT TIME I WANT TO HAIL A TAXI
© 1980 PAWS, INC. All Rights Reserved.

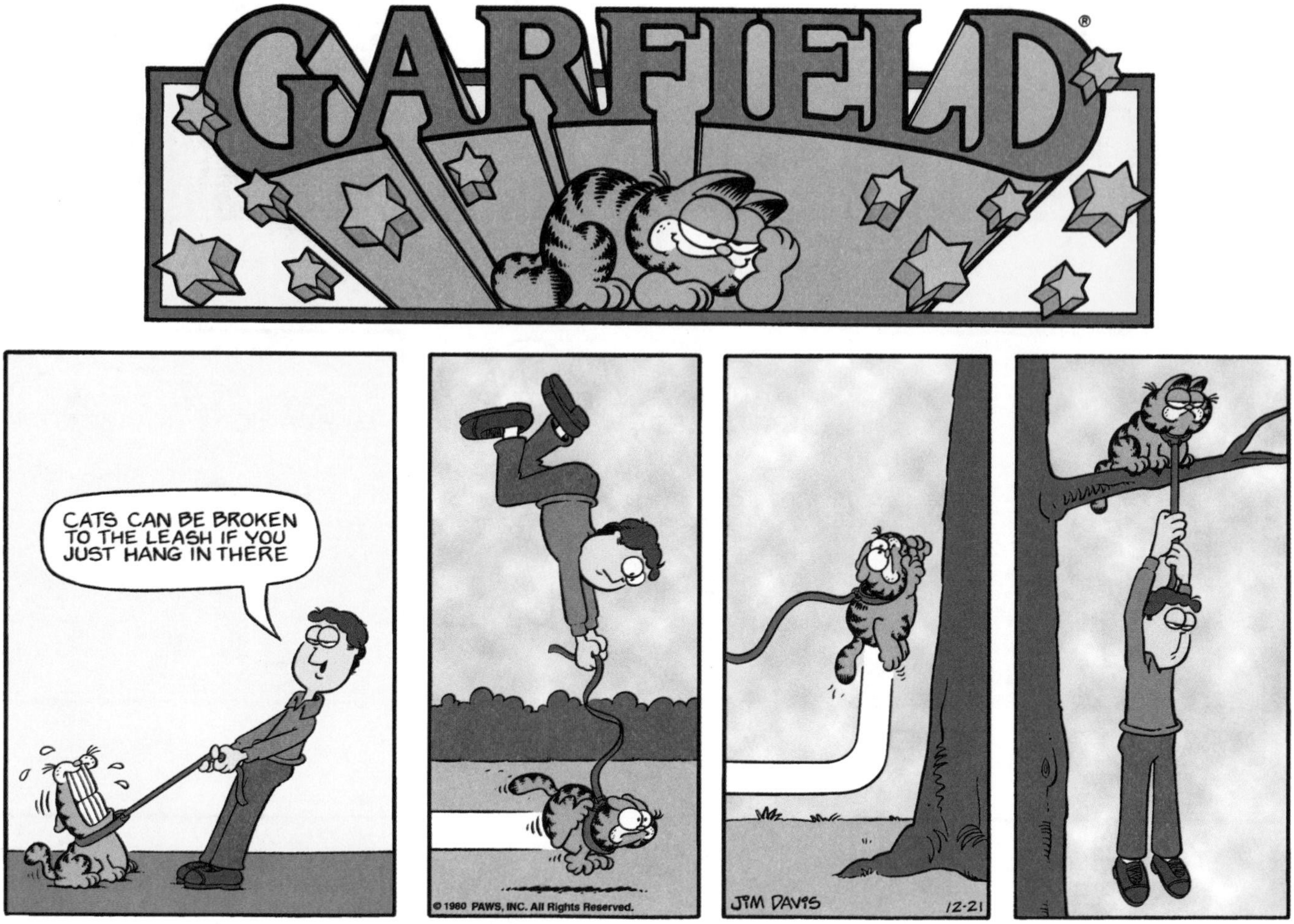
GARFIELD®
CATS CAN BE BROKEN TO THE LEASH IF YOU JUST HANG IN THERE
© 1980 PAWS, INC. All Rights Reserved.
JIM DAVIS
12-21

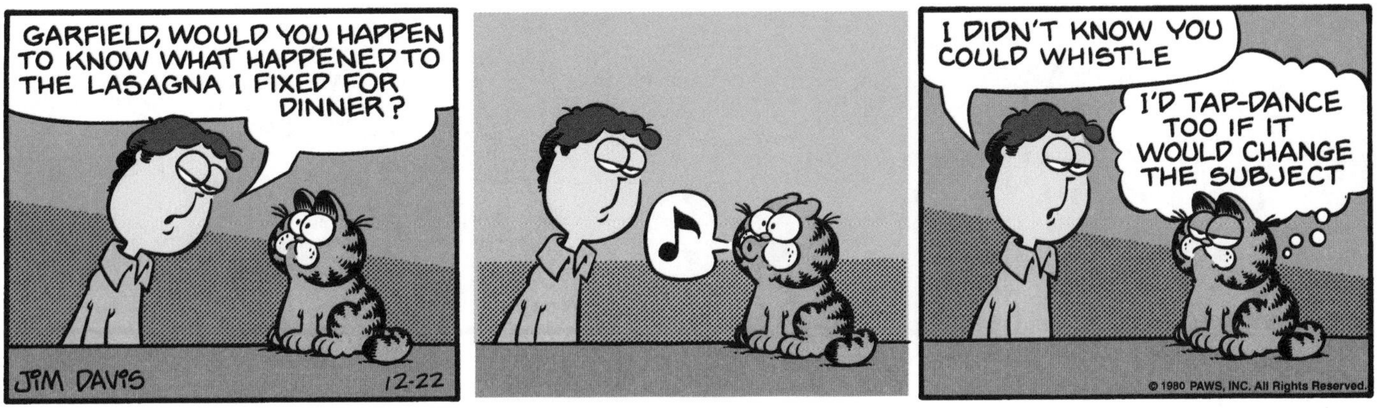
GARFIELD, WOULD YOU HAPPEN TO KNOW WHAT HAPPENED TO THE LASAGNA I FIXED FOR DINNER?
JIM DAVIS
12-22
I DIDN'T KNOW YOU COULD WHISTLE
I'D TAP-DANCE TOO IF IT WOULD CHANGE THE SUBJECT
© 1980 PAWS, INC. All Rights Reserved.

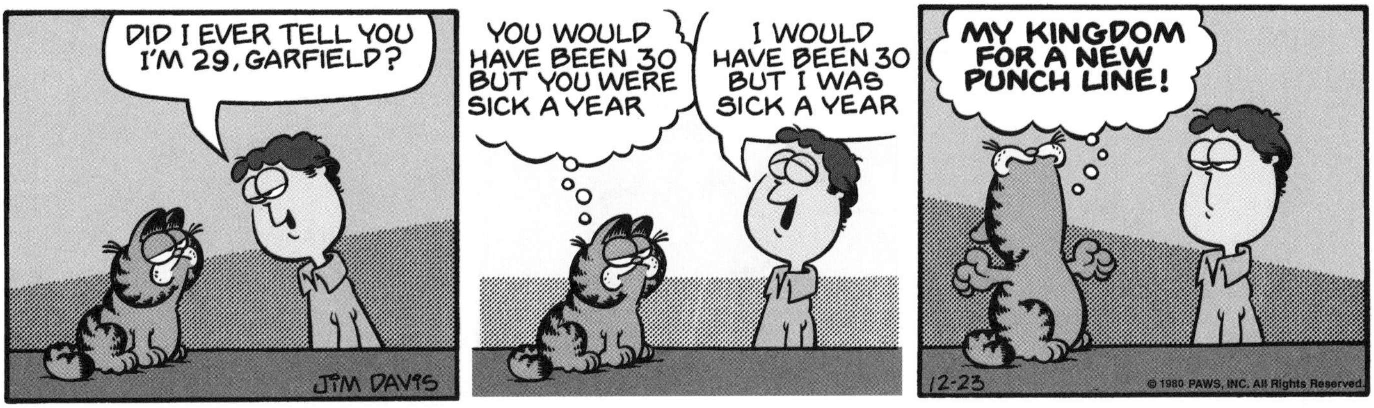
DID I EVER TELL YOU I'M 29, GARFIELD?
JIM DAVIS
YOU WOULD HAVE BEEN 30 BUT YOU WERE SICK A YEAR
I WOULD HAVE BEEN 30 BUT I WAS SICK A YEAR
MY KINGDOM FOR A NEW PUNCH LINE!
12-23
© 1980 PAWS, INC. All Rights Reserved.

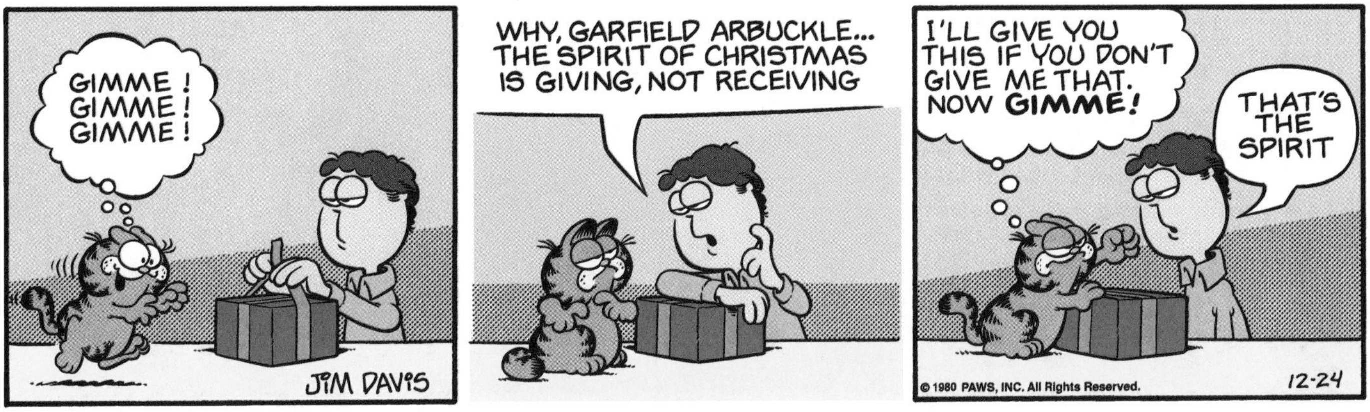
GIMME! GIMME! GIMME!
JIM DAVIS
WHY, GARFIELD ARBUCKLE... THE SPIRIT OF CHRISTMAS IS GIVING, NOT RECEIVING
I'LL GIVE YOU THIS IF YOU DON'T GIVE ME THAT. NOW **GIMME!**
THAT'S THE SPIRIT
© 1980 PAWS, INC. All Rights Reserved.
12-24

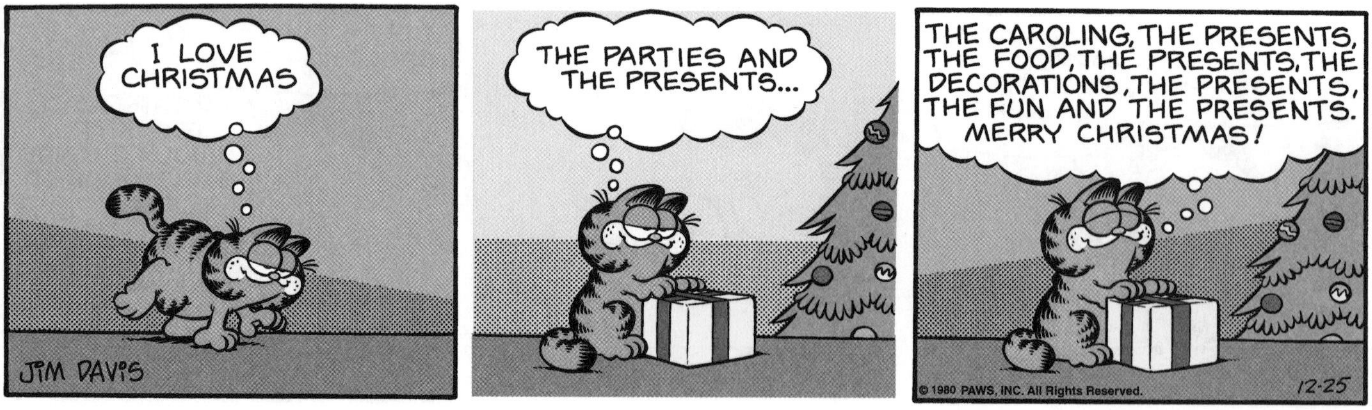
I LOVE CHRISTMAS
JIM DAVIS
THE PARTIES AND THE PRESENTS...
THE CAROLING, THE PRESENTS, THE FOOD, THE PRESENTS, THE DECORATIONS, THE PRESENTS, THE FUN AND THE PRESENTS. MERRY CHRISTMAS!
© 1980 PAWS, INC. All Rights Reserved.
12-25

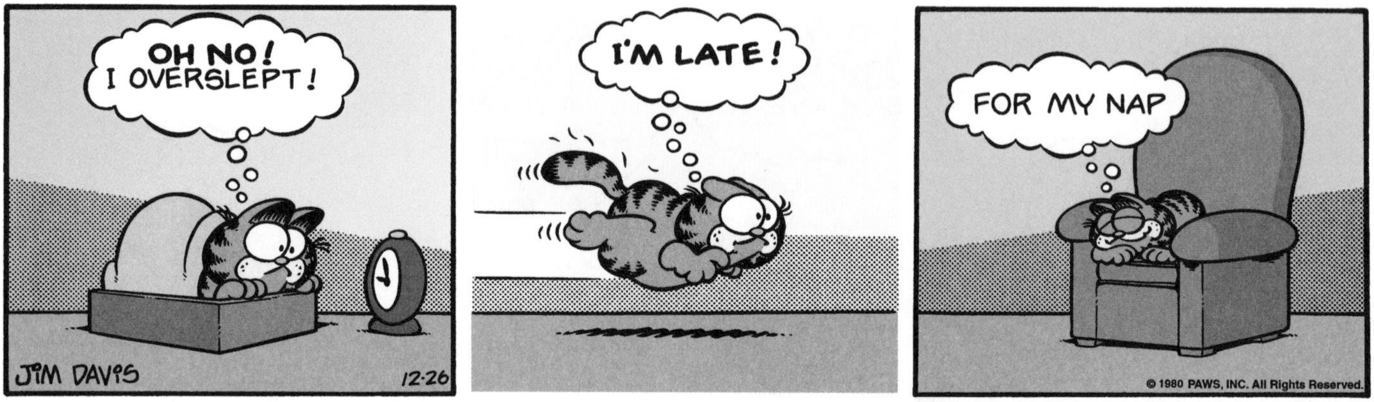
OH NO! I OVERSLEPT!
JIM DAVIS
12-26
I'M LATE!
FOR MY NAP
© 1980 PAWS, INC. All Rights Reserved.

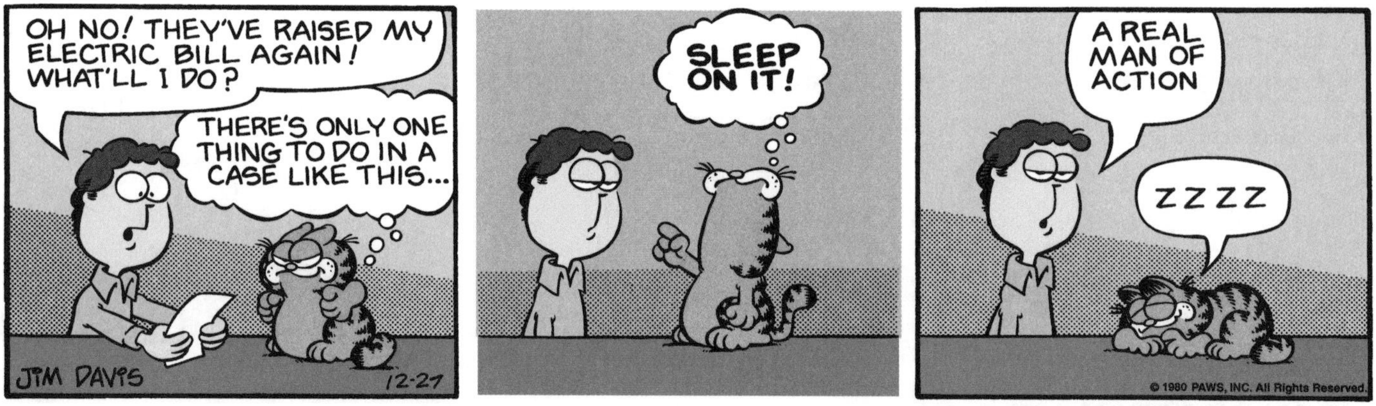
OH NO! THEY'VE RAISED MY ELECTRIC BILL AGAIN! WHAT'LL I DO?
THERE'S ONLY ONE THING TO DO IN A CASE LIKE THIS...
JIM DAVIS
12-27
SLEEP ON IT!
A REAL MAN OF ACTION
ZZZZ
© 1980 PAWS, INC. All Rights Reserved.

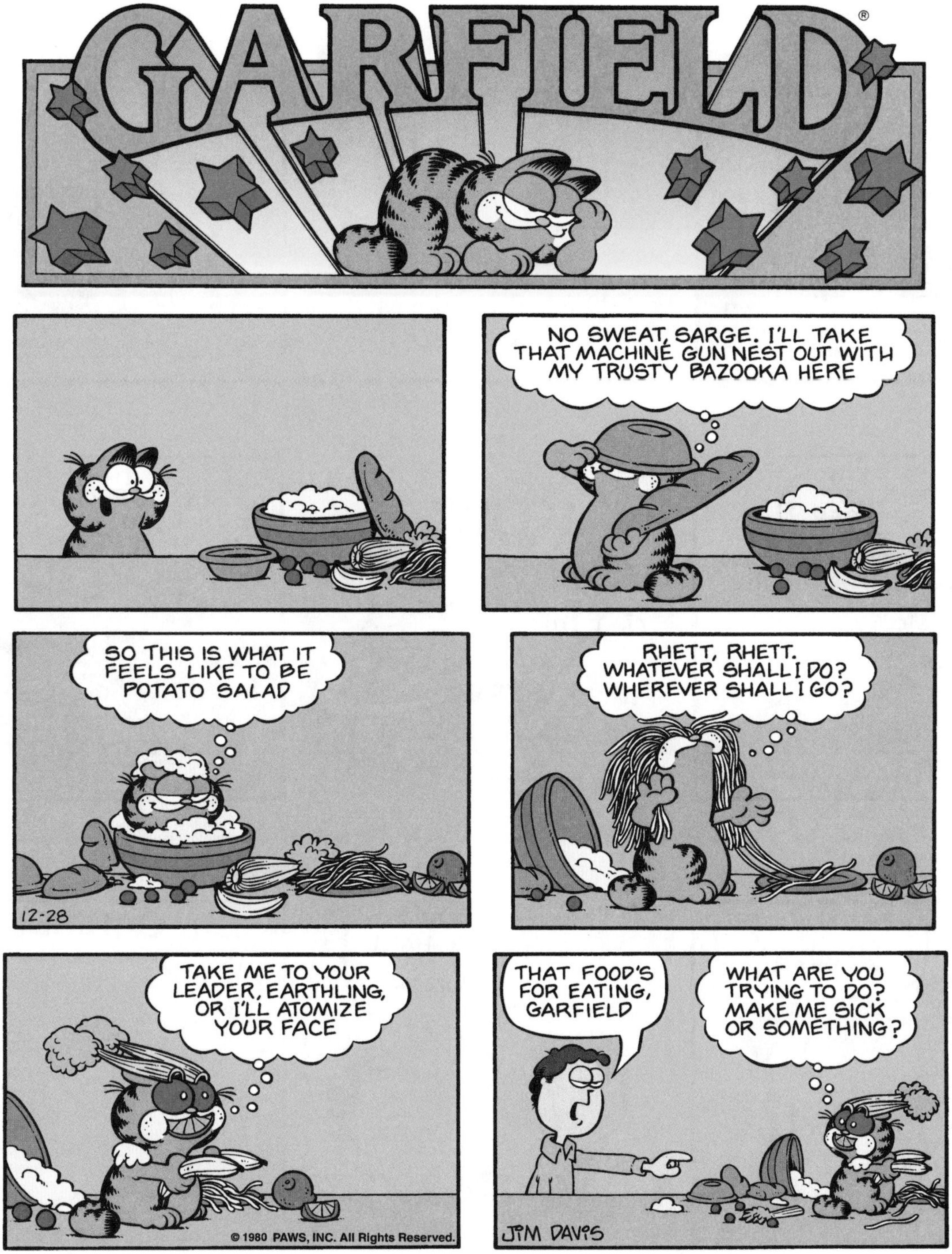
GARFIELD
NO SWEAT, SARGE. I'LL TAKE THAT MACHINE GUN NEST OUT WITH MY TRUSTY BAZOOKA HERE
SO THIS IS WHAT IT FEELS LIKE TO BE POTATO SALAD
12-28
RHETT, RHETT. WHATEVER SHALL I DO? WHEREVER SHALL I GO?
TAKE ME TO YOUR LEADER, EARTHLING, OR I'LL ATOMIZE YOUR FACE
© 1980 PAWS, INC. All Rights Reserved.
THAT FOOD'S FOR EATING, GARFIELD
WHAT ARE YOU TRYING TO DO? MAKE ME SICK OR SOMETHING?
JIM DAVIS

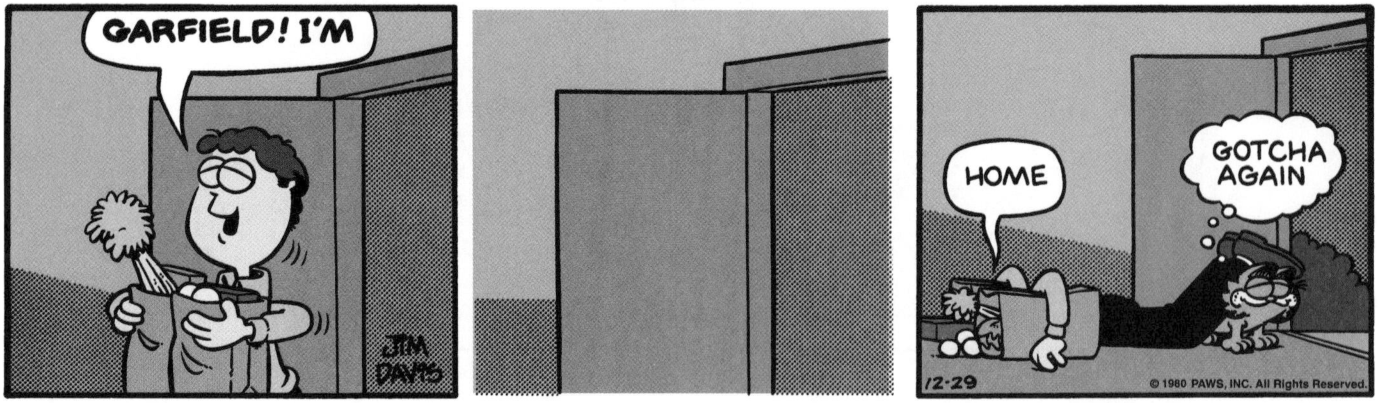
GARFIELD! I'M
HOME
GOTCHA AGAIN
JIM DAVIS
12-29
© 1980 PAWS, INC. All Rights Reserved.

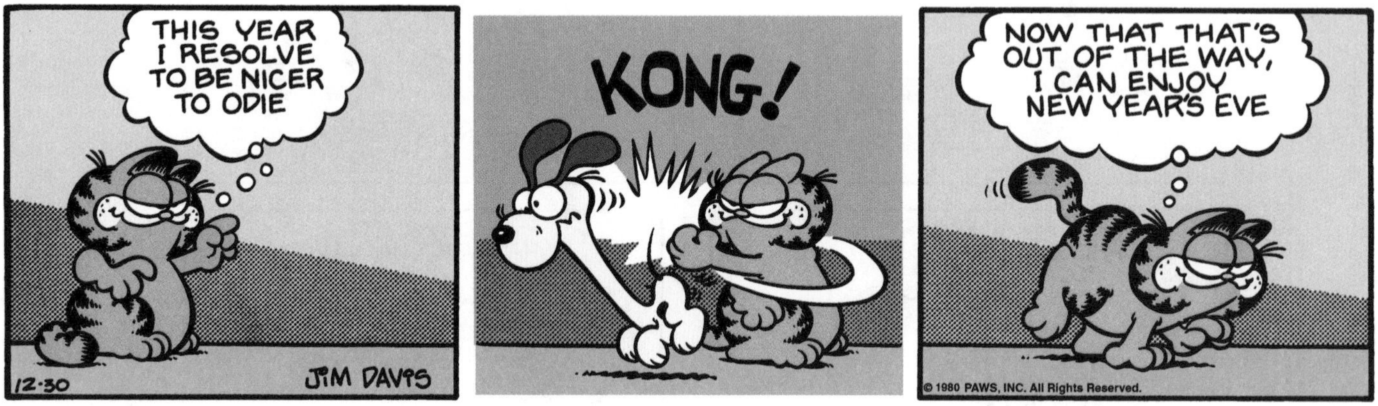
THIS YEAR I RESOLVE TO BE NICER TO ODIE
12-30
JIM DAVIS
KONG!
NOW THAT THAT'S OUT OF THE WAY, I CAN ENJOY NEW YEAR'S EVE
© 1980 PAWS, INC. All Rights Reserved.

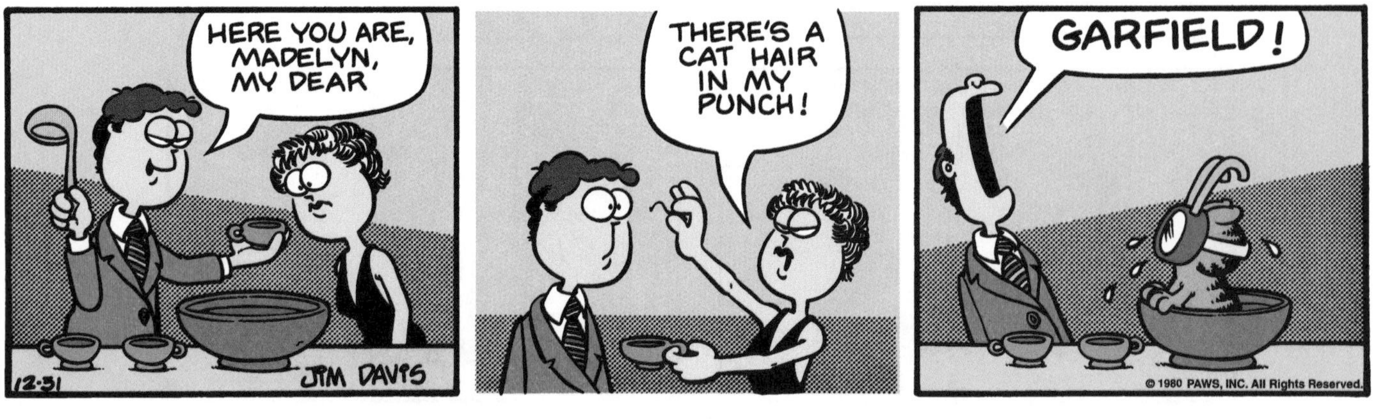
HERE YOU ARE, MADELYN, MY DEAR
12-31
JIM DAVIS
THERE'S A CAT HAIR IN MY PUNCH!
GARFIELD!
© 1980 PAWS, INC. All Rights Reserved.

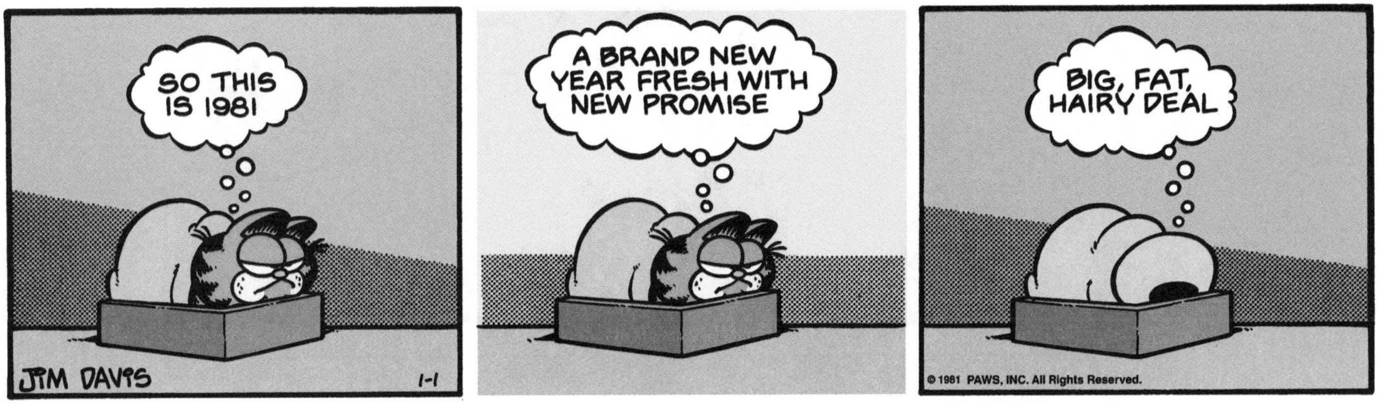
SO THIS IS 1981
A BRAND NEW YEAR FRESH WITH NEW PROMISE
BIG, FAT, HAIRY DEAL
JIM DAVIS
1-1
© 1981 PAWS, INC. All Rights Reserved.

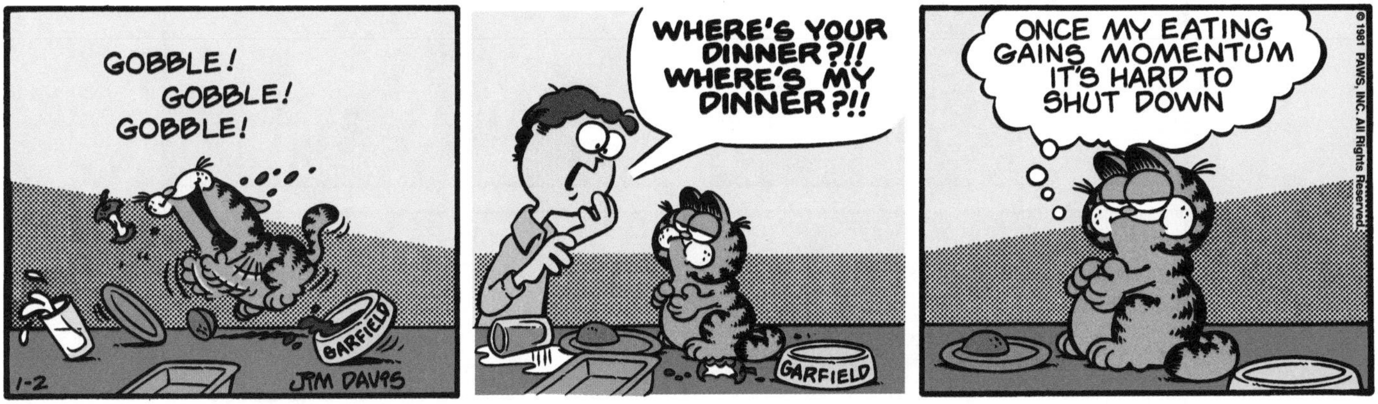
GOBBLE! GOBBLE! GOBBLE!
BARFIELD
1-2
JIM DAVIS
WHERE'S YOUR DINNER?!! WHERE'S MY DINNER?!!
GARFIELD
ONCE MY EATING GAINS MOMENTUM IT'S HARD TO SHUT DOWN
© 1981 PAWS, INC. All Rights Reserved.

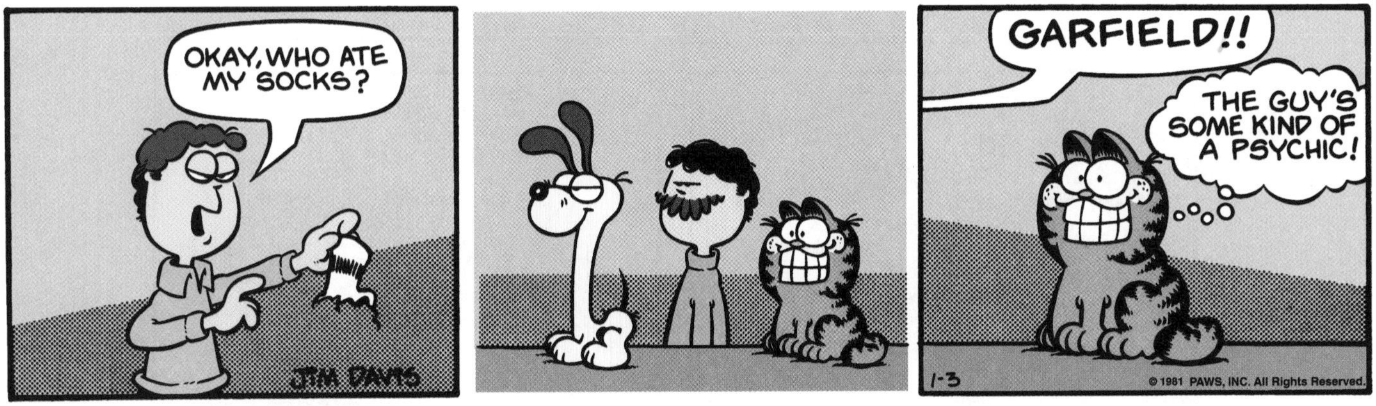
OKAY, WHO ATE MY SOCKS?
JIM DAVIS
GARFIELD!!
THE GUY'S SOME KIND OF A PSYCHIC!
1-3
© 1981 PAWS, INC. All Rights Reserved.

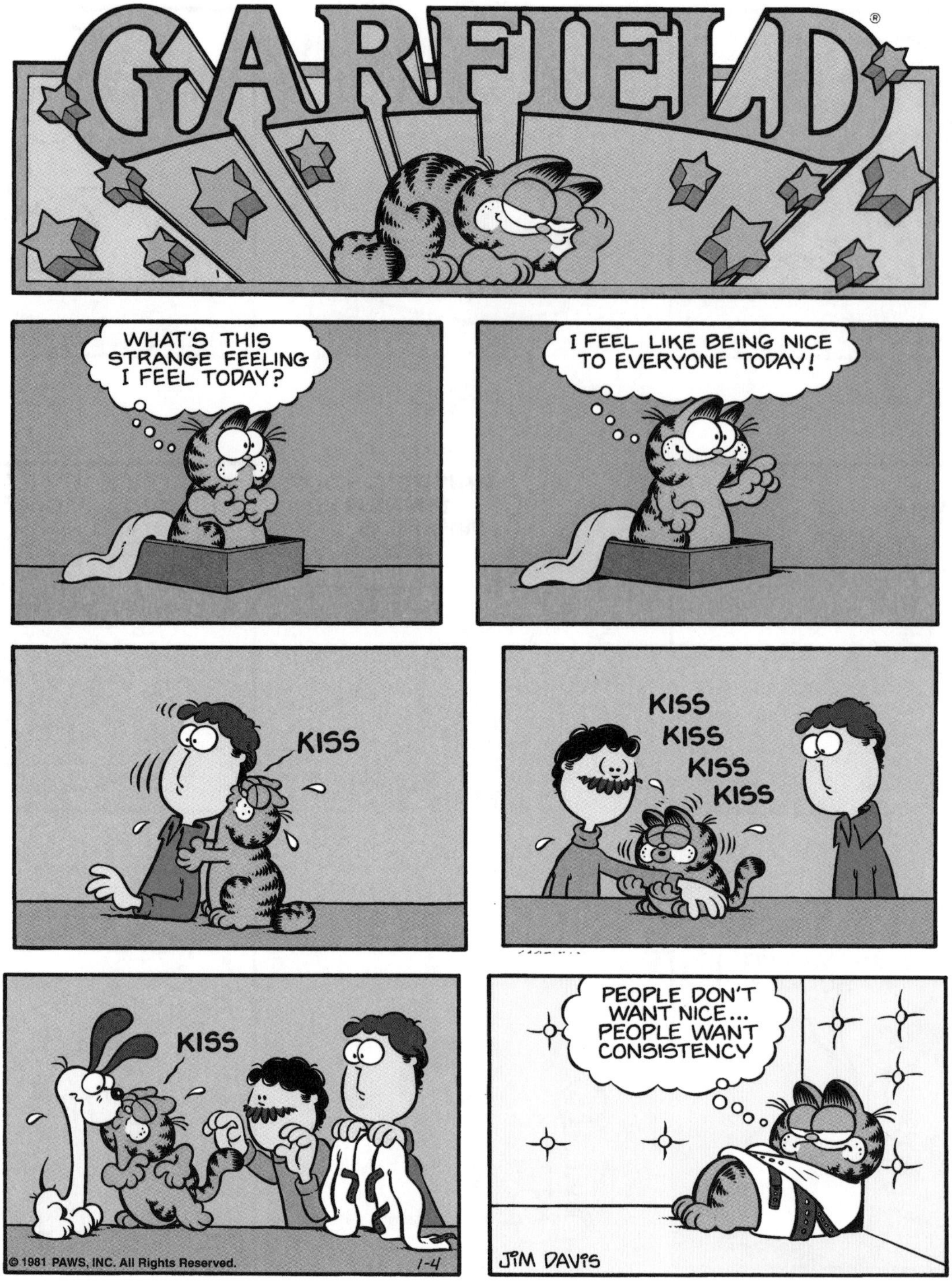
GARFIELD®
WHAT'S THIS STRANGE FEELING I FEEL TODAY?
I FEEL LIKE BEING NICE TO EVERYONE TODAY!
KISS
KISS KISS KISS KISS
KISS
PEOPLE DON'T WANT NICE... PEOPLE WANT CONSISTENCY
© 1981 PAWS, INC. All Rights Reserved.
1-4
JIM DAVIS

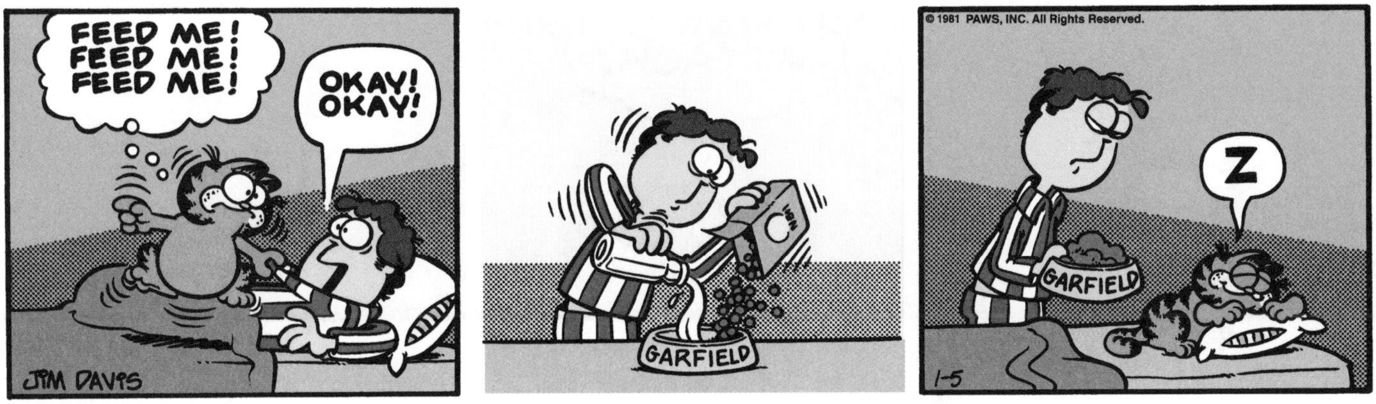
FEED ME! FEED ME! FEED ME!
OKAY! OKAY!
GARFIELD
© 1981 PAWS, INC. All Rights Reserved.
GARFIELD
Z
JIM DAVIS
1-5

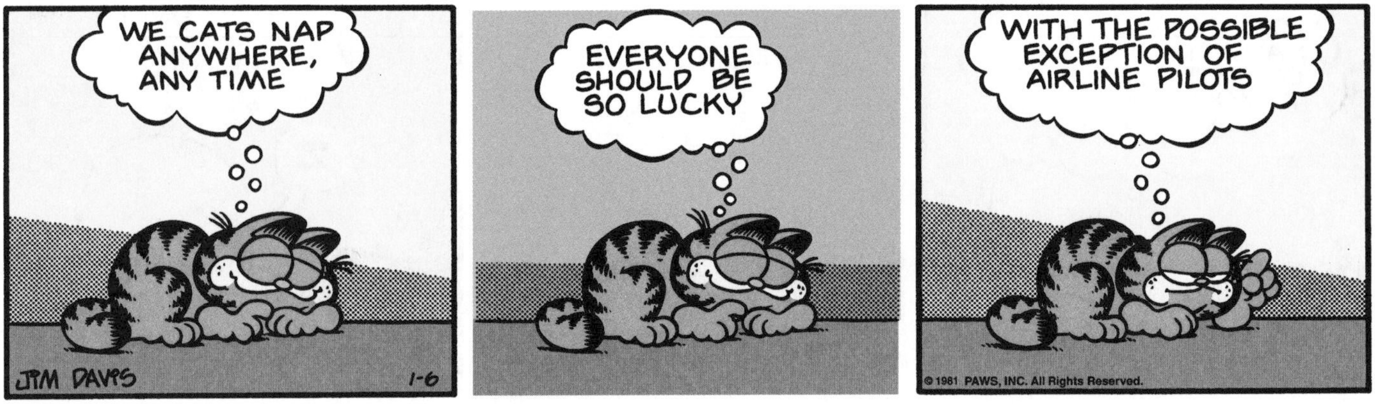
WE CATS NAP ANYWHERE, ANY TIME
EVERYONE SHOULD BE SO LUCKY
WITH THE POSSIBLE EXCEPTION OF AIRLINE PILOTS
JIM DAVIS
1-6
© 1981 PAWS, INC. All Rights Reserved.

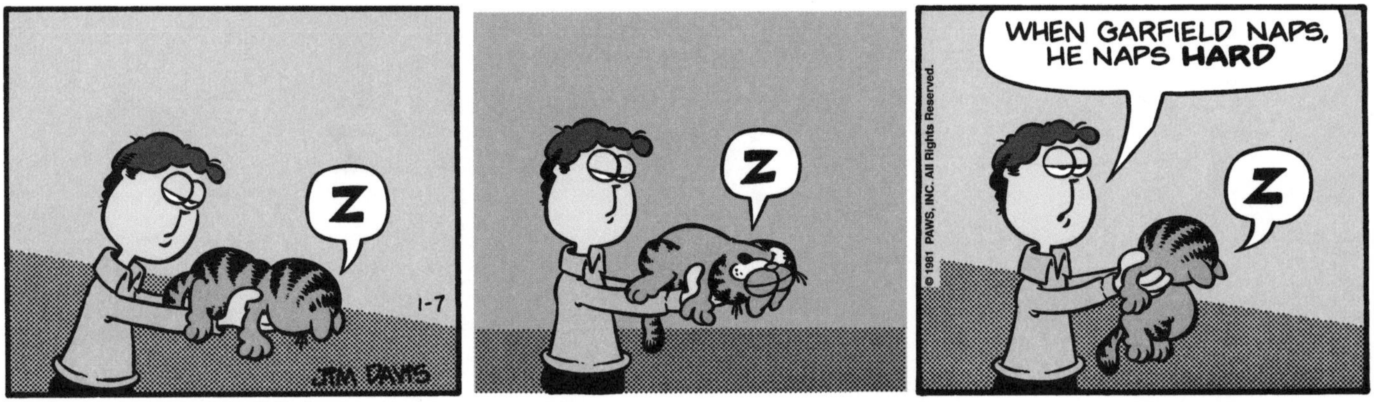
Z
1-7
JIM DAVIS
Z
© 1981 PAWS, INC. All Rights Reserved.
WHEN GARFIELD NAPS, HE NAPS **HARD**
Z

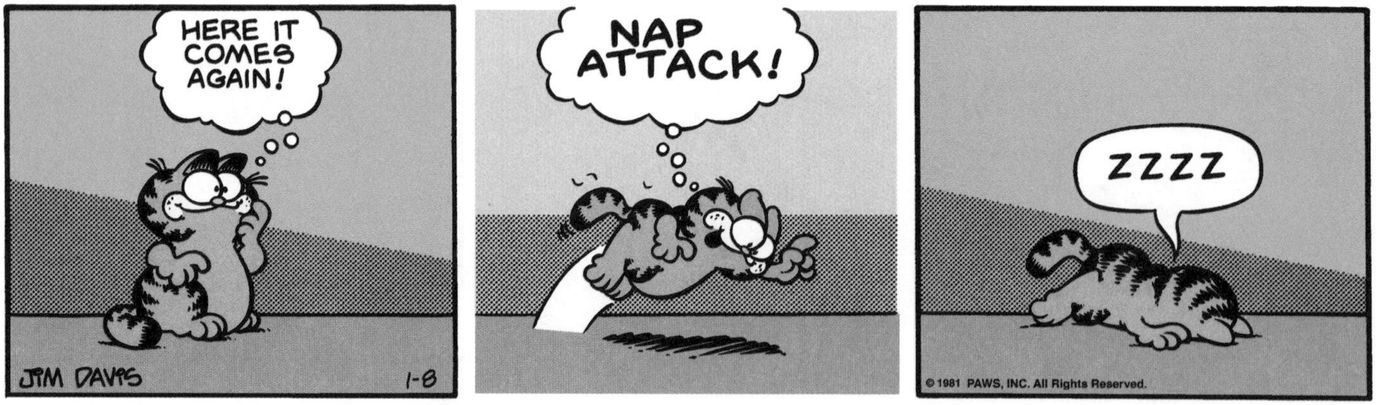
HERE IT COMES AGAIN!
JIM DAVIS
1-8
NAP ATTACK!
ZZZZ
© 1981 PAWS, INC. All Rights Reserved.

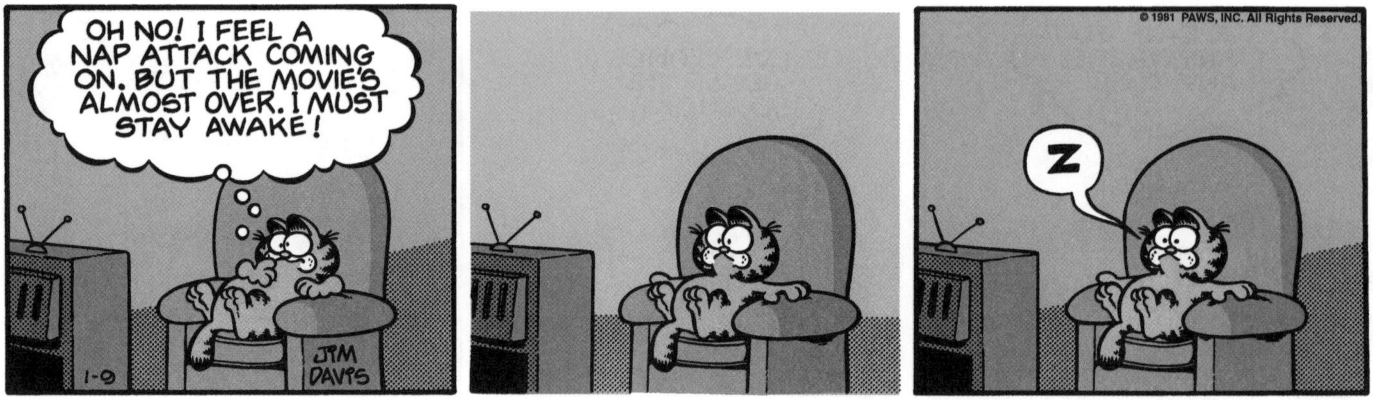
OH NO! I FEEL A NAP ATTACK COMING ON. BUT THE MOVIE'S ALMOST OVER. I MUST STAY AWAKE!
1-9
JIM DAVIS
© 1981 PAWS, INC. All Rights Reserved.
Z

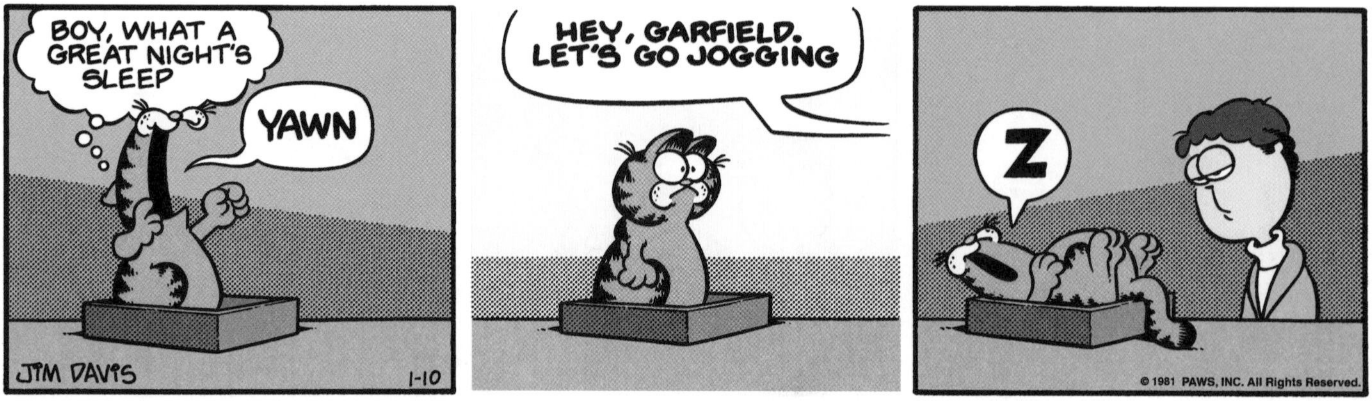
BOY, WHAT A GREAT NIGHT'S SLEEP
YAWN
JIM DAVIS
1-10
HEY, GARFIELD. LET'S GO JOGGING
Z
© 1981 PAWS, INC. All Rights Reserved.

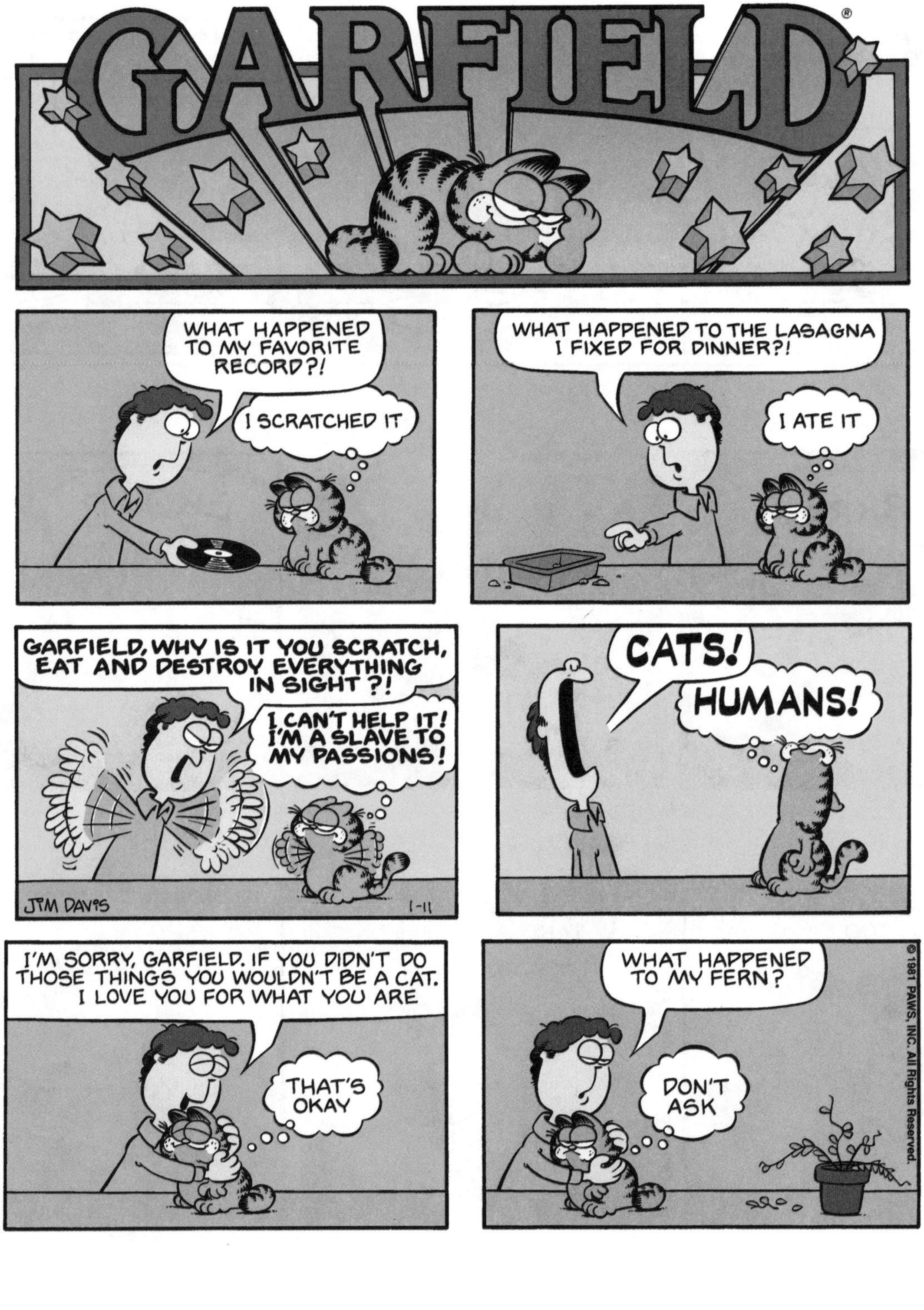
GARFIELD®
WHAT HAPPENED TO MY FAVORITE RECORD?!
I SCRATCHED IT
WHAT HAPPENED TO THE LASAGNA I FIXED FOR DINNER?!
I ATE IT
GARFIELD, WHY IS IT YOU SCRATCH, EAT AND DESTROY EVERYTHING IN SIGHT?!
I CAN'T HELP IT! I'M A SLAVE TO MY PASSIONS!
JIM DAVIS
1-11
CATS!
HUMANS!
I'M SORRY, GARFIELD. IF YOU DIDN'T DO THOSE THINGS YOU WOULDN'T BE A CAT. I LOVE YOU FOR WHAT YOU ARE
THAT'S OKAY
WHAT HAPPENED TO MY FERN?
DON'T ASK

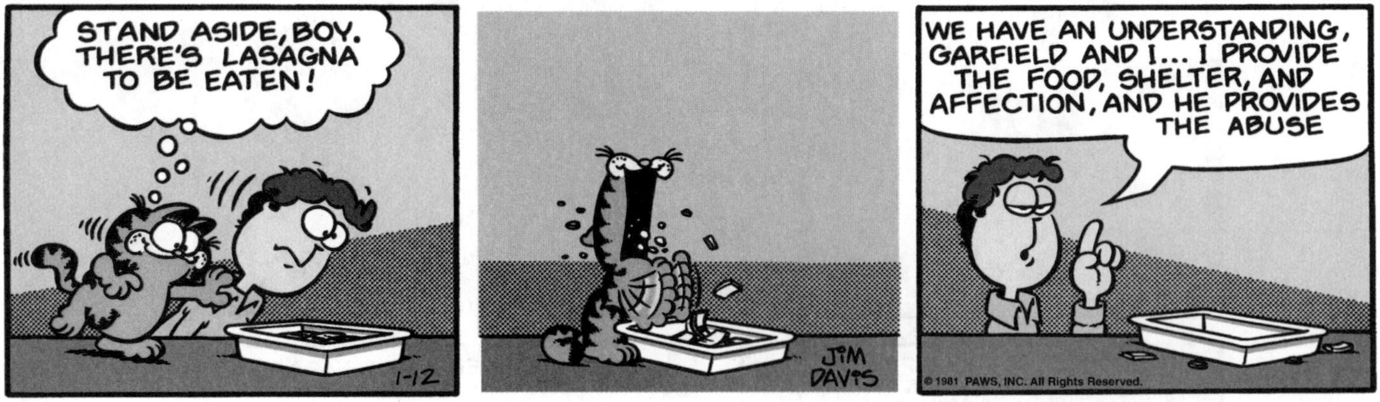
STAND ASIDE, BOY. THERE'S LASAGNA TO BE EATEN!
1-12
JIM DAVIS
WE HAVE AN UNDERSTANDING, GARFIELD AND I... I PROVIDE THE FOOD, SHELTER, AND AFFECTION, AND HE PROVIDES THE ABUSE
© 1981 PAWS, INC. All Rights Reserved.

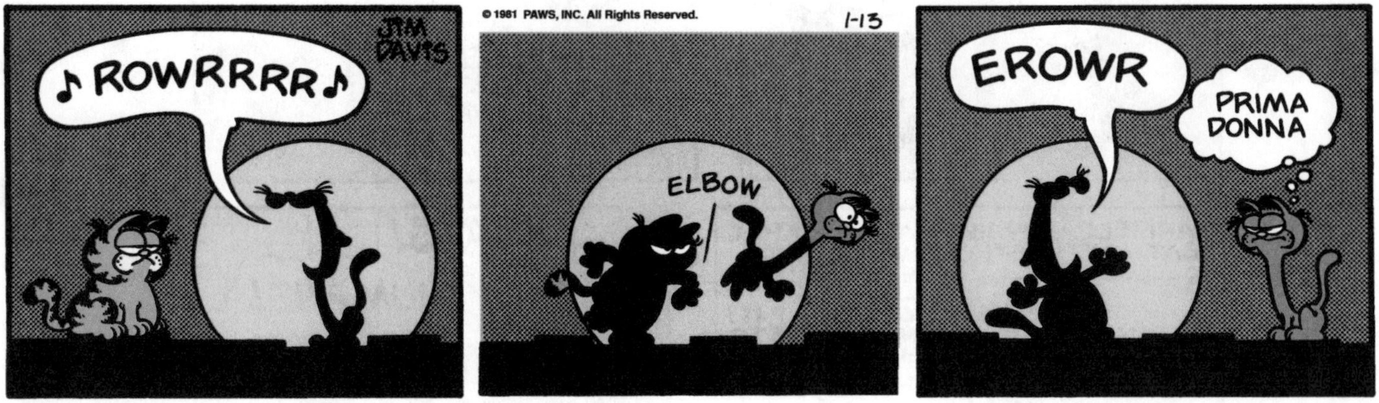
JIM DAVIS
♪ ROWRRRR ♪
© 1981 PAWS, INC. All Rights Reserved.
1-13
ELBOW
EROWR
PRIMA DONNA

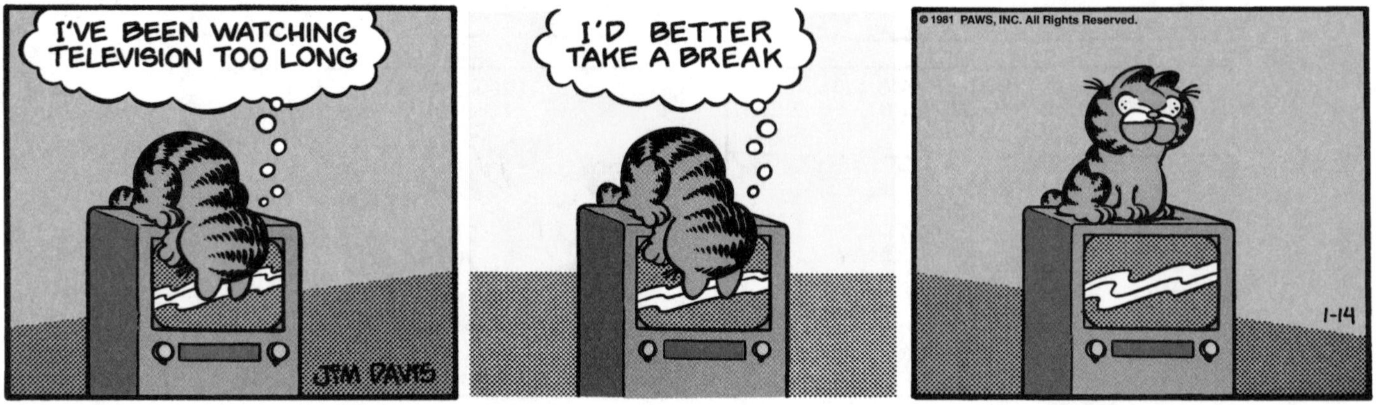
I'VE BEEN WATCHING TELEVISION TOO LONG
JIM DAVIS
I'D BETTER TAKE A BREAK
© 1981 PAWS, INC. All Rights Reserved.
1-14

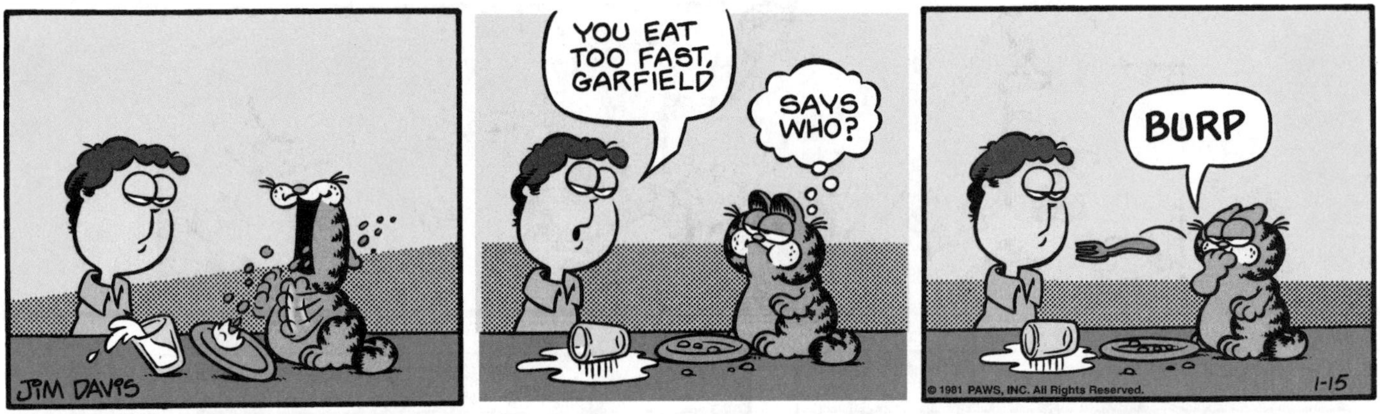
JIM DAVIS
YOU EAT TOO FAST, GARFIELD
SAYS WHO?
BURP
© 1981 PAWS, INC. All Rights Reserved.
1-15

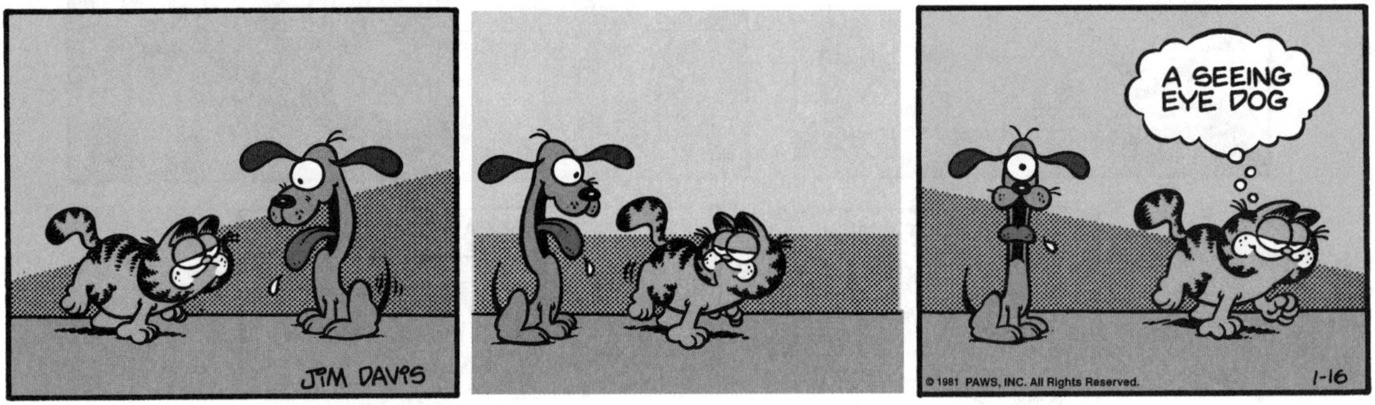
JIM DAVIS
A SEEING EYE DOG
© 1981 PAWS, INC. All Rights Reserved.
1-16

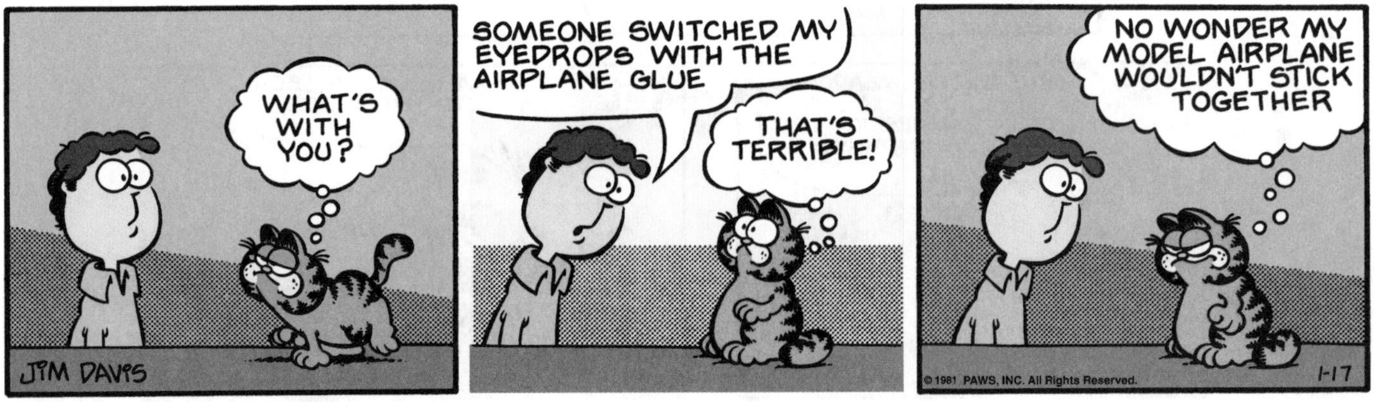
JIM DAVIS
WHAT'S WITH YOU?
SOMEONE SWITCHED MY EYEDROPS WITH THE AIRPLANE GLUE
THAT'S TERRIBLE!
NO WONDER MY MODEL AIRPLANE WOULDN'T STICK TOGETHER
© 1981 PAWS, INC. All Rights Reserved.
1-17

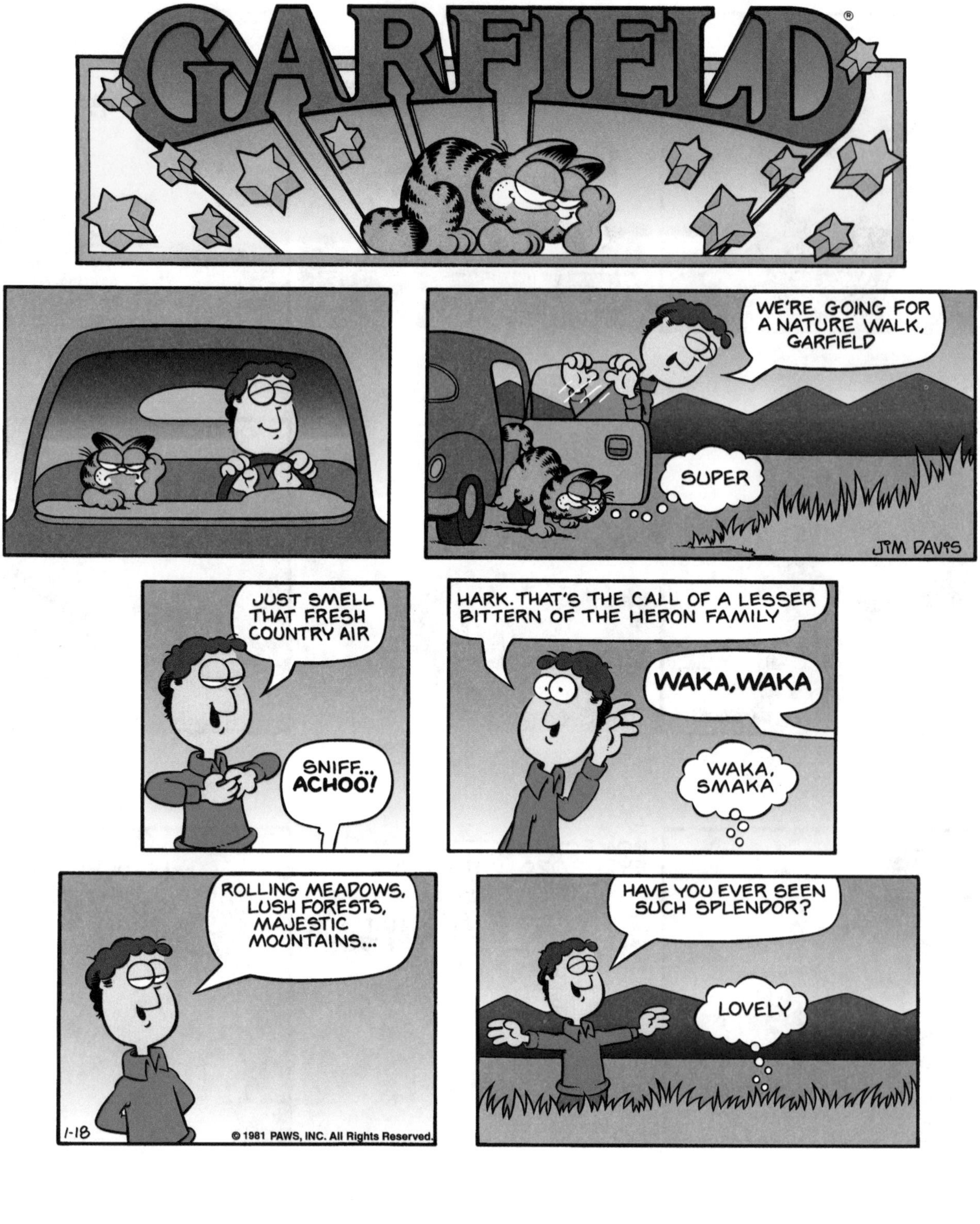
GARFIELD
WE'RE GOING FOR A NATURE WALK, GARFIELD
SUPER
JIM DAVIS
JUST SMELL THAT FRESH COUNTRY AIR
SNIFF... ACHOO!
HARK. THAT'S THE CALL OF A LESSER BITTERN OF THE HERON FAMILY
WAKA, WAKA
WAKA, SMAKA
ROLLING MEADOWS, LUSH FORESTS, MAJESTIC MOUNTAINS...
1-18
© 1981 PAWS, INC. All Rights Reserved.
HAVE YOU EVER SEEN SUCH SPLENDOR?
LOVELY

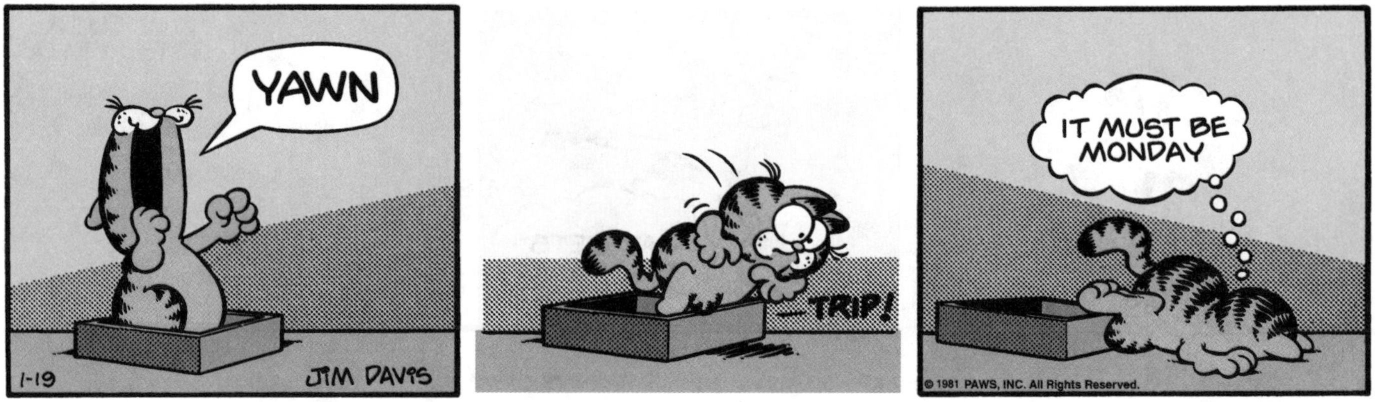
YAWN
1-19
JIM DAVIS
TRIP!
IT MUST BE MONDAY
© 1981 PAWS, INC. All Rights Reserved.

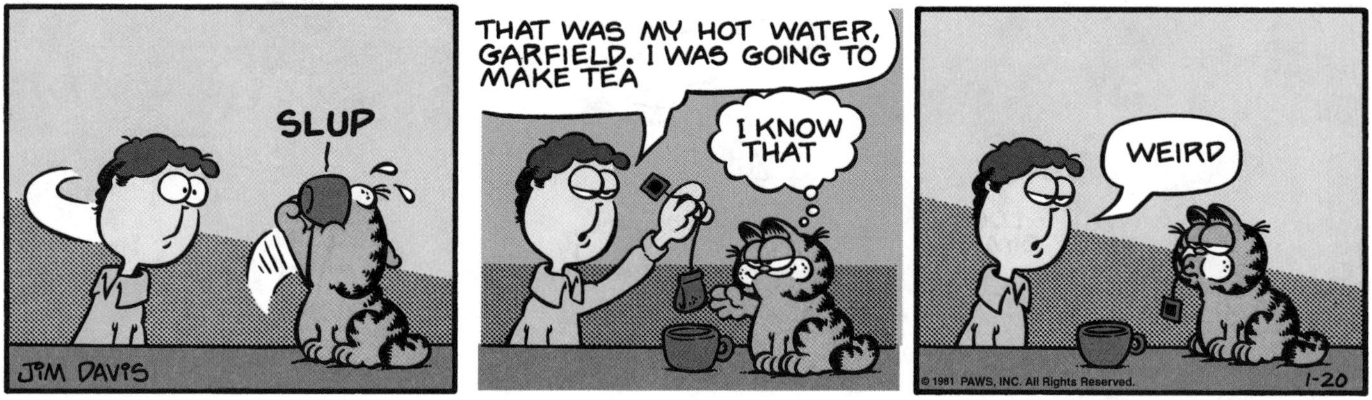
SLUP
JIM DAVIS
THAT WAS MY HOT WATER, GARFIELD. I WAS GOING TO MAKE TEA
I KNOW THAT
WEIRD
© 1981 PAWS, INC. All Rights Reserved.
1-20

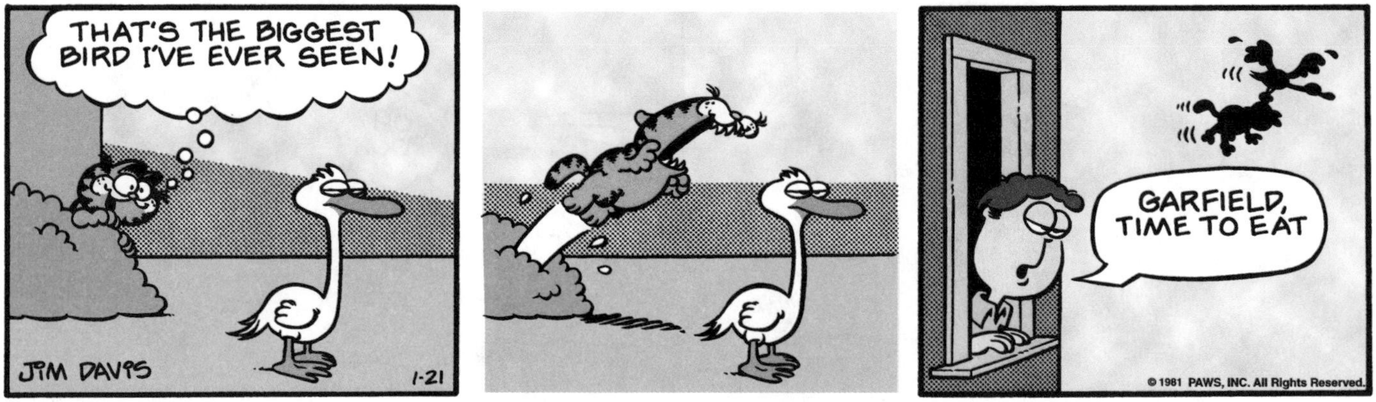
THAT'S THE BIGGEST BIRD I'VE EVER SEEN!
JIM DAVIS
1-21
GARFIELD, TIME TO EAT
© 1981 PAWS, INC. All Rights Reserved.

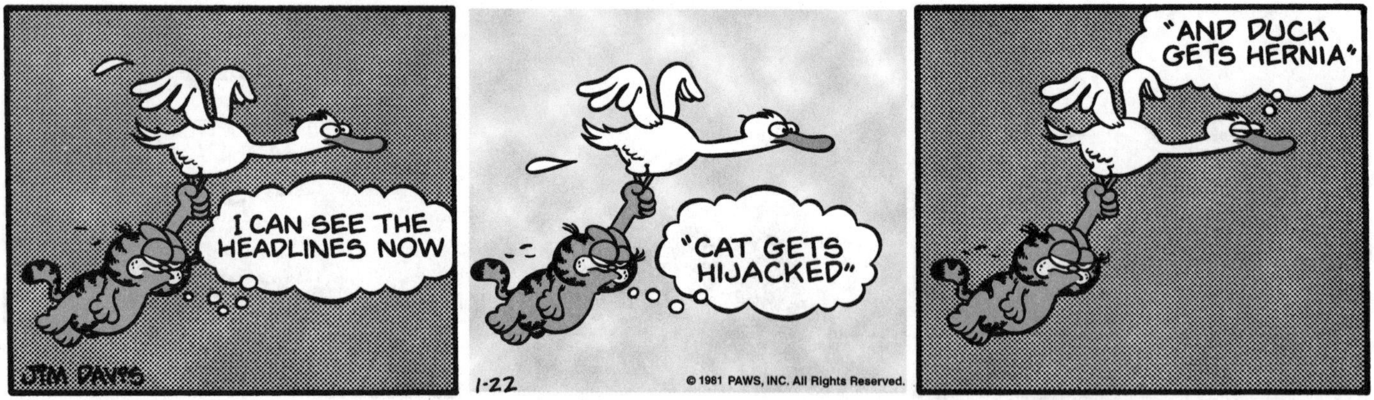
I CAN SEE THE HEADLINES NOW
JIM DAVIS
"CAT GETS HIJACKED"
1-22
© 1981 PAWS, INC. All Rights Reserved.
"AND DUCK GETS HERNIA"

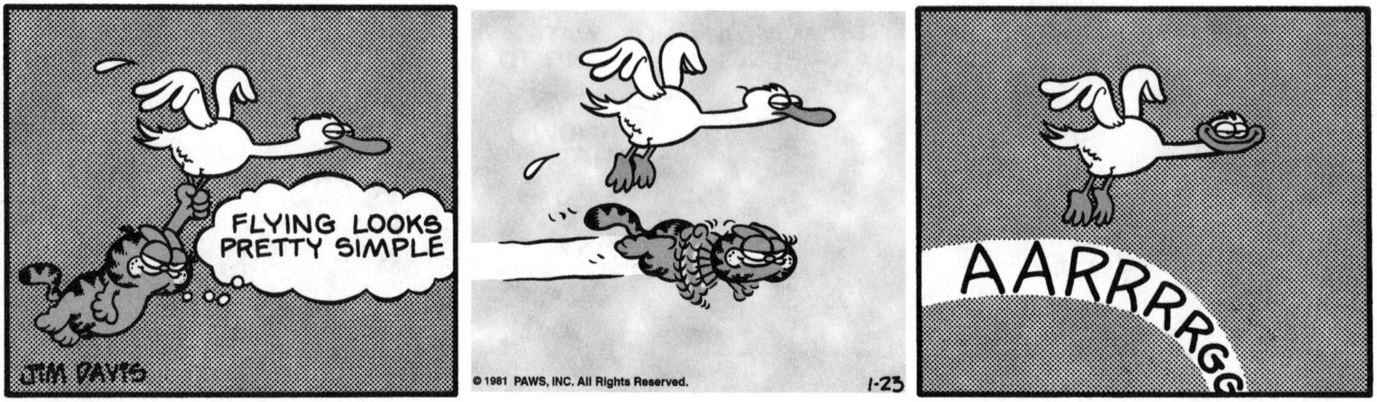
FLYING LOOKS PRETTY SIMPLE
JIM DAVIS
© 1981 PAWS, INC. All Rights Reserved.
1-23
AARRRRRG

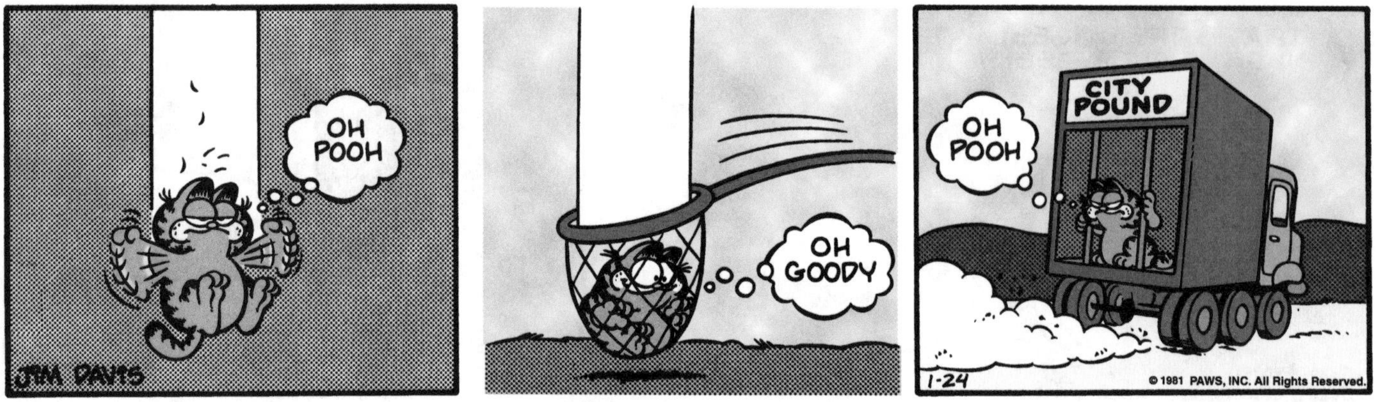
OH POOH
JIM DAVIS
OH GOODY
CITY POUND
OH POOH
1-24
© 1981 PAWS, INC. All Rights Reserved.

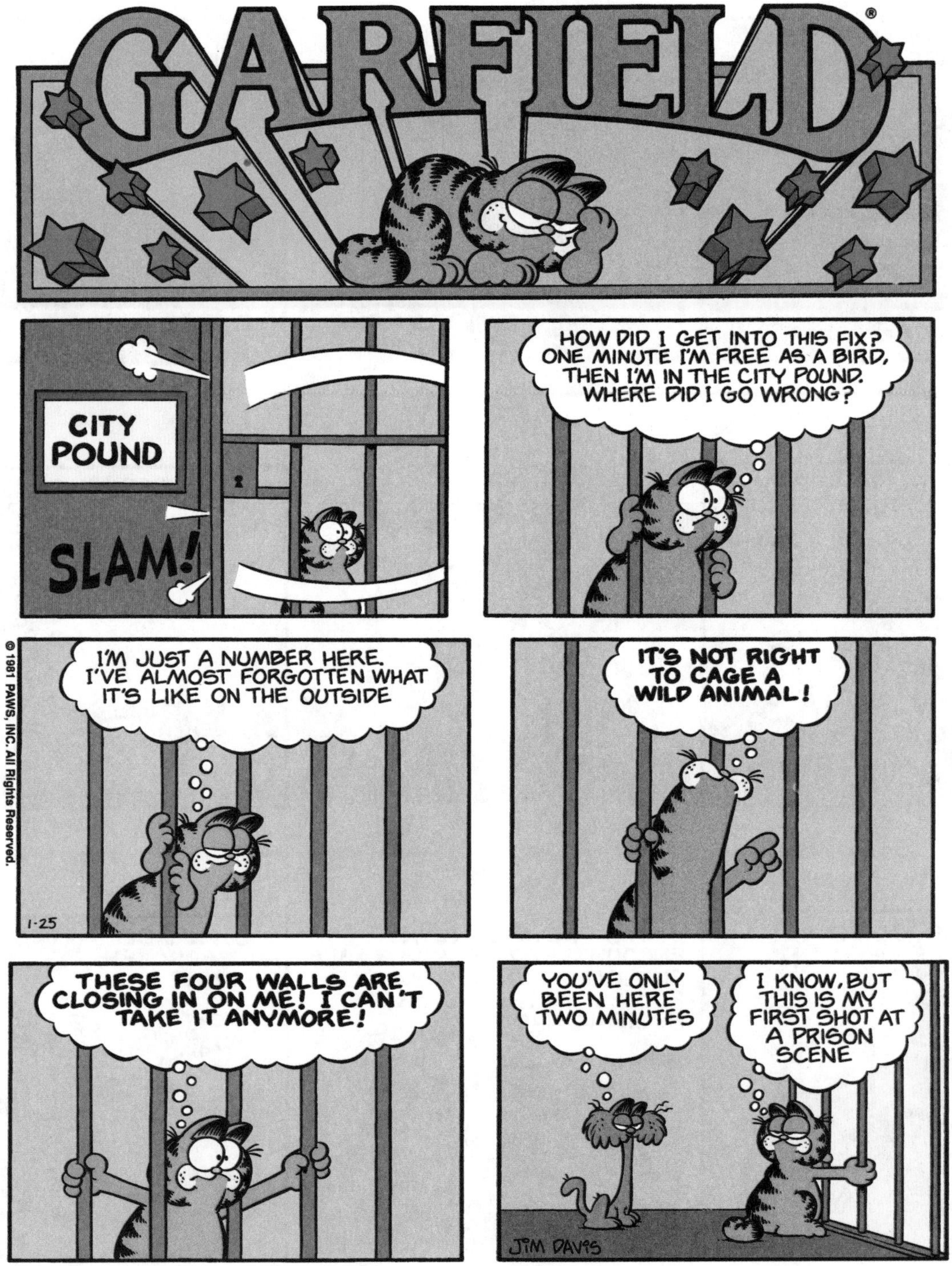
GARFIELD
CITY POUND
SLAM!
HOW DID I GET INTO THIS FIX? ONE MINUTE I'M FREE AS A BIRD, THEN I'M IN THE CITY POUND. WHERE DID I GO WRONG?
I'M JUST A NUMBER HERE. I'VE ALMOST FORGOTTEN WHAT IT'S LIKE ON THE OUTSIDE
IT'S NOT RIGHT TO CAGE A WILD ANIMAL!
THESE FOUR WALLS ARE CLOSING IN ON ME! I CAN'T TAKE IT ANYMORE!
YOU'VE ONLY BEEN HERE TWO MINUTES
I KNOW, BUT THIS IS MY FIRST SHOT AT A PRISON SCENE
1-25
JIM DAVIS

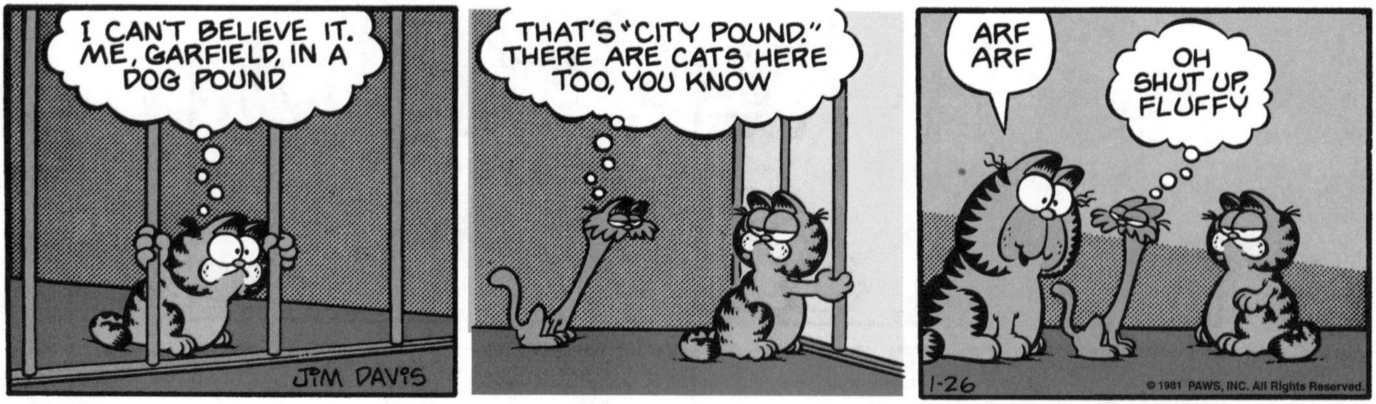
I CAN'T BELIEVE IT. ME, GARFIELD, IN A DOG POUND
JIM DAVIS
THAT'S "CITY POUND." THERE ARE CATS HERE TOO, YOU KNOW
ARF ARF
OH SHUT UP, FLUFFY
1-26
© 1981 PAWS, INC. All Rights Reserved.

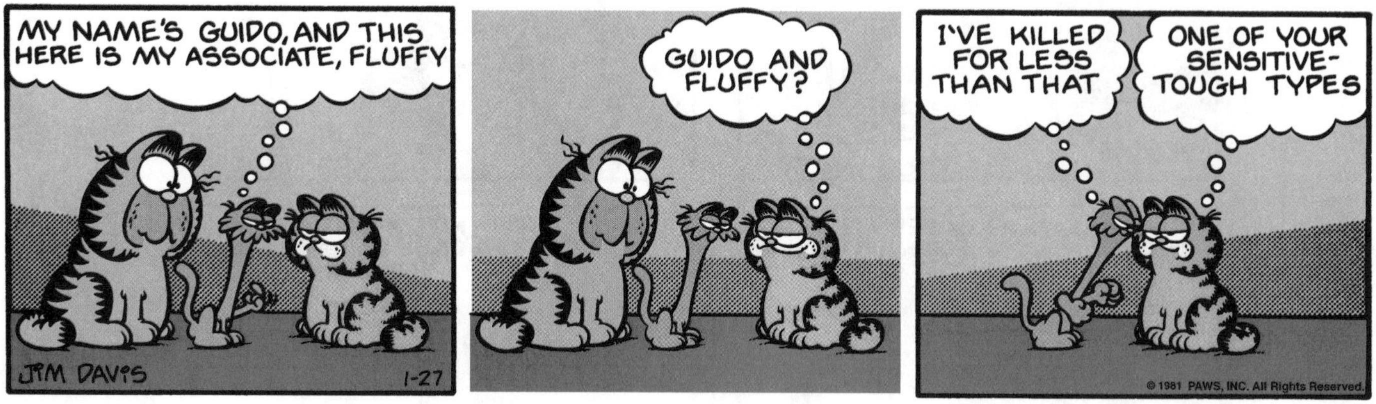
MY NAME'S GUIDO, AND THIS HERE IS MY ASSOCIATE, FLUFFY
JIM DAVIS
1-27
GUIDO AND FLUFFY?
I'VE KILLED FOR LESS THAN THAT
ONE OF YOUR SENSITIVE-TOUGH TYPES
© 1981 PAWS, INC. All Rights Reserved.

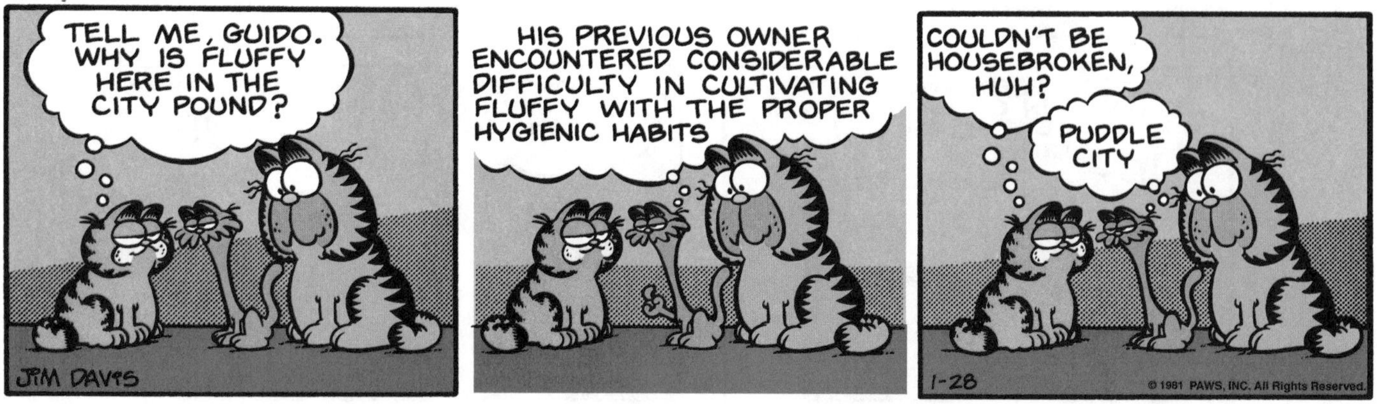
TELL ME, GUIDO. WHY IS FLUFFY HERE IN THE CITY POUND?
JIM DAVIS
HIS PREVIOUS OWNER ENCOUNTERED CONSIDERABLE DIFFICULTY IN CULTIVATING FLUFFY WITH THE PROPER HYGIENIC HABITS
COULDN'T BE HOUSEBROKEN, HUH?
PUDDLE CITY
1-28
© 1981 PAWS, INC. All Rights Reserved.

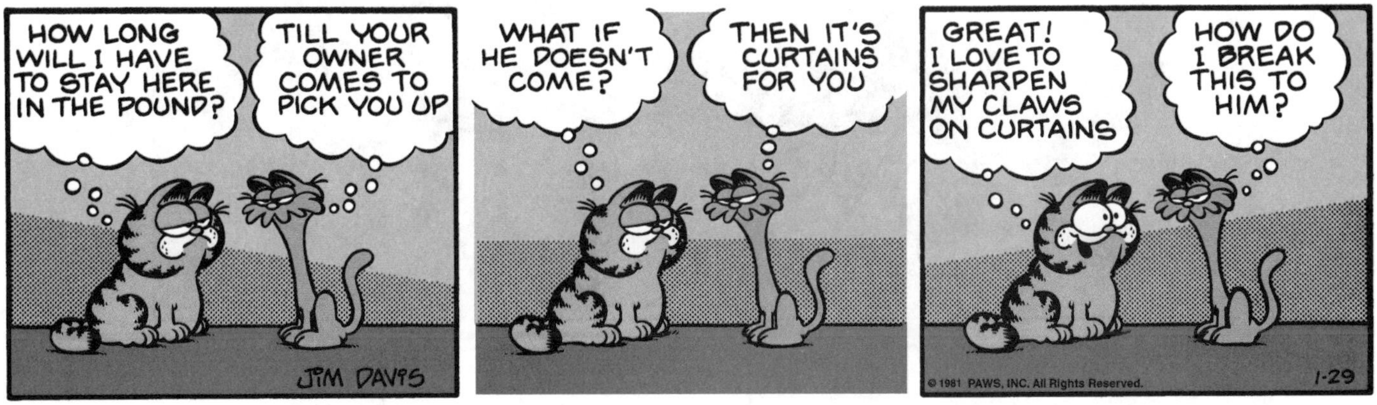
HOW LONG WILL I HAVE TO STAY HERE IN THE POUND?
TILL YOUR OWNER COMES TO PICK YOU UP
WHAT IF HE DOESN'T COME?
THEN IT'S CURTAINS FOR YOU
GREAT! I LOVE TO SHARPEN MY CLAWS ON CURTAINS
HOW DO I BREAK THIS TO HIM?
JIM DAVIS
© 1981 PAWS, INC. All Rights Reserved.
1-29

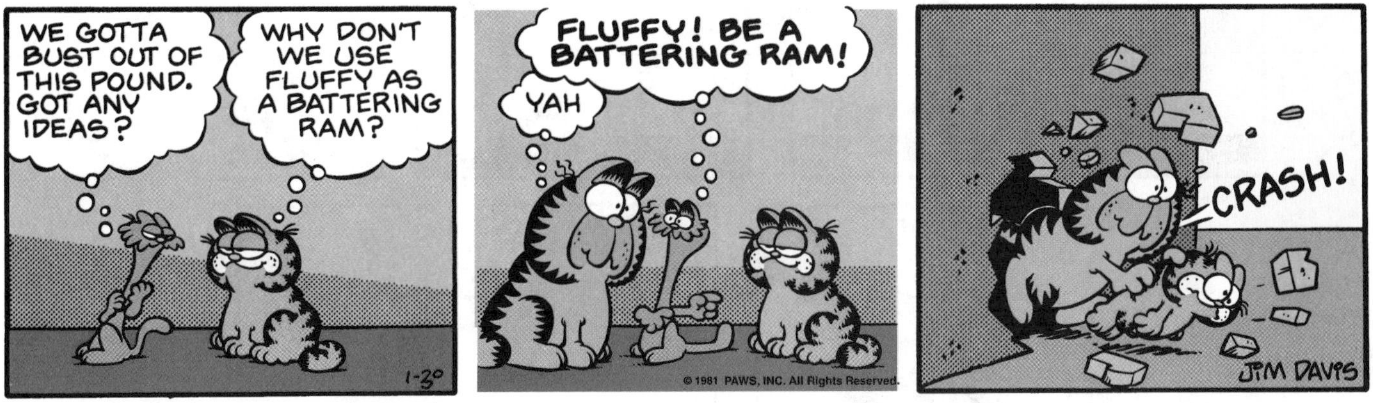
WE GOTTA BUST OUT OF THIS POUND. GOT ANY IDEAS?
WHY DON'T WE USE FLUFFY AS A BATTERING RAM?
1-30
FLUFFY! BE A BATTERING RAM!
YAH
© 1981 PAWS, INC. All Rights Reserved.
CRASH!
JIM DAVIS

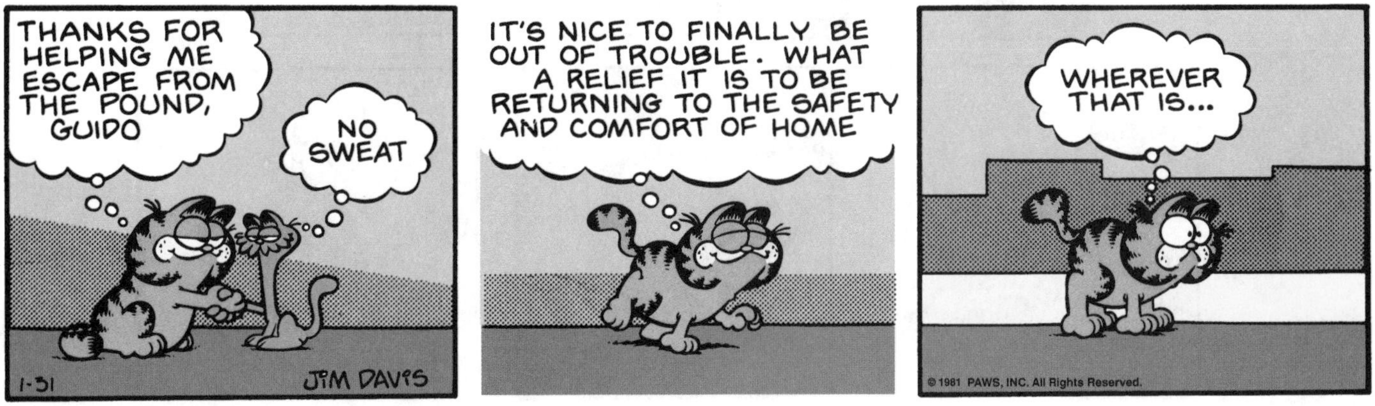
THANKS FOR HELPING ME ESCAPE FROM THE POUND, GUIDO
NO SWEAT
1-31
JIM DAVIS
IT'S NICE TO FINALLY BE OUT OF TROUBLE. WHAT A RELIEF IT IS TO BE RETURNING TO THE SAFETY AND COMFORT OF HOME
WHEREVER THAT IS...
© 1981 PAWS, INC. All Rights Reserved.

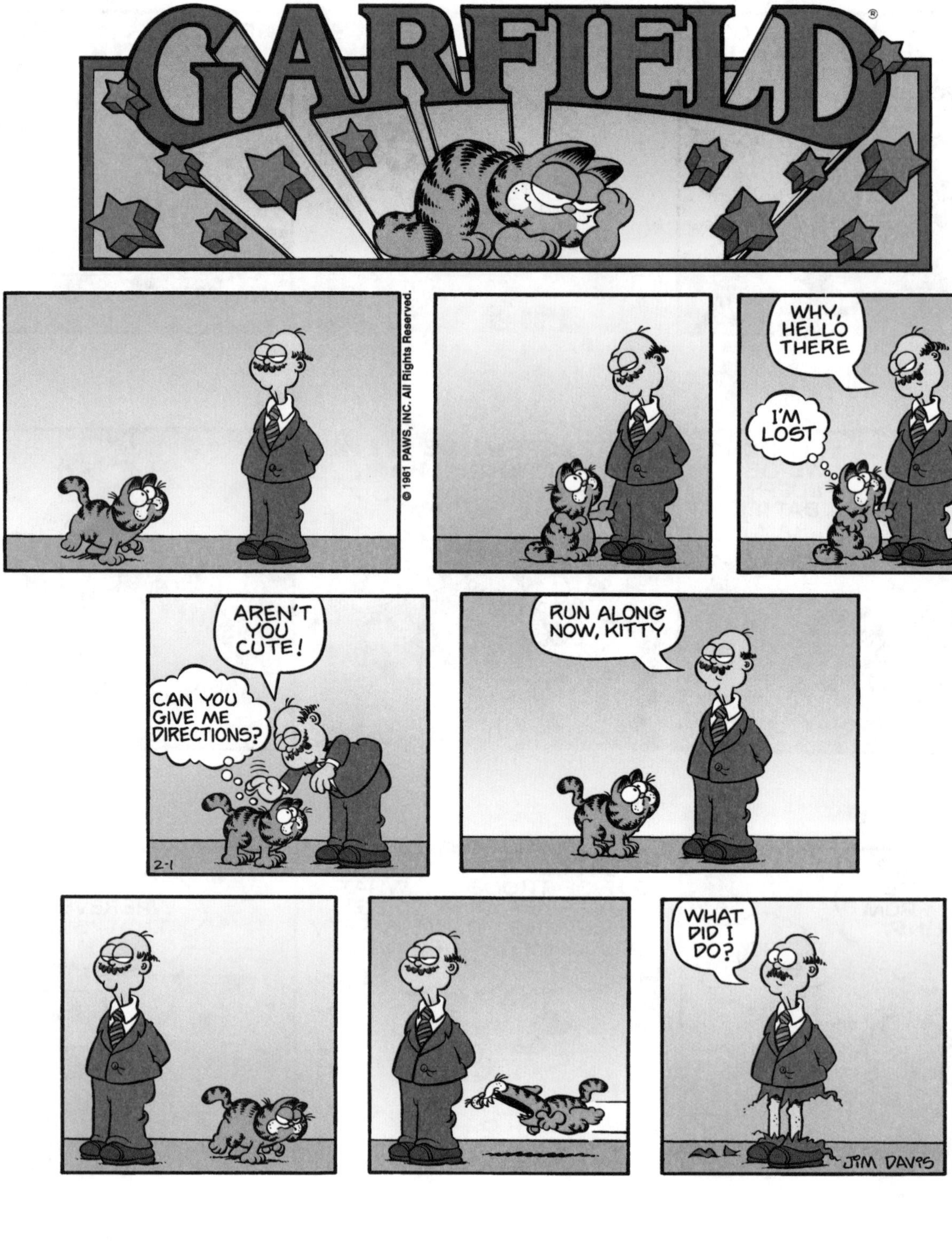
GARFIELD®
© 1981 PAWS, INC. All Rights Reserved.
WHY, HELLO THERE
I'M LOST
AREN'T YOU CUTE!
CAN YOU GIVE ME DIRECTIONS?
2-1
RUN ALONG NOW, KITTY
WHAT DID I DO?
JIM DAVIS

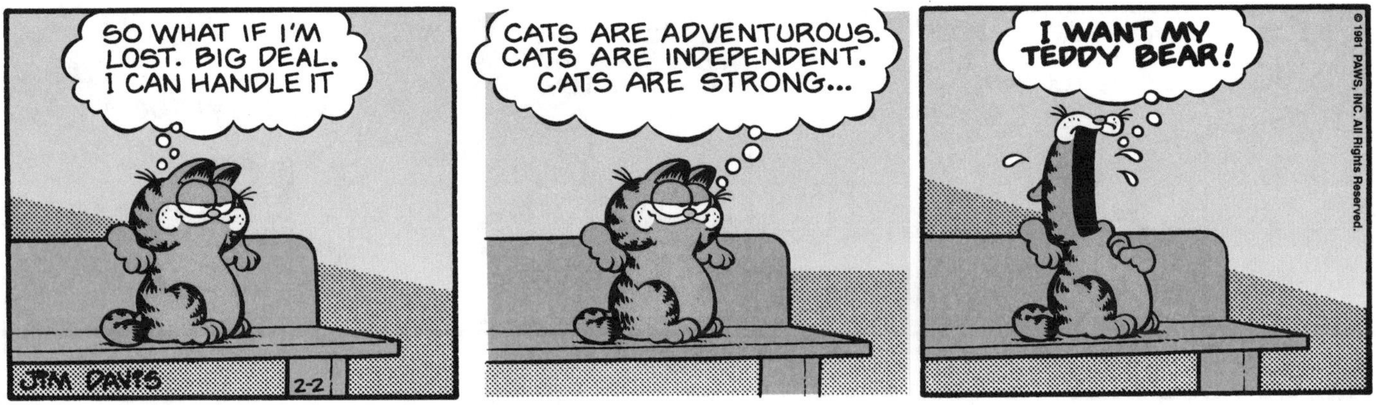
SO WHAT IF I'M LOST. BIG DEAL. I CAN HANDLE IT
JIM DAVIS
2-2
CATS ARE ADVENTUROUS. CATS ARE INDEPENDENT. CATS ARE STRONG...
I WANT MY TEDDY BEAR!
© 1981 PAWS, INC. All Rights Reserved.

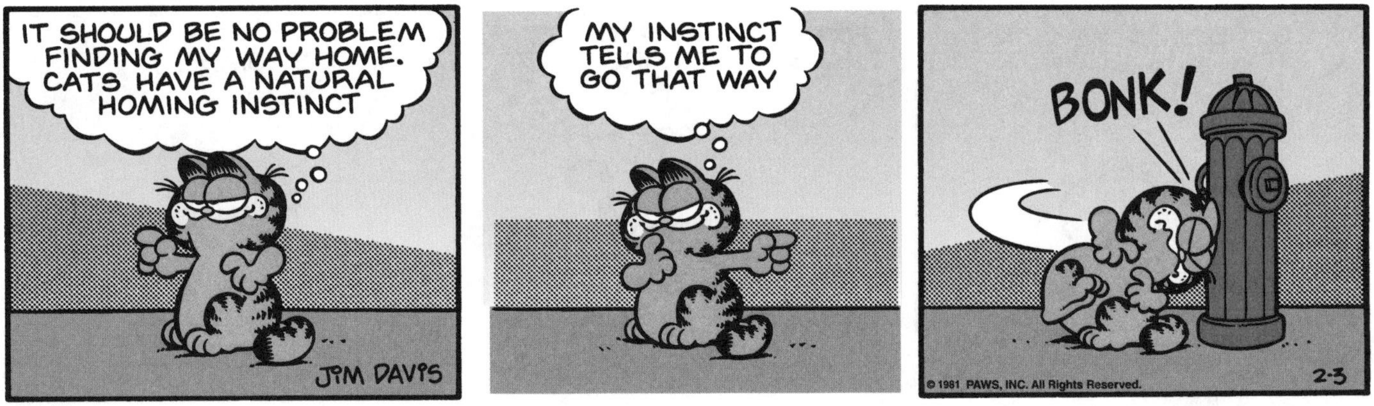
IT SHOULD BE NO PROBLEM FINDING MY WAY HOME. CATS HAVE A NATURAL HOMING INSTINCT
JIM DAVIS
MY INSTINCT TELLS ME TO GO THAT WAY
BONK!
© 1981 PAWS, INC. All Rights Reserved.
2-3

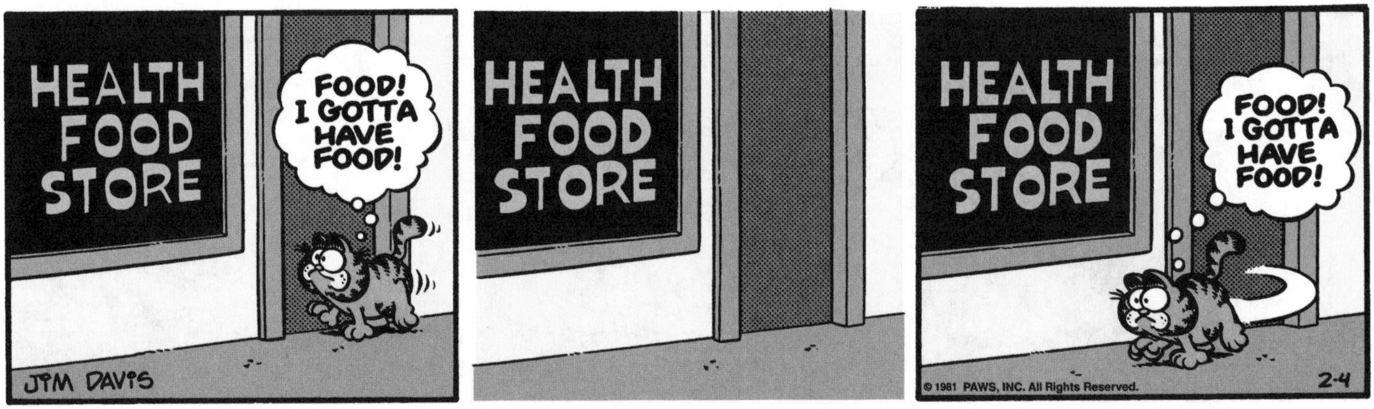
HEALTH FOOD STORE
FOOD! I GOTTA HAVE FOOD!
JIM DAVIS
HEALTH FOOD STORE
HEALTH FOOD STORE
FOOD! I GOTTA HAVE FOOD!
© 1981 PAWS, INC. All Rights Reserved.
2-4

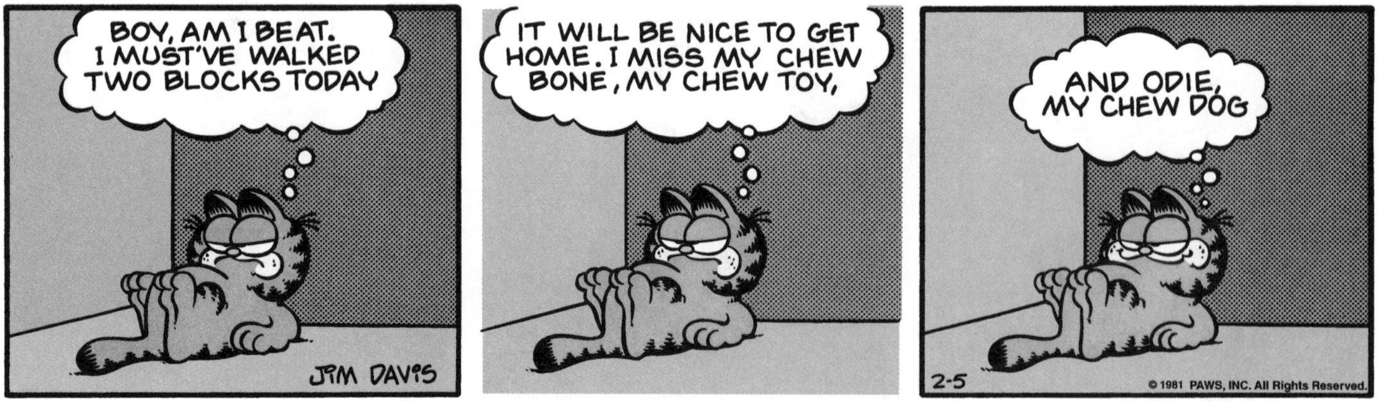
BOY, AM I BEAT. I MUST'VE WALKED TWO BLOCKS TODAY
JIM DAVIS
IT WILL BE NICE TO GET HOME. I MISS MY CHEW BONE, MY CHEW TOY,
AND ODIE, MY CHEW DOG
2-5
© 1981 PAWS, INC. All Rights Reserved.

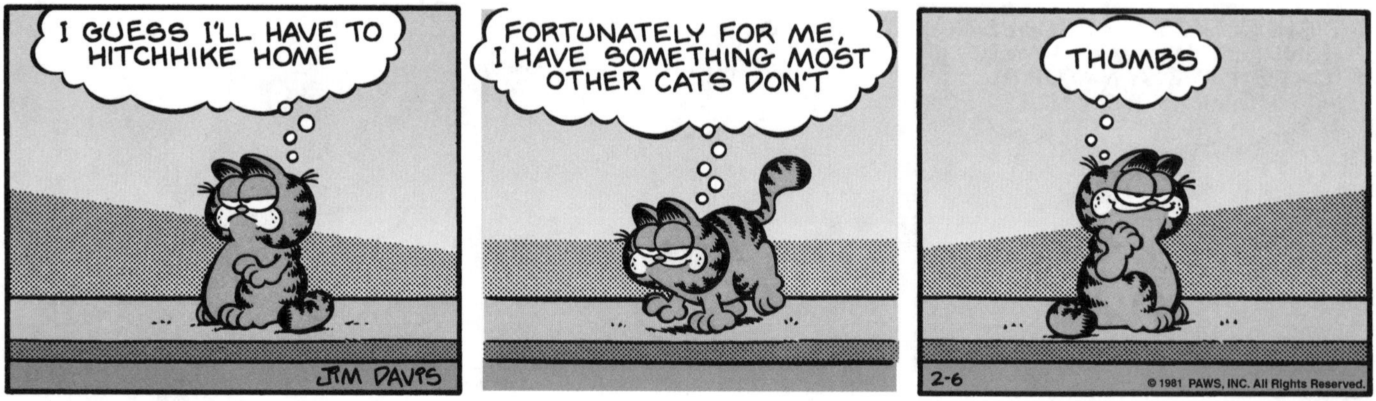
I GUESS I'LL HAVE TO HITCHHIKE HOME
JIM DAVIS
FORTUNATELY FOR ME, I HAVE SOMETHING MOST OTHER CATS DON'T
THUMBS
2-6
© 1981 PAWS, INC. All Rights Reserved.

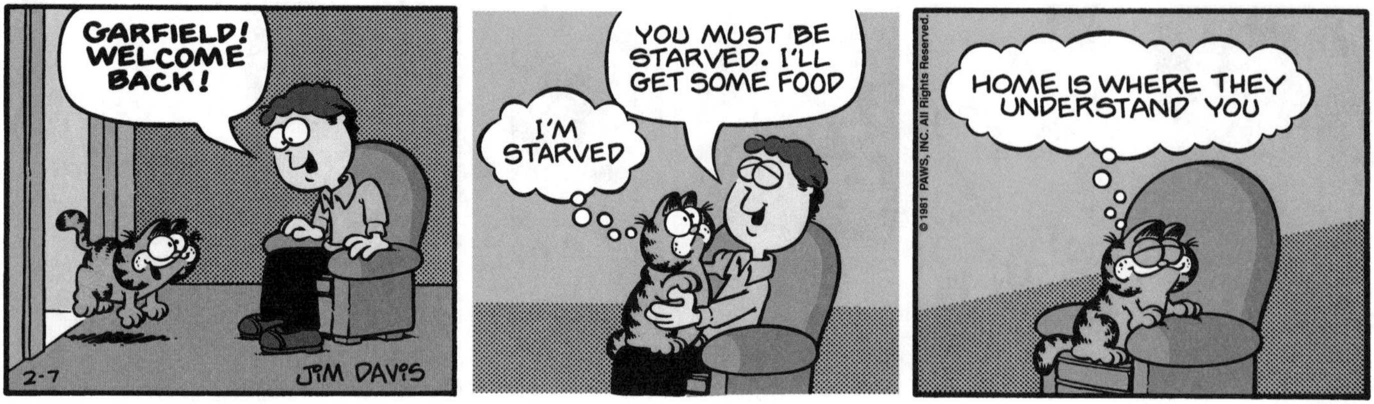
GARFIELD! WELCOME BACK!
2-7
JIM DAVIS
YOU MUST BE STARVED. I'LL GET SOME FOOD
I'M STARVED
© 1981 PAWS, INC. All Rights Reserved.
HOME IS WHERE THEY UNDERSTAND YOU

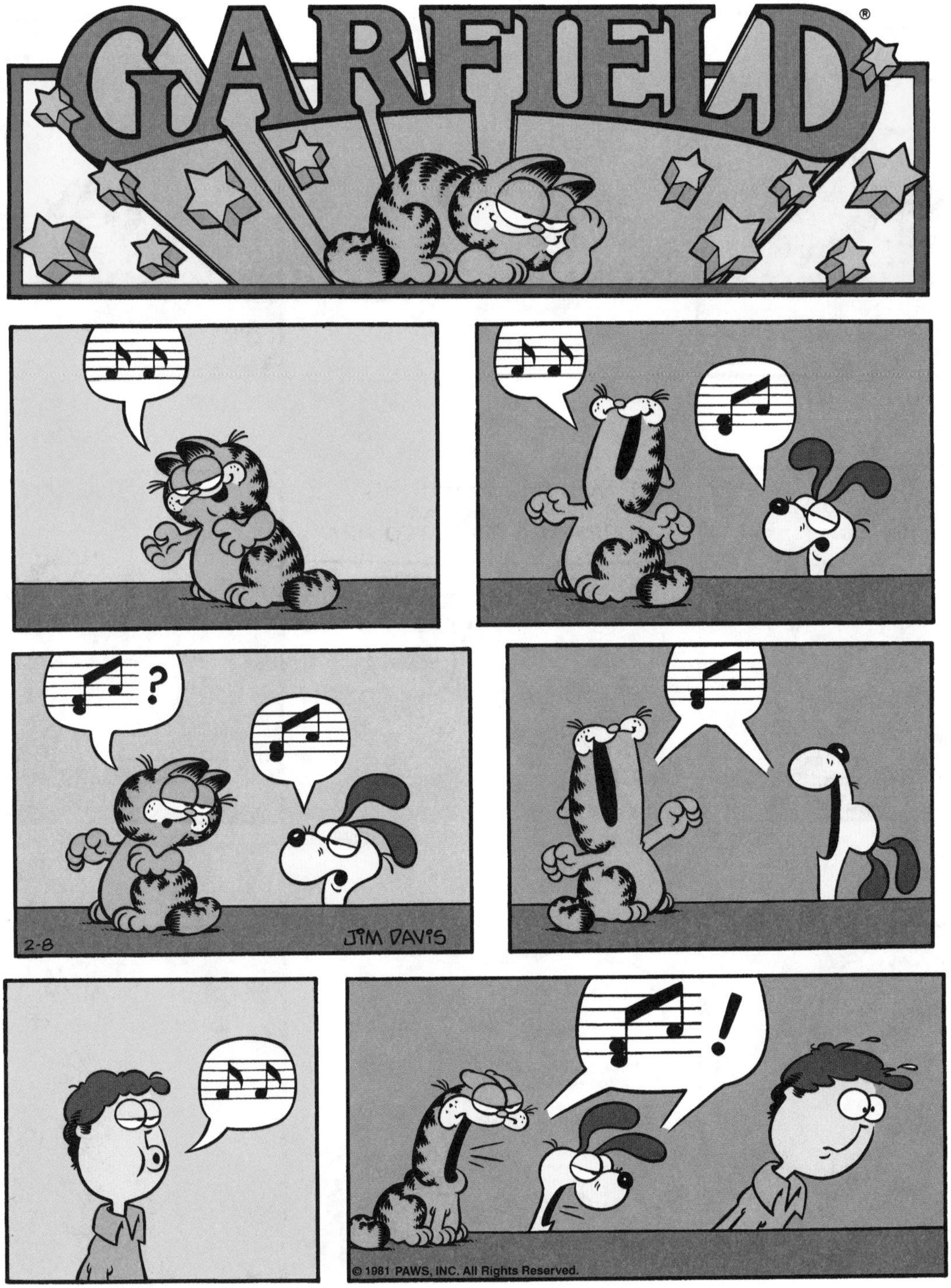
GARFIELD®
?
2-8
JIM DAVIS
!
© 1981 PAWS, INC. All Rights Reserved.

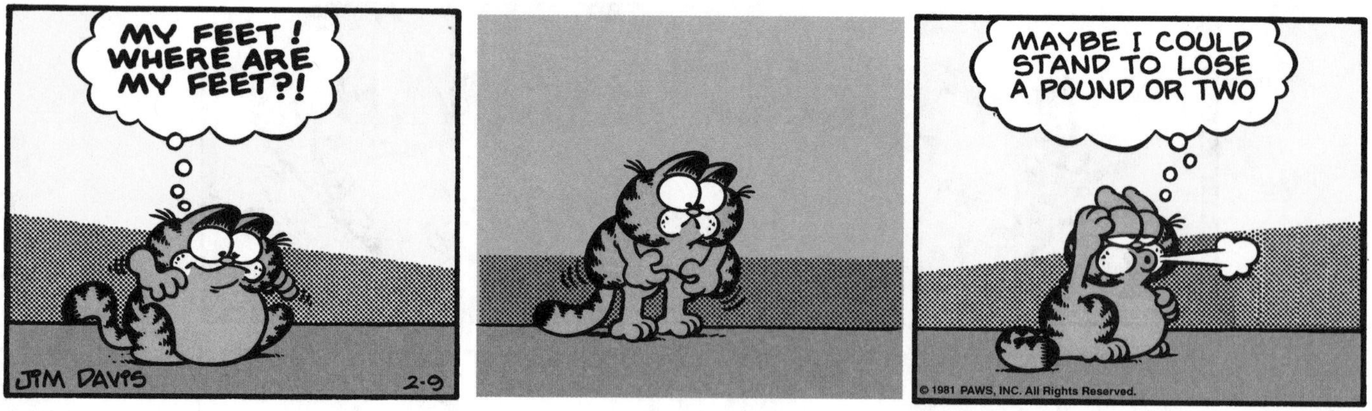
MY FEET! WHERE ARE MY FEET?!
JIM DAVIS
2-9
MAYBE I COULD STAND TO LOSE A POUND OR TWO
© 1981 PAWS, INC. All Rights Reserved.

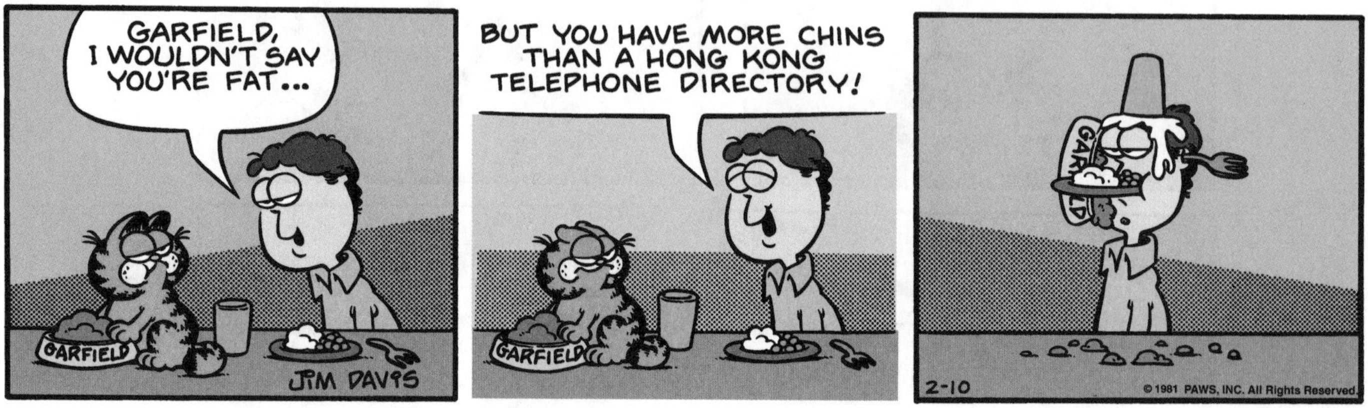
GARFIELD, I WOULDN'T SAY YOU'RE FAT...
GARFIELD
JIM DAVIS
BUT YOU HAVE MORE CHINS THAN A HONG KONG TELEPHONE DIRECTORY!
GARFIELD
2-10
© 1981 PAWS, INC. All Rights Reserved.

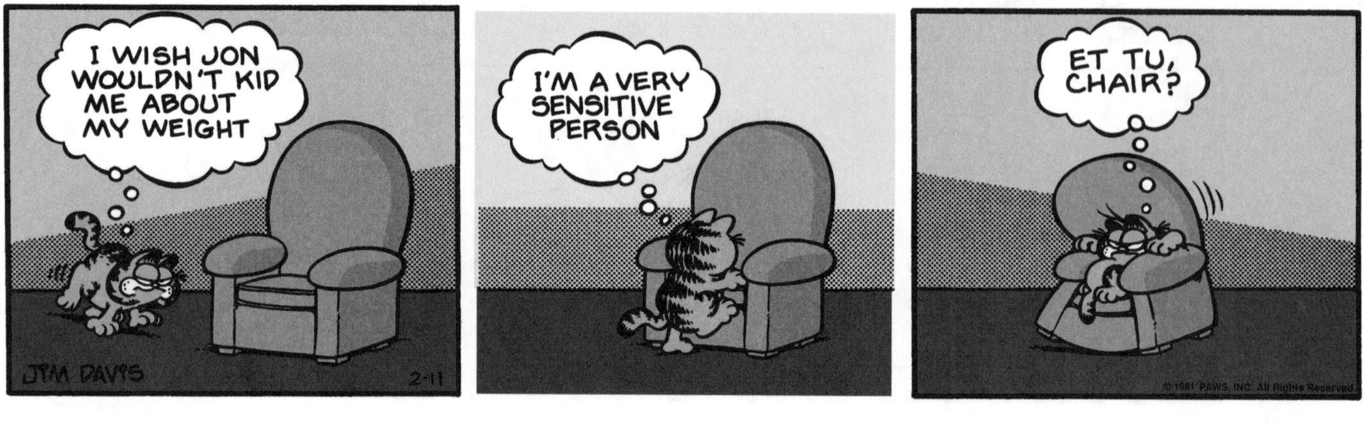
I WISH JON WOULDN'T KID ME ABOUT MY WEIGHT
JIM DAVIS
2-11
I'M A VERY SENSITIVE PERSON
ET TU, CHAIR?
© 1981 PAWS, INC. All Rights Reserved.

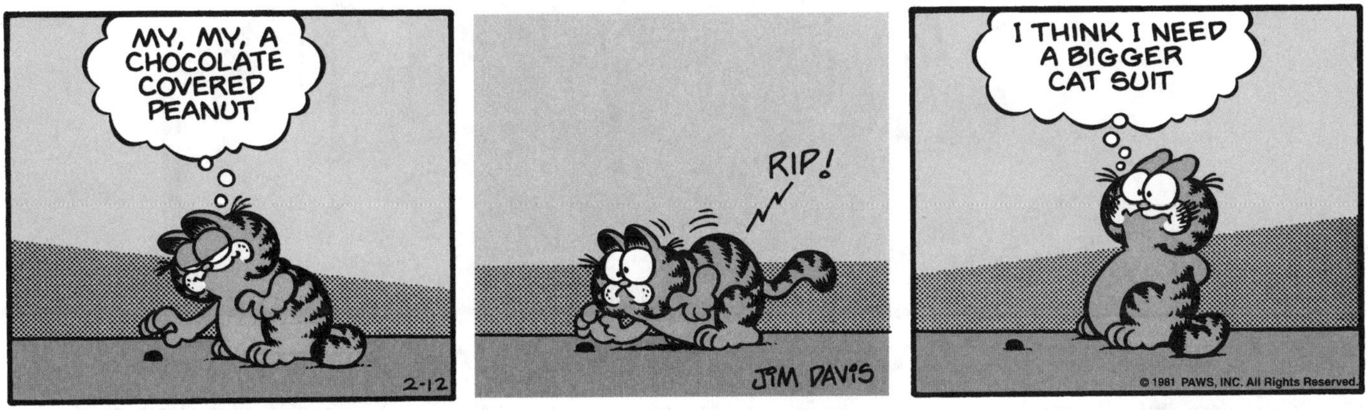
MY, MY, A CHOCOLATE COVERED PEANUT
2-12
RIP!
JIM DAVIS
I THINK I NEED A BIGGER CAT SUIT
© 1981 PAWS, INC. All Rights Reserved.

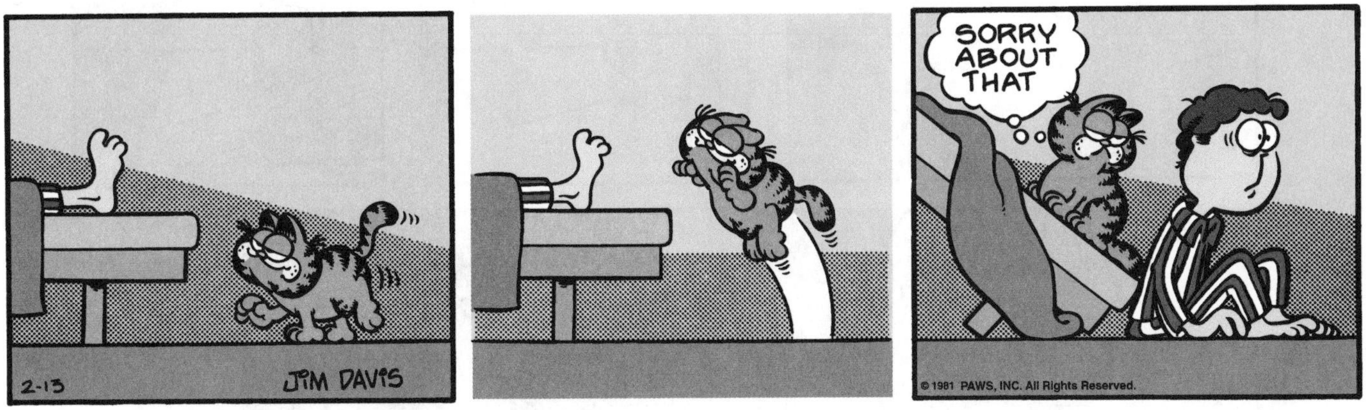
2-13
JIM DAVIS
SORRY ABOUT THAT
© 1981 PAWS, INC. All Rights Reserved.

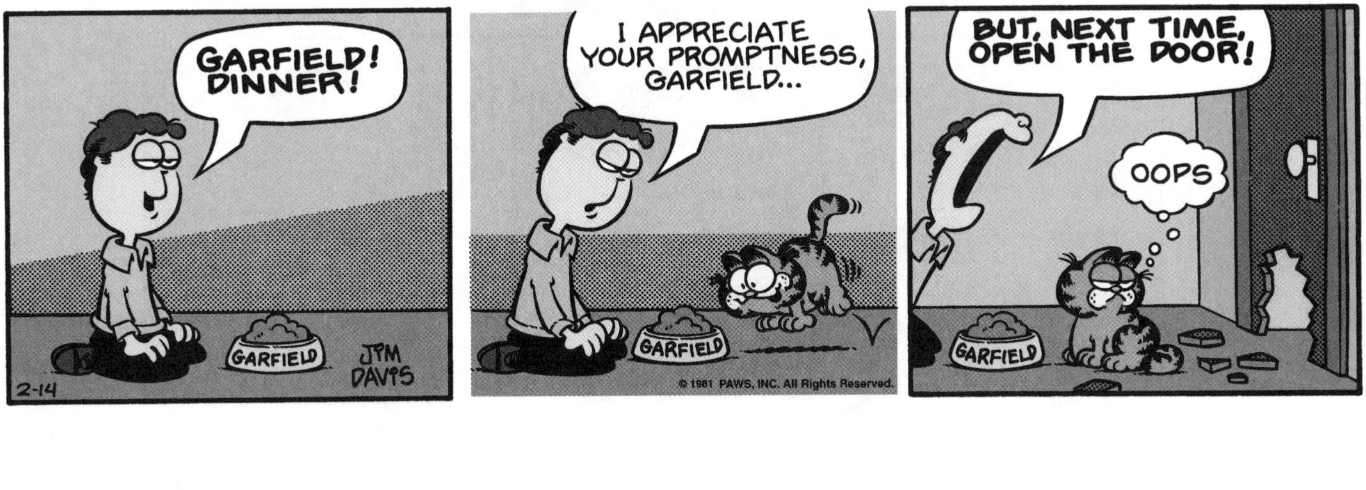
GARFIELD! DINNER!
GARFIELD
JIM DAVIS
2-14
I APPRECIATE YOUR PROMPTNESS, GARFIELD...
GARFIELD
© 1981 PAWS, INC. All Rights Reserved.
BUT, NEXT TIME, OPEN THE DOOR!
OOPS
GARFIELD

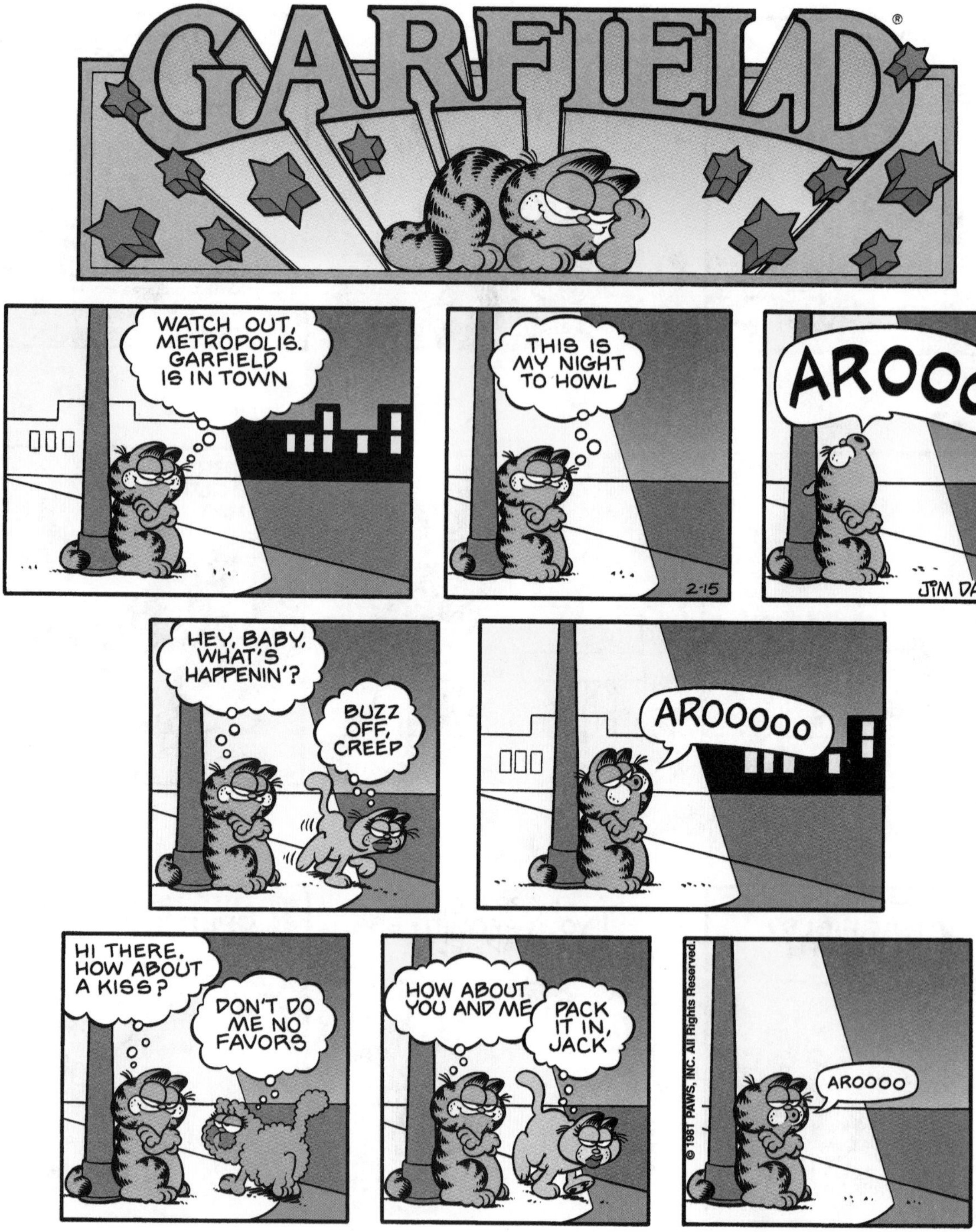
GARFIELD
WATCH OUT, METROPOLIS. GARFIELD IS IN TOWN
THIS IS MY NIGHT TO HOWL
2-15
AROOO
JIM DAVIS
HEY, BABY, WHAT'S HAPPENIN'?
BUZZ OFF, CREEP
AROOOOO
HI THERE. HOW ABOUT A KISS?
DON'T DO ME NO FAVORS
HOW ABOUT YOU AND ME
PACK IT IN, JACK
© 1981 PAWS, INC. All Rights Reserved.
AROOOO

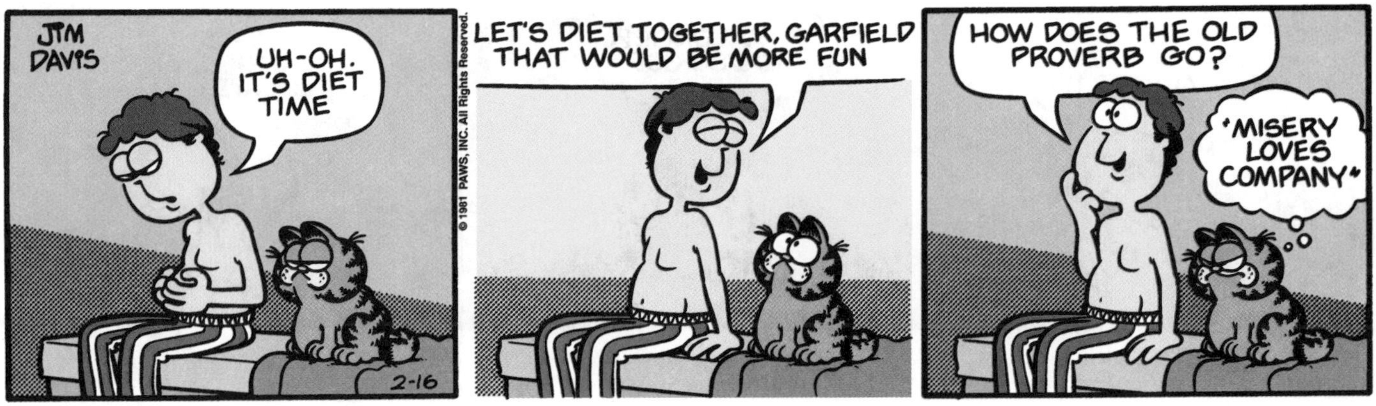
JIM DAVIS
UH-OH. IT'S DIET TIME
2-16
© 1981 PAWS, INC. All Rights Reserved.
LET'S DIET TOGETHER, GARFIELD THAT WOULD BE MORE FUN
HOW DOES THE OLD PROVERB GO?
"MISERY LOVES COMPANY"

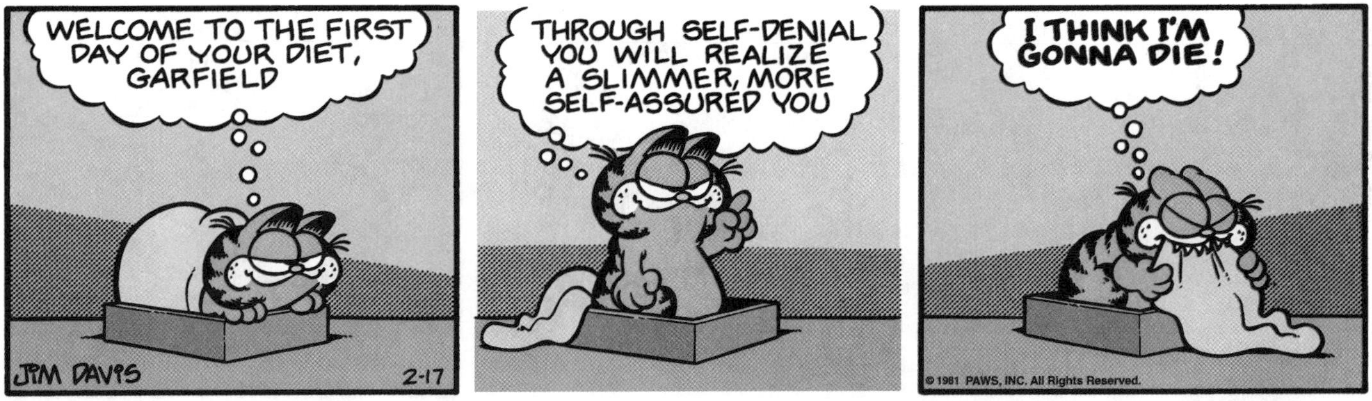
WELCOME TO THE FIRST DAY OF YOUR DIET, GARFIELD
JIM DAVIS
2-17
THROUGH SELF-DENIAL YOU WILL REALIZE A SLIMMER, MORE SELF-ASSURED YOU
I THINK I'M GONNA DIE!
© 1981 PAWS, INC. All Rights Reserved.

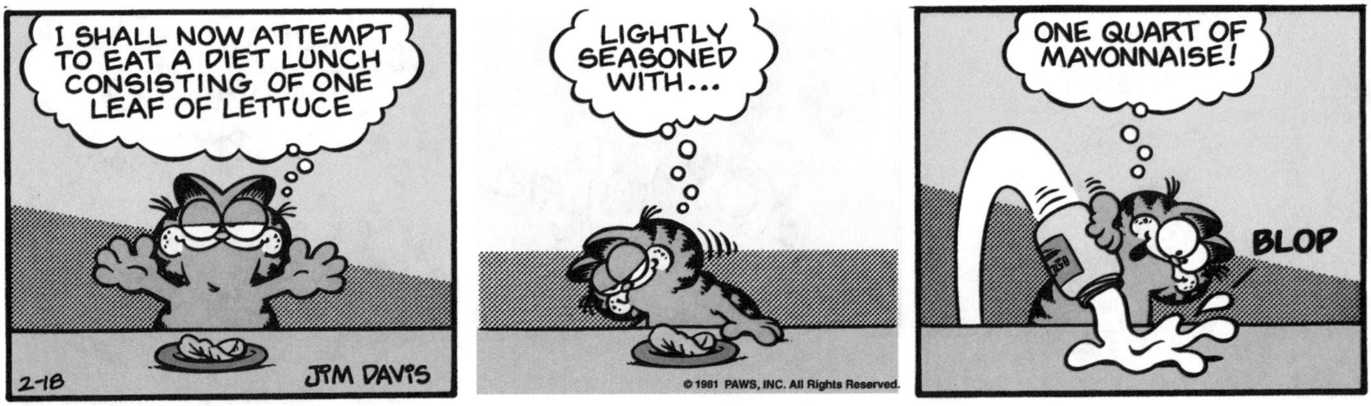
I SHALL NOW ATTEMPT TO EAT A DIET LUNCH CONSISTING OF ONE LEAF OF LETTUCE
2-18
JIM DAVIS
LIGHTLY SEASONED WITH...
© 1981 PAWS, INC. All Rights Reserved.
ONE QUART OF MAYONNAISE!
BLOP

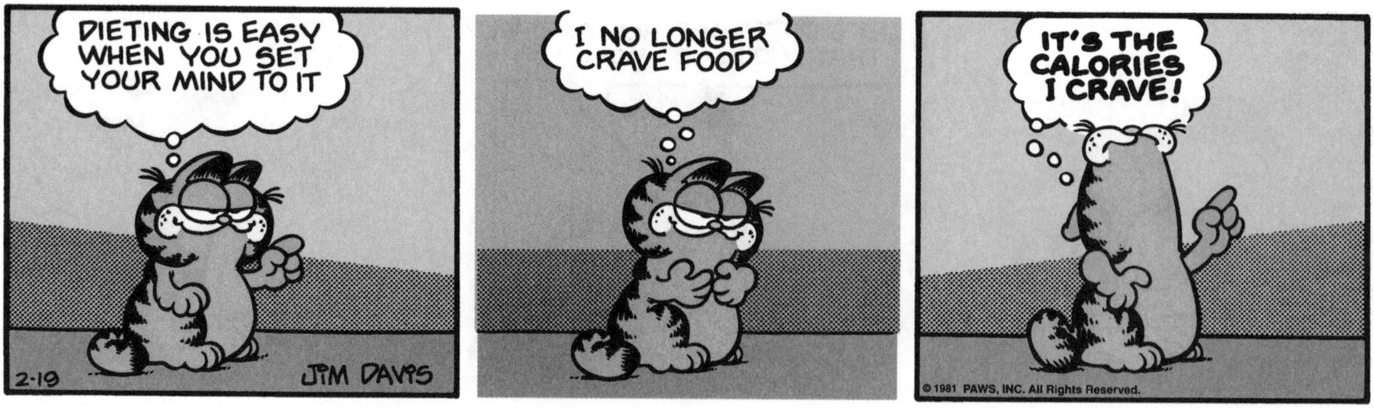
DIETING IS EASY WHEN YOU SET YOUR MIND TO IT
2-19
JIM DAVIS
I NO LONGER CRAVE FOOD
IT'S THE CALORIES I CRAVE!
© 1981 PAWS, INC. All Rights Reserved.

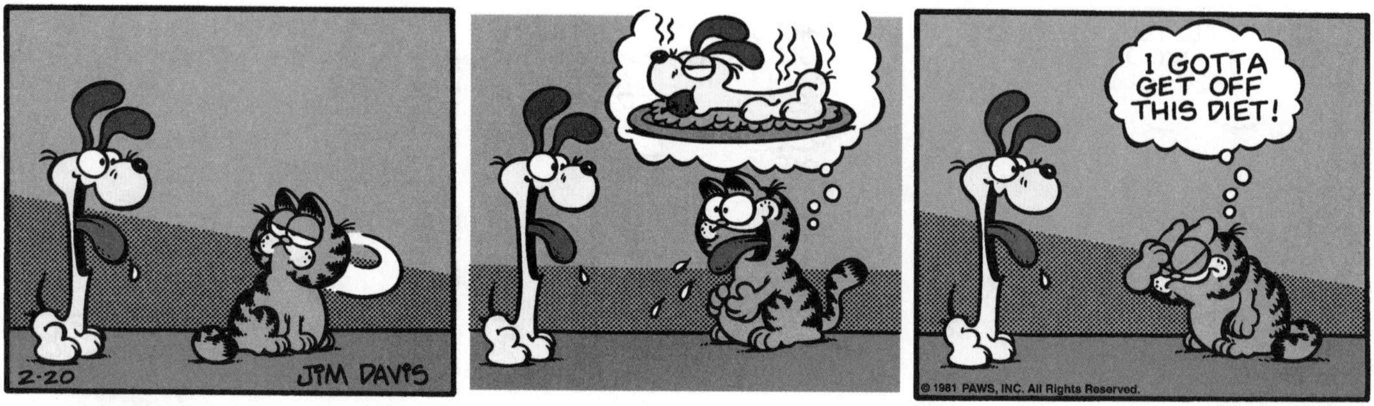
2-20
JIM DAVIS
I GOTTA GET OFF THIS DIET!
© 1981 PAWS, INC. All Rights Reserved.

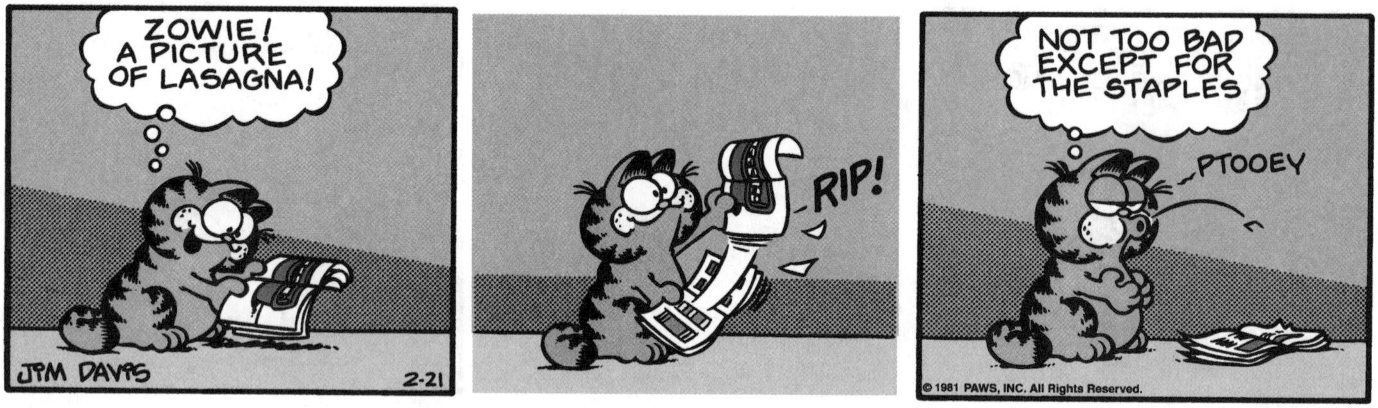
ZOWIE! A PICTURE OF LASAGNA!
JIM DAVIS
2-21
RIP!
NOT TOO BAD EXCEPT FOR THE STAPLES
PTOOEY
© 1981 PAWS, INC. All Rights Reserved.

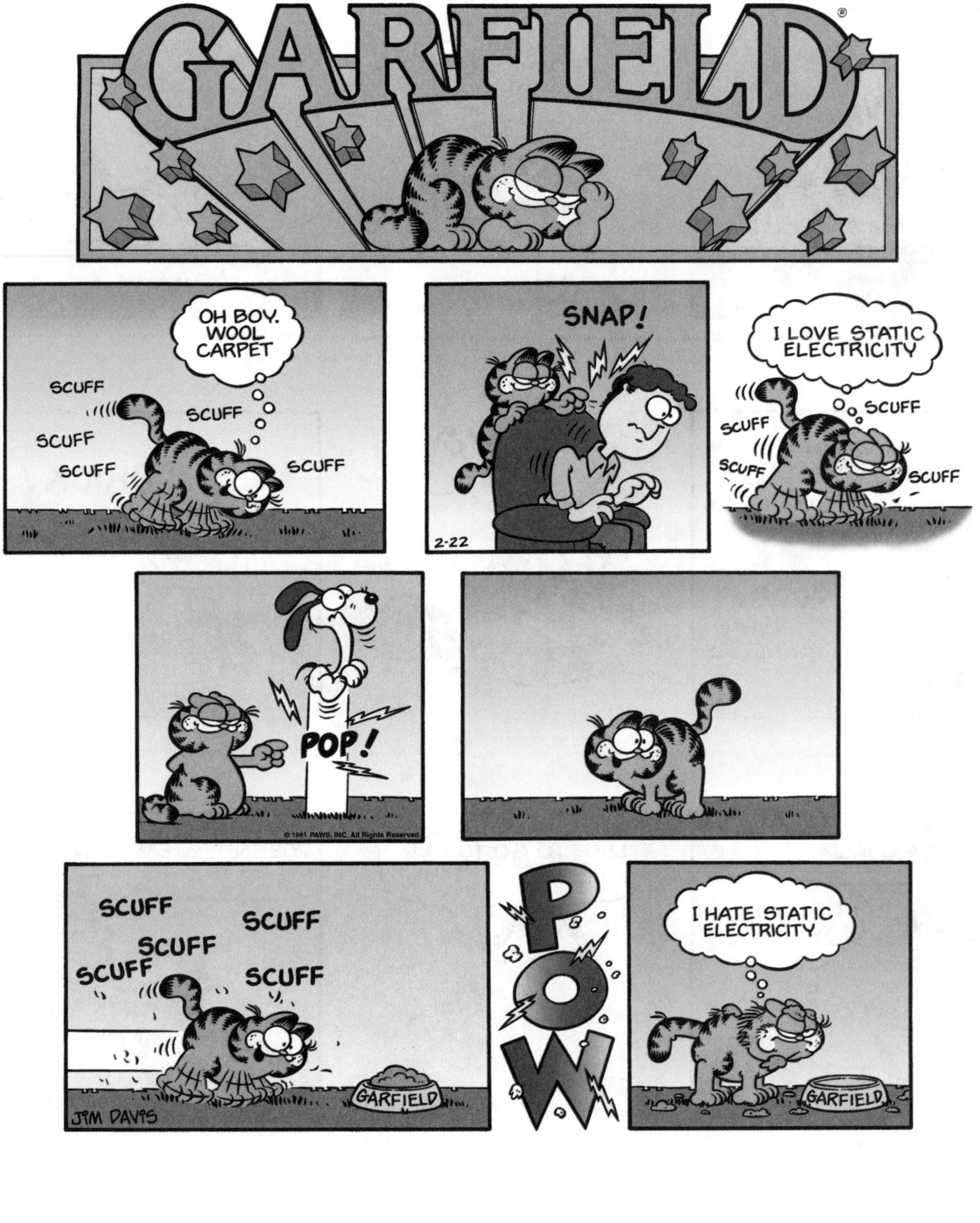
GARFIELD®
OH BOY. WOOL CARPET
SCUFF
SCUFF
SCUFF
SCUFF
SCUFF
SNAP!
2-22
I LOVE STATIC ELECTRICITY
SCUFF
SCUFF
SCUFF
SCUFF
POP!
© 1981 PAWS, INC. All Rights Reserved.
SCUFF
SCUFF
SCUFF
SCUFF
SCUFF
GARFIELD
JIM DAVIS
POW
I HATE STATIC ELECTRICITY
GARFIELD

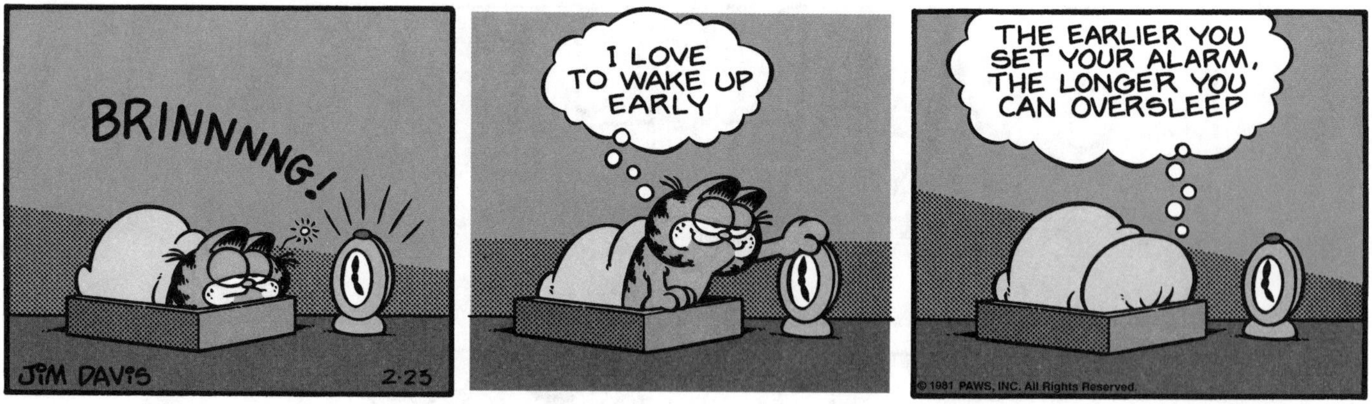
BRINNNNG!
JIM DAVIS
2-23
I LOVE TO WAKE UP EARLY
THE EARLIER YOU SET YOUR ALARM, THE LONGER YOU CAN OVERSLEEP
© 1981 PAWS, INC. All Rights Reserved.

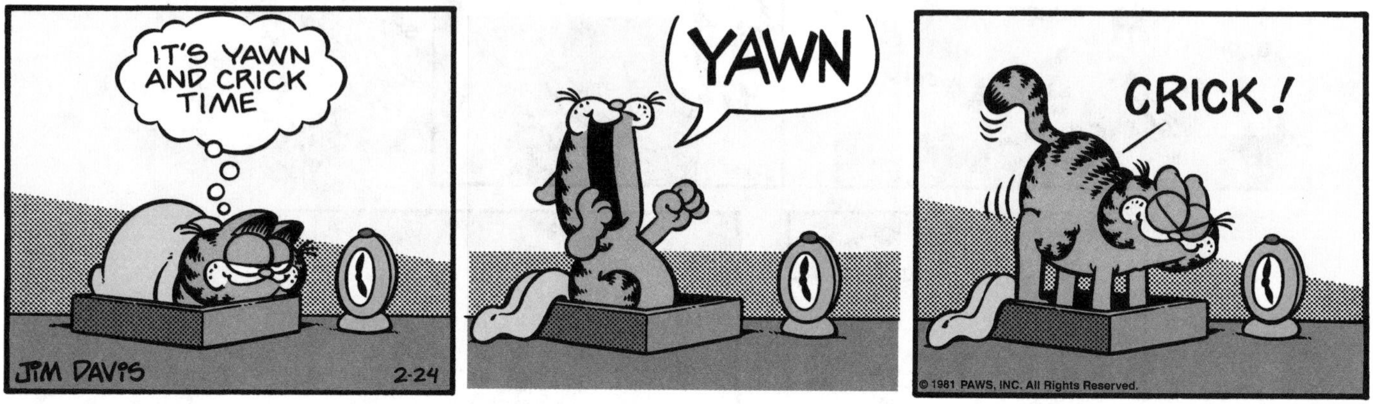
IT'S YAWN AND CRICK TIME
JIM DAVIS
2-24
YAWN
CRICK!
© 1981 PAWS, INC. All Rights Reserved.

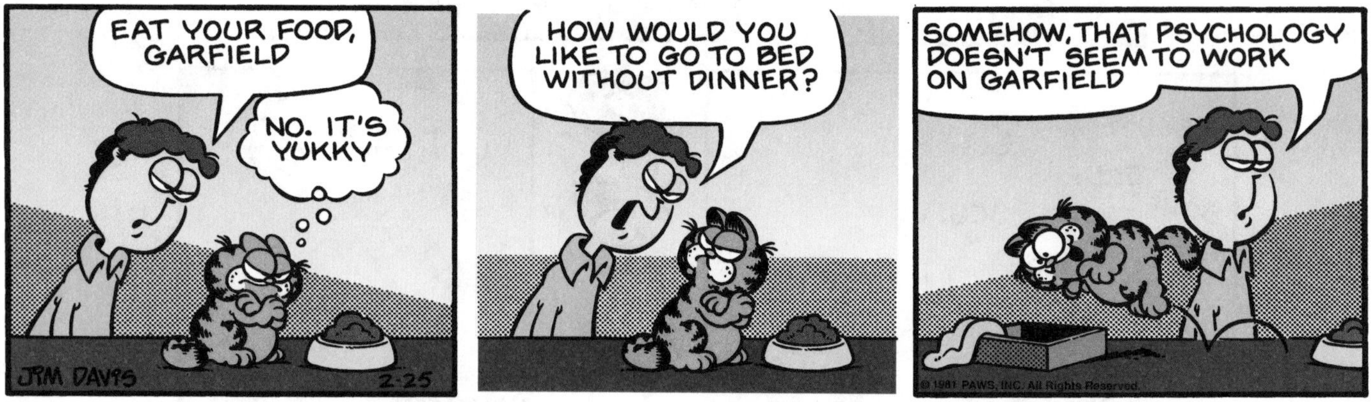
EAT YOUR FOOD, GARFIELD
NO. IT'S YUKKY
JIM DAVIS
2-25
HOW WOULD YOU LIKE TO GO TO BED WITHOUT DINNER?
SOMEHOW, THAT PSYCHOLOGY DOESN'T SEEM TO WORK ON GARFIELD
© 1981 PAWS, INC. All Rights Reserved.

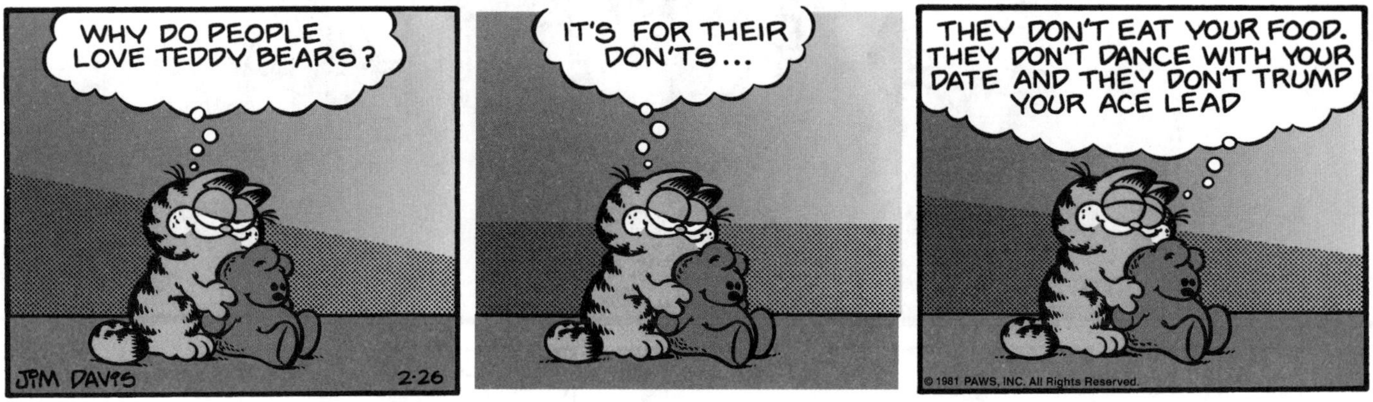
WHY DO PEOPLE LOVE TEDDY BEARS?
JIM DAVIS
2·26
IT'S FOR THEIR DON'TS...
THEY DON'T EAT YOUR FOOD. THEY DON'T DANCE WITH YOUR DATE AND THEY DON'T TRUMP YOUR ACE LEAD
© 1981 PAWS, INC. All Rights Reserved.

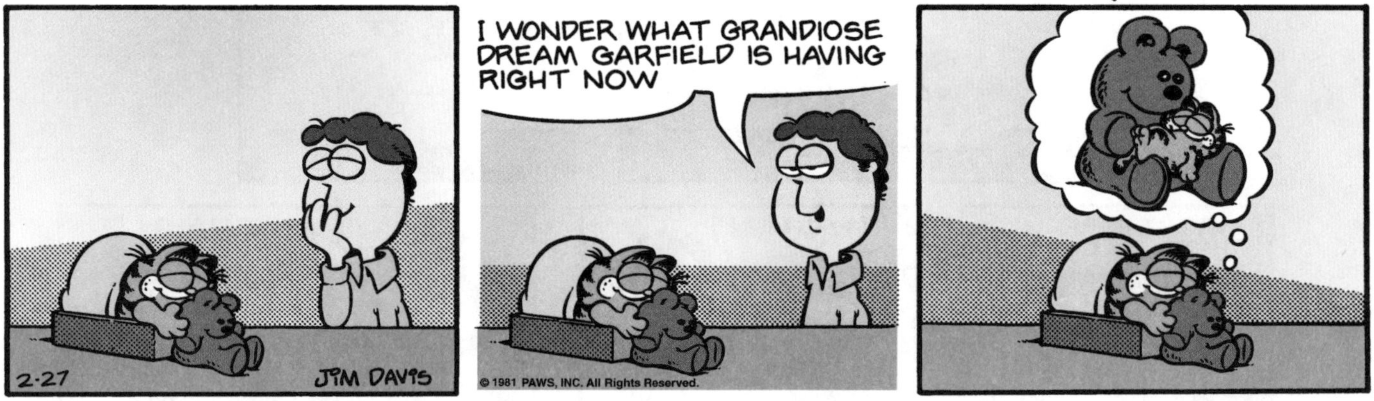
2·27
JIM DAVIS
I WONDER WHAT GRANDIOSE DREAM GARFIELD IS HAVING RIGHT NOW
© 1981 PAWS, INC. All Rights Reserved.

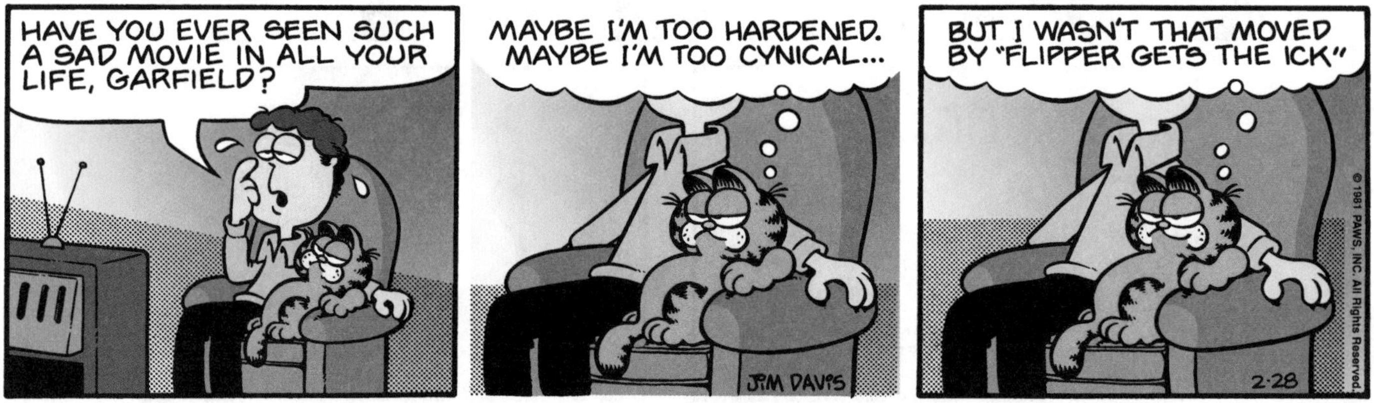
HAVE YOU EVER SEEN SUCH A SAD MOVIE IN ALL YOUR LIFE, GARFIELD?
MAYBE I'M TOO HARDENED. MAYBE I'M TOO CYNICAL...
JIM DAVIS
BUT I WASN'T THAT MOVED BY "FLIPPER GETS THE ICK"
2·28
© 1981 PAWS, INC. All Rights Reserved.

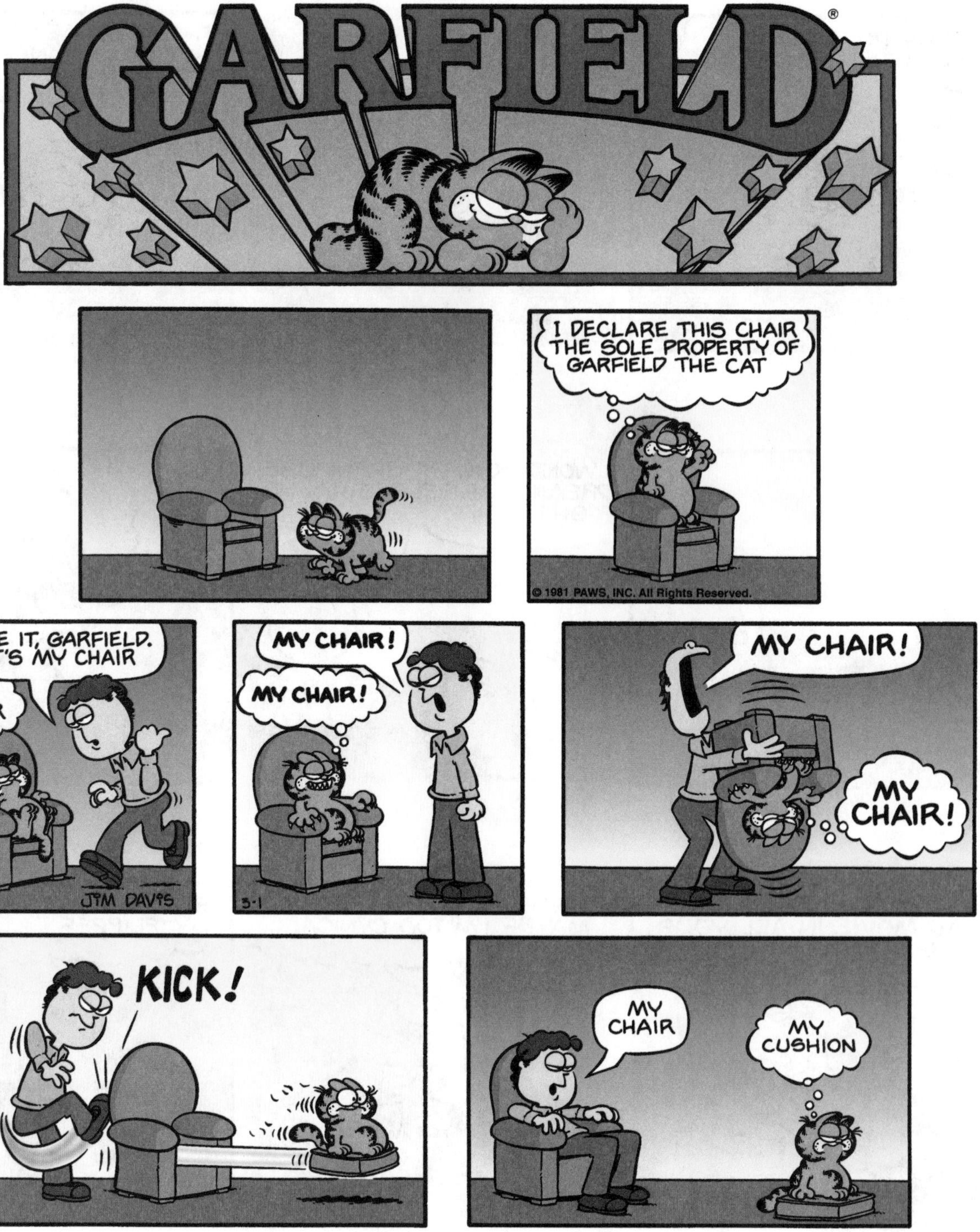
GARFIELD
I DECLARE THIS CHAIR THE SOLE PROPERTY OF GARFIELD THE CAT
© 1981 PAWS, INC. All Rights Reserved.
MOVE IT, GARFIELD. THAT'S MY CHAIR
MY CHAIR
JIM DAVIS
MY CHAIR!
MY CHAIR!
3-1
MY CHAIR!
MY CHAIR!
KICK!
MY CHAIR
MY CUSHION

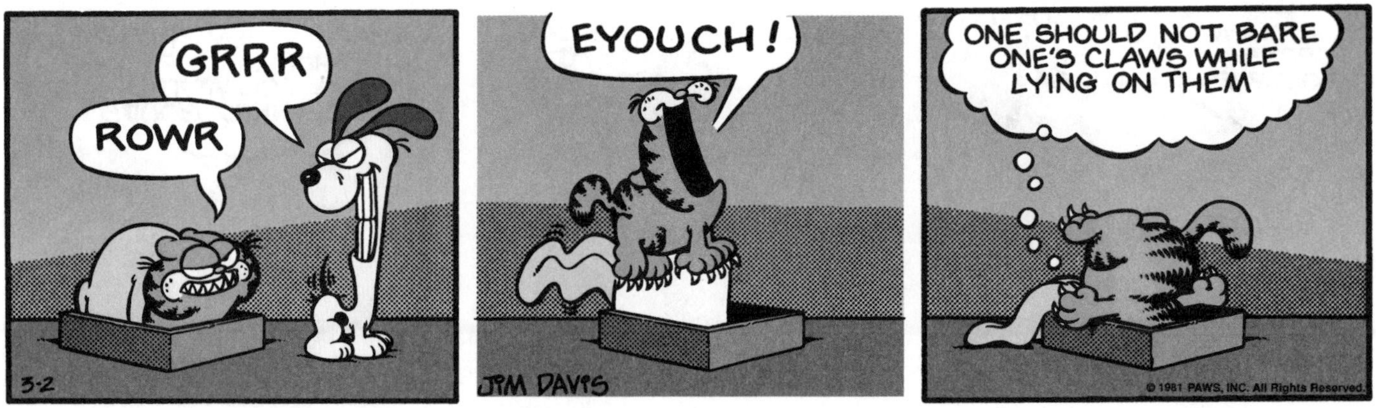
GRRR
ROWR
3-2
EYOUCH!
JIM DAVIS
ONE SHOULD NOT BARE ONE'S CLAWS WHILE LYING ON THEM
© 1981 PAWS, INC. All Rights Reserved.

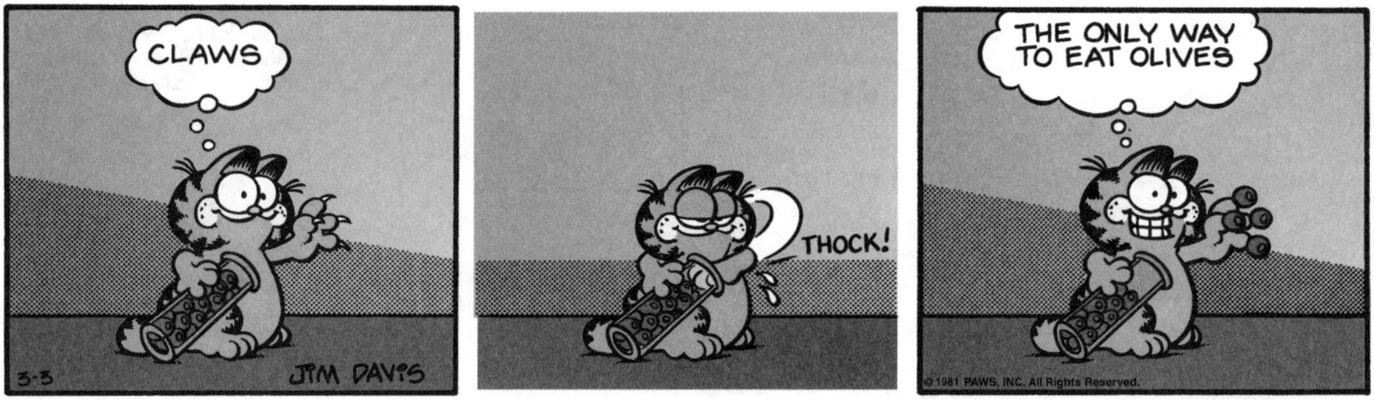
CLAWS
3-3
JIM DAVIS
THOCK!
THE ONLY WAY TO EAT OLIVES
© 1981 PAWS, INC. All Rights Reserved.

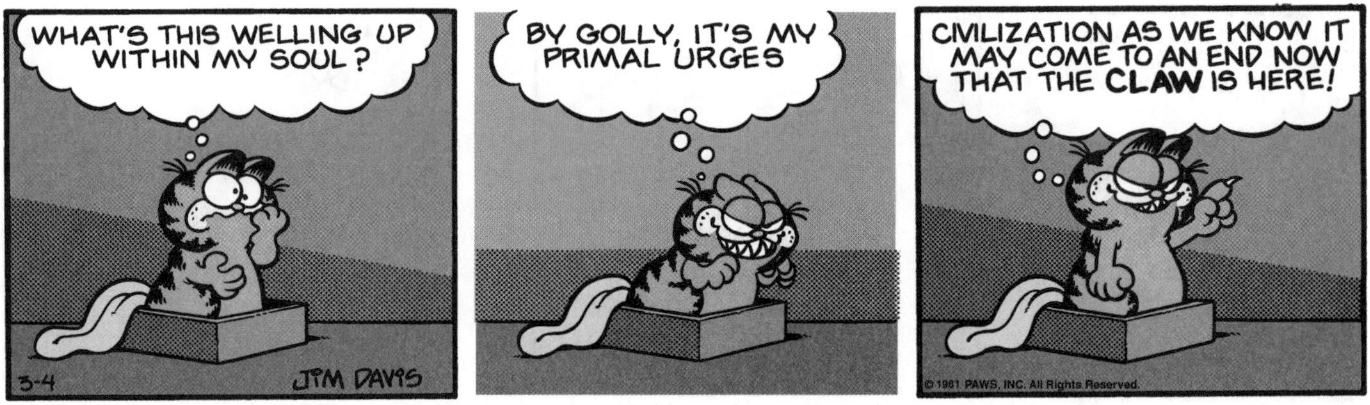
WHAT'S THIS WELLING UP WITHIN MY SOUL?
3-4
JIM DAVIS
BY GOLLY, IT'S MY PRIMAL URGES
CIVILIZATION AS WE KNOW IT MAY COME TO AN END NOW THAT THE **CLAW** IS HERE!
© 1981 PAWS, INC. All Rights Reserved.

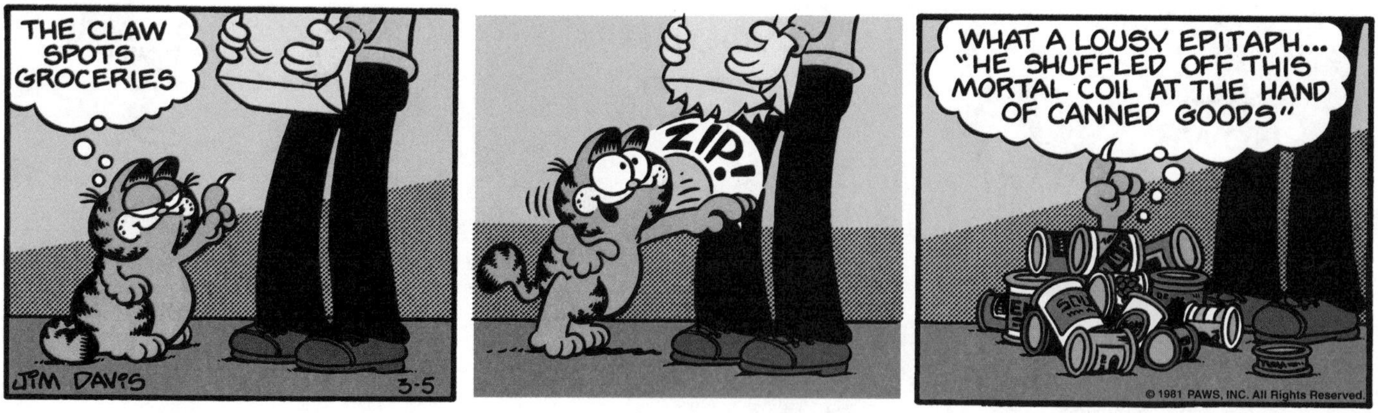
THE CLAW SPOTS GROCERIES
JIM DAVIS
3-5
ZIP!
WHAT A LOUSY EPITAPH... "HE SHUFFLED OFF THIS MORTAL COIL AT THE HAND OF CANNED GOODS"
© 1981 PAWS, INC. All Rights Reserved.

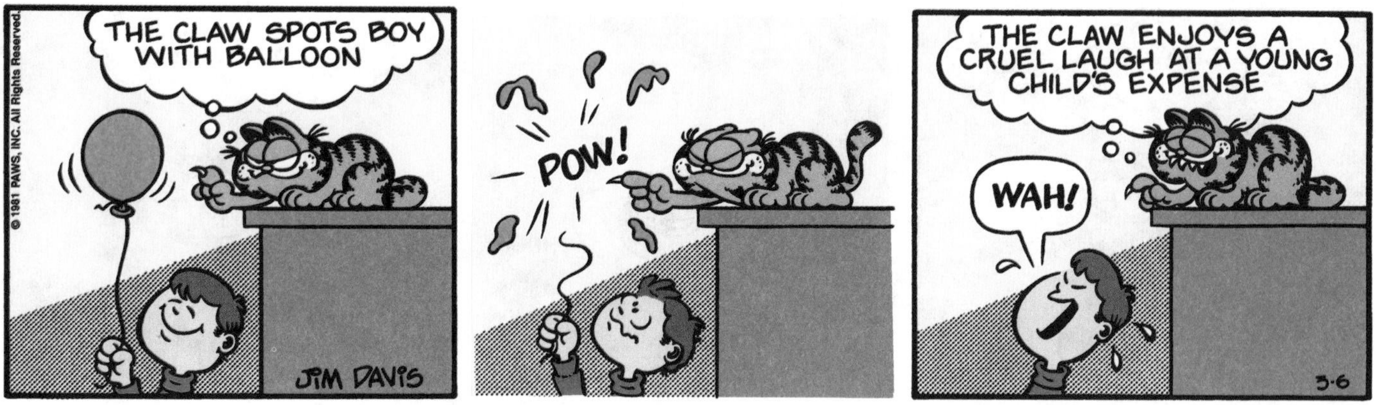
© 1981 PAWS, INC. All Rights Reserved.
THE CLAW SPOTS BOY WITH BALLOON
JIM DAVIS
POW!
THE CLAW ENJOYS A CRUEL LAUGH AT A YOUNG CHILD'S EXPENSE
WAH!
3-6

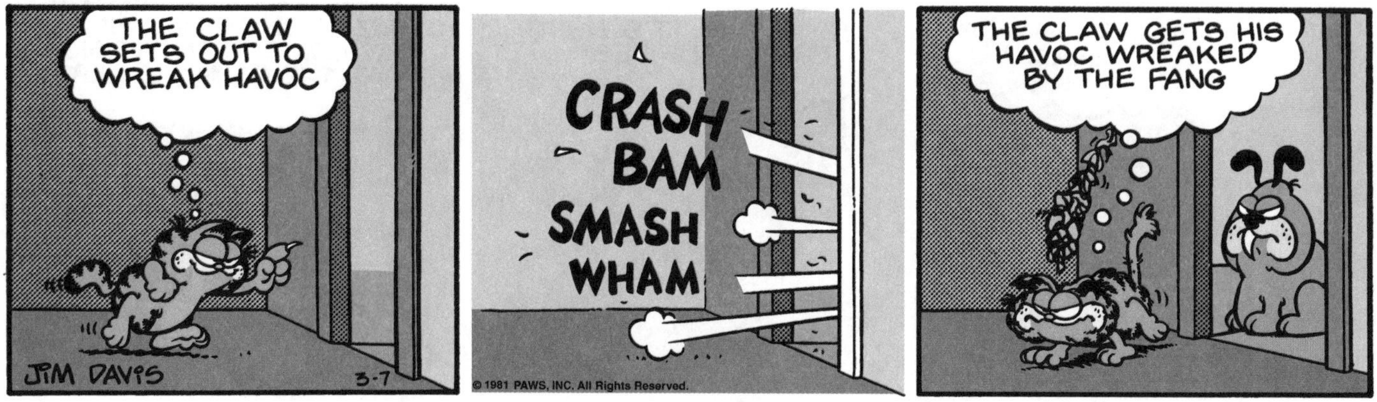
THE CLAW SETS OUT TO WREAK HAVOC
JIM DAVIS
3-7
CRASH
BAM
SMASH
WHAM
© 1981 PAWS, INC. All Rights Reserved.
THE CLAW GETS HIS HAVOC WREAKED BY THE FANG

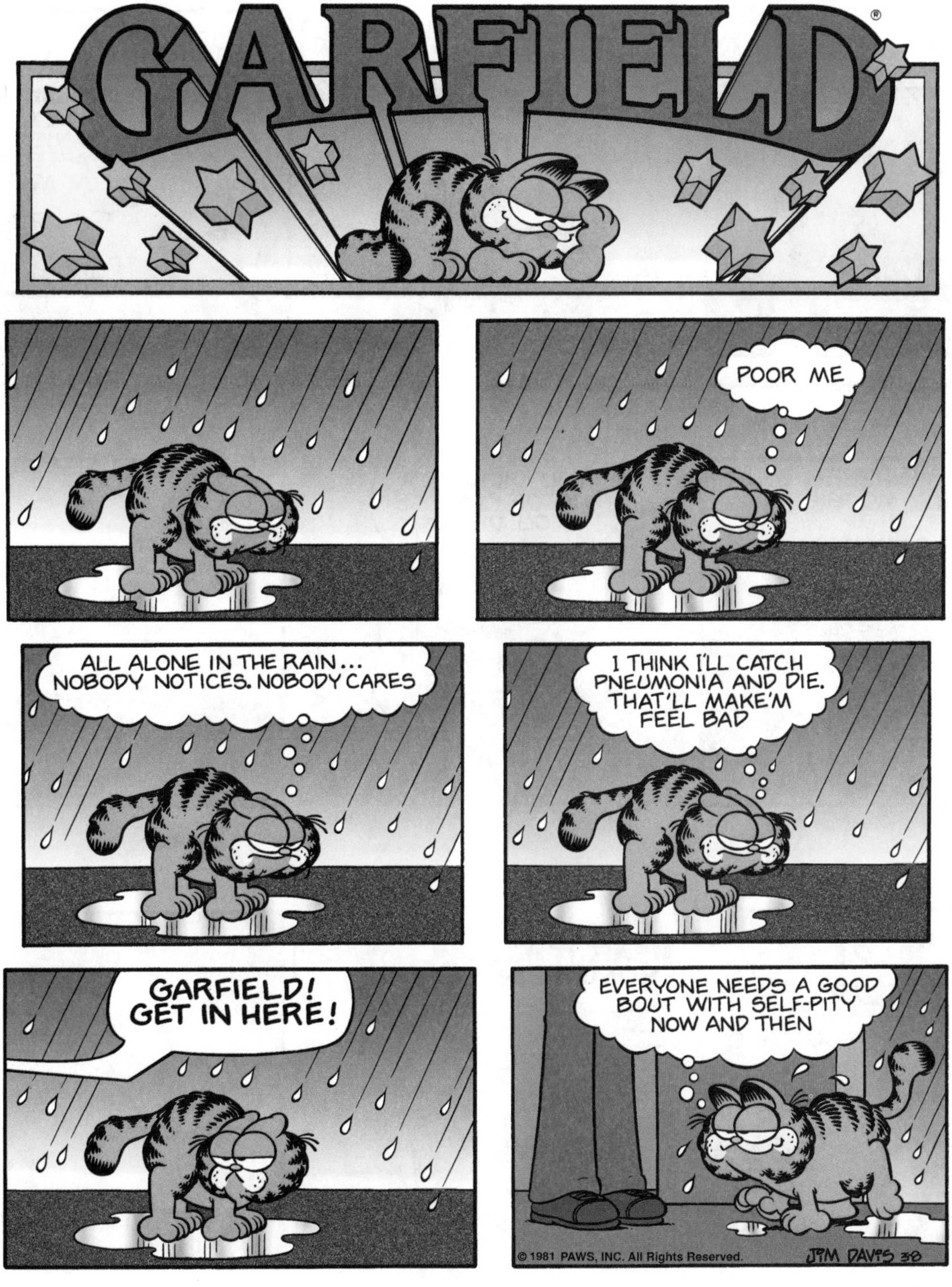
GARFIELD®
POOR ME
ALL ALONE IN THE RAIN... NOBODY NOTICES. NOBODY CARES
I THINK I'LL CATCH PNEUMONIA AND DIE. THAT'LL MAKE'M FEEL BAD
GARFIELD! GET IN HERE!
EVERYONE NEEDS A GOOD BOUT WITH SELF-PITY NOW AND THEN
© 1981 PAWS, INC. All Rights Reserved.
JIM DAVIS 3-8

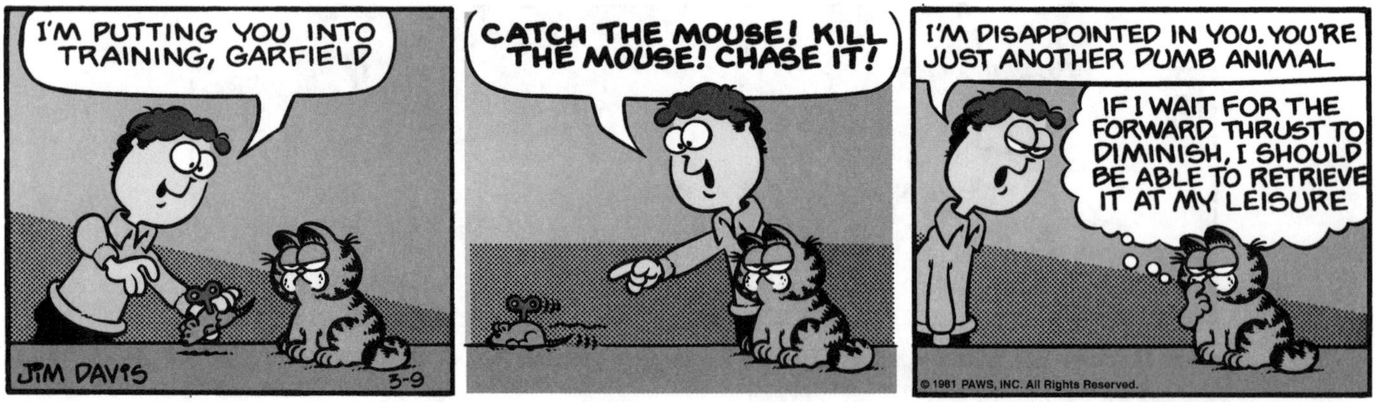
I'M PUTTING YOU INTO TRAINING, GARFIELD
JIM DAVIS
3-9
CATCH THE MOUSE! KILL THE MOUSE! CHASE IT!
I'M DISAPPOINTED IN YOU. YOU'RE JUST ANOTHER DUMB ANIMAL
IF I WAIT FOR THE FORWARD THRUST TO DIMINISH, I SHOULD BE ABLE TO RETRIEVE IT AT MY LEISURE
© 1981 PAWS, INC. All Rights Reserved.

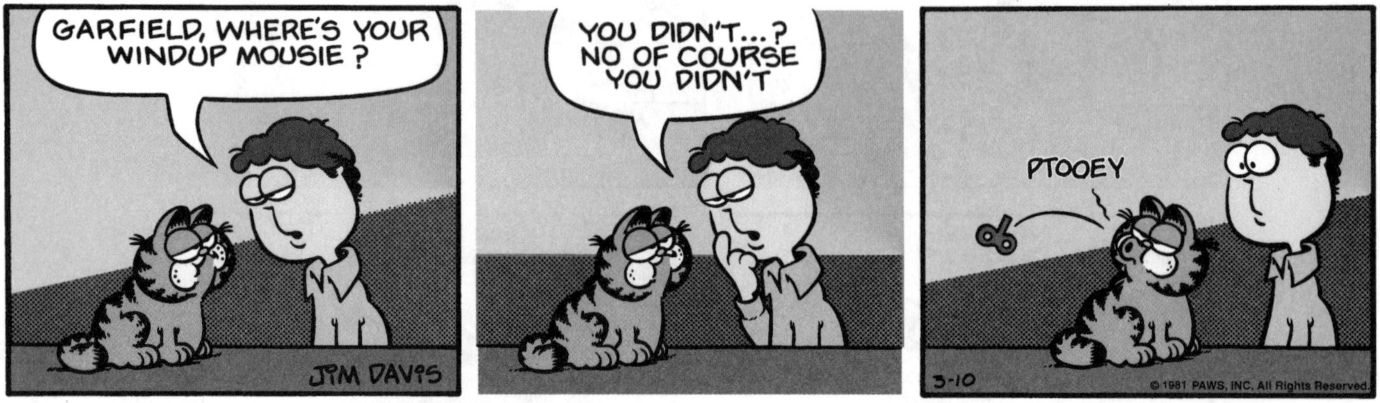
GARFIELD, WHERE'S YOUR WINDUP MOUSIE ?
JIM DAVIS
YOU DIDN'T...? NO OF COURSE YOU DIDN'T
PTOOEY
3-10
© 1981 PAWS, INC. All Rights Reserved.

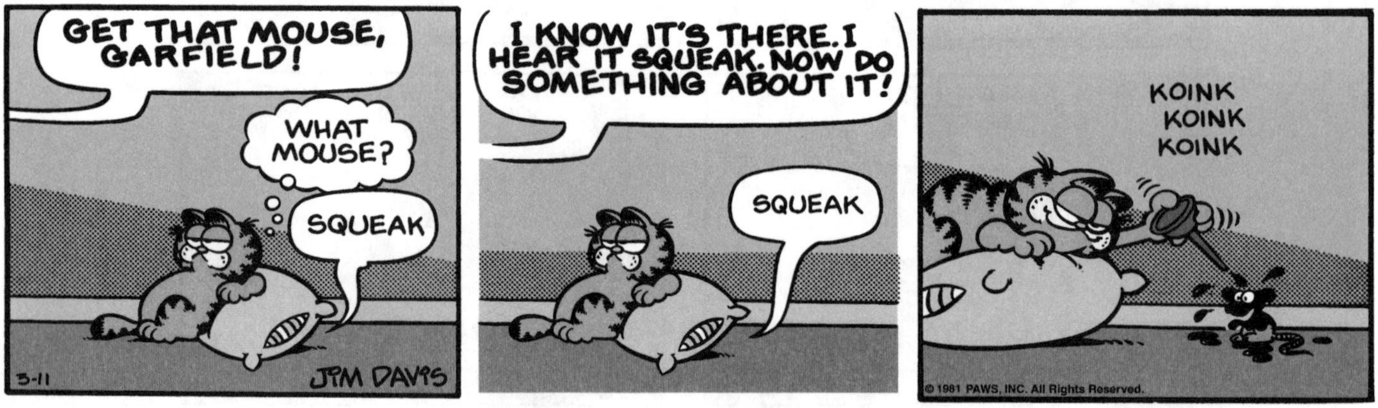
GET THAT MOUSE, GARFIELD!
WHAT MOUSE?
SQUEAK
3-11
JIM DAVIS
I KNOW IT'S THERE. I HEAR IT SQUEAK. NOW DO SOMETHING ABOUT IT!
SQUEAK
KOINK
KOINK
KOINK
© 1981 PAWS, INC. All Rights Reserved.

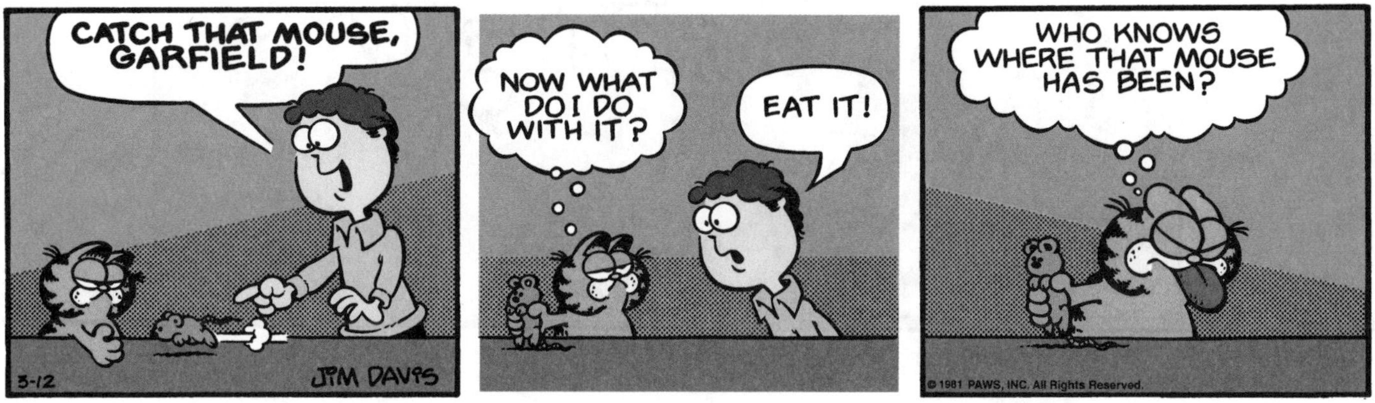
CATCH THAT MOUSE, GARFIELD!
NOW WHAT DO I DO WITH IT?
EAT IT!
WHO KNOWS WHERE THAT MOUSE HAS BEEN?
3-12
JIM DAVIS
© 1981 PAWS, INC. All Rights Reserved.

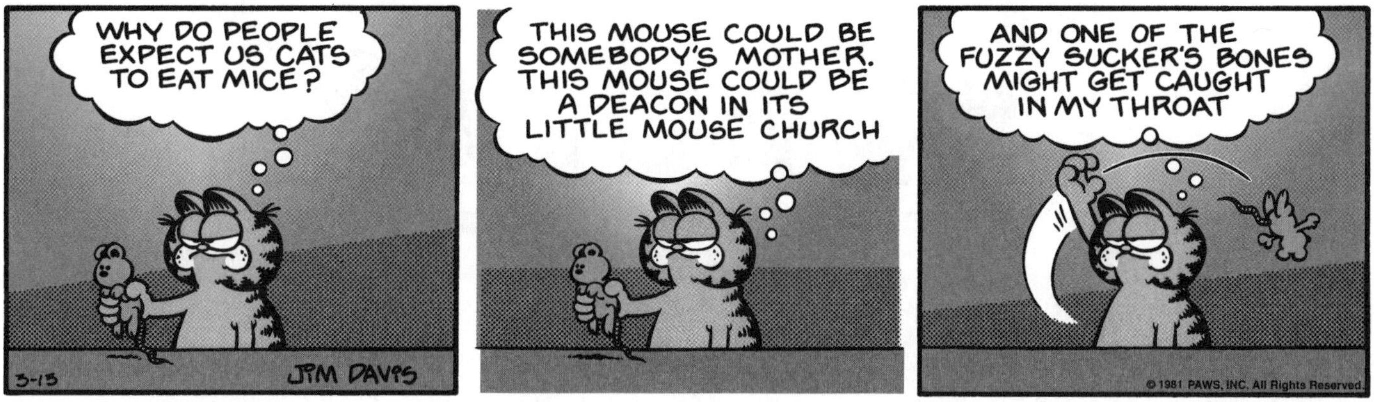
WHY DO PEOPLE EXPECT US CATS TO EAT MICE?
THIS MOUSE COULD BE SOMEBODY'S MOTHER. THIS MOUSE COULD BE A DEACON IN ITS LITTLE MOUSE CHURCH
AND ONE OF THE FUZZY SUCKER'S BONES MIGHT GET CAUGHT IN MY THROAT
3-13
JIM DAVIS
© 1981 PAWS, INC. All Rights Reserved.

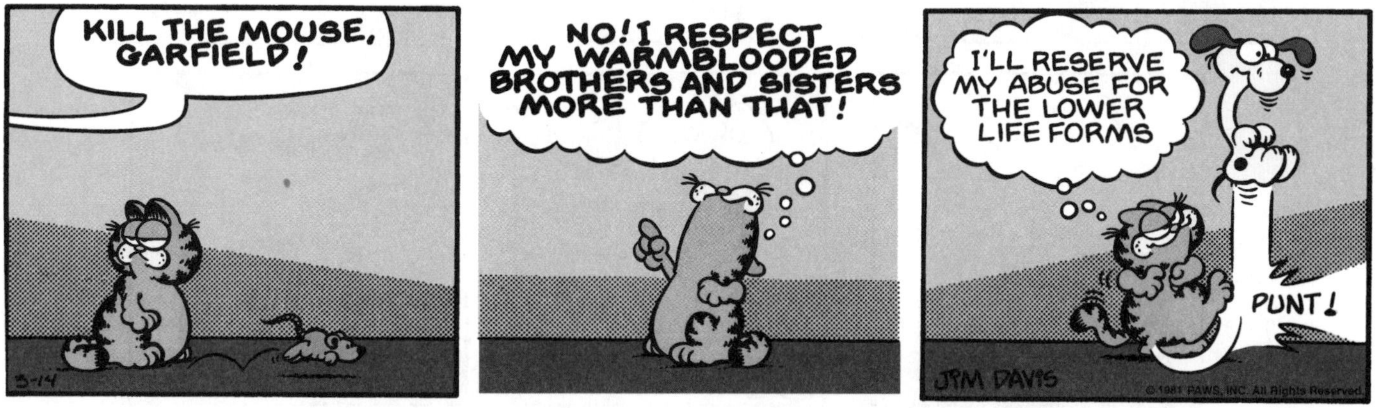
KILL THE MOUSE, GARFIELD!
NO! I RESPECT MY WARMBLOODED BROTHERS AND SISTERS MORE THAN THAT!
I'LL RESERVE MY ABUSE FOR THE LOWER LIFE FORMS
PUNT!
3-14
JIM DAVIS
© 1981 PAWS, INC. All Rights Reserved.

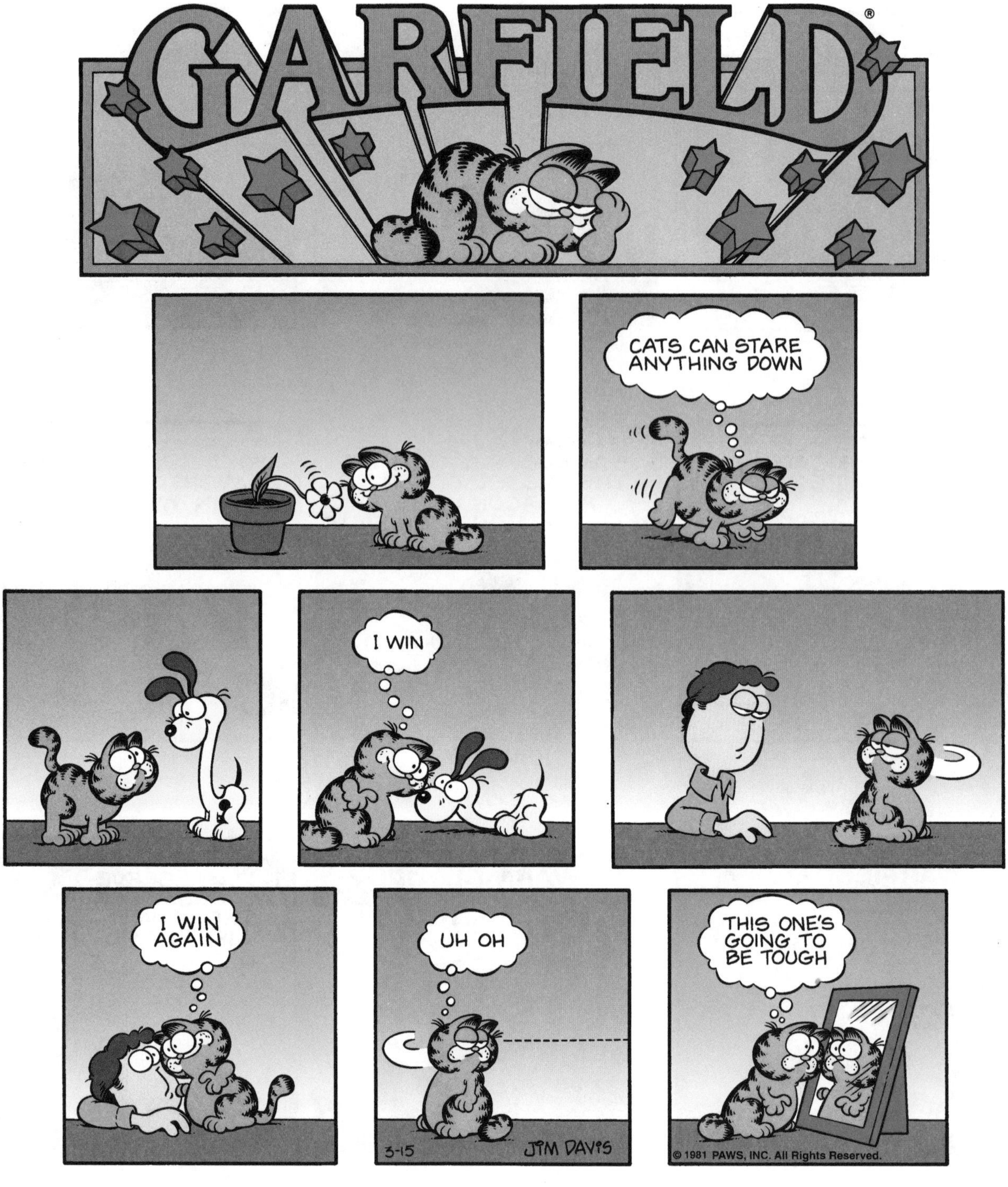
GARFIELD
CATS CAN STARE ANYTHING DOWN
I WIN
I WIN AGAIN
UH OH
THIS ONE'S GOING TO BE TOUGH
3-15
JIM DAVIS
© 1981 PAWS, INC. All Rights Reserved.

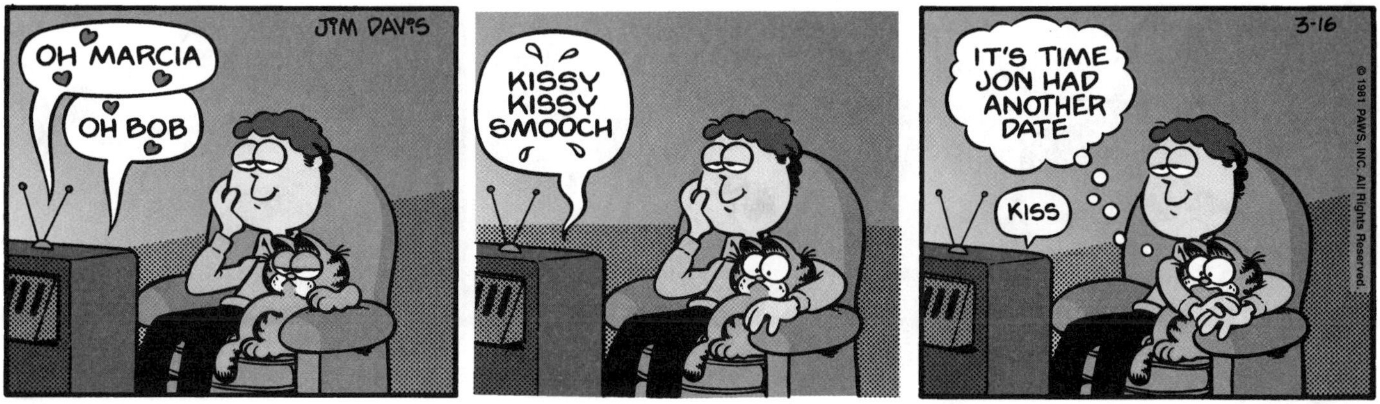
JIM DAVIS
OH MARCIA
OH BOB
KISSY KISSY SMOOCH
3-16
IT'S TIME JON HAD ANOTHER DATE
KISS
© 1981 PAWS, INC. All Rights Reserved.

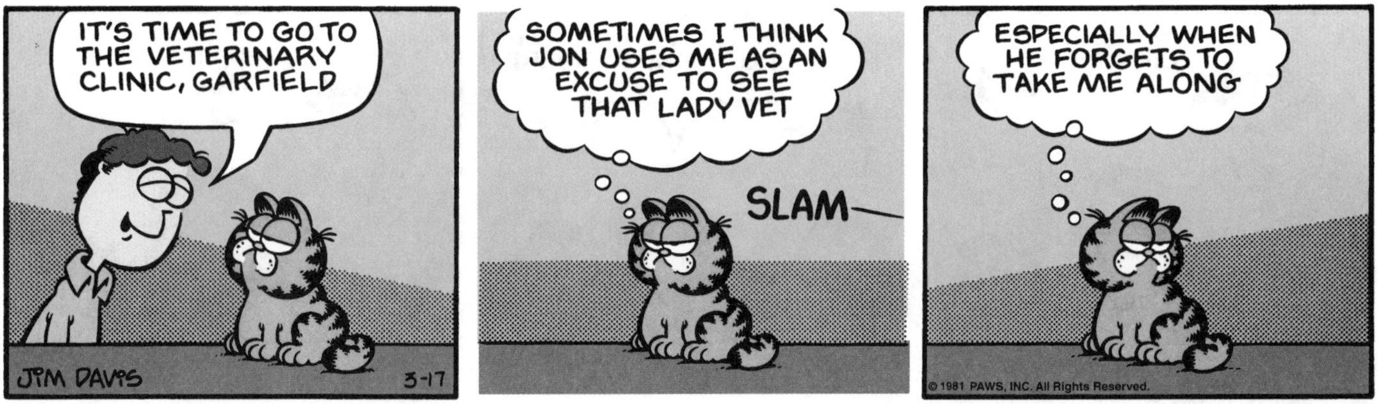
IT'S TIME TO GO TO THE VETERINARY CLINIC, GARFIELD
JIM DAVIS
3-17
SOMETIMES I THINK JON USES ME AS AN EXCUSE TO SEE THAT LADY VET
SLAM
ESPECIALLY WHEN HE FORGETS TO TAKE ME ALONG
© 1981 PAWS, INC. All Rights Reserved.

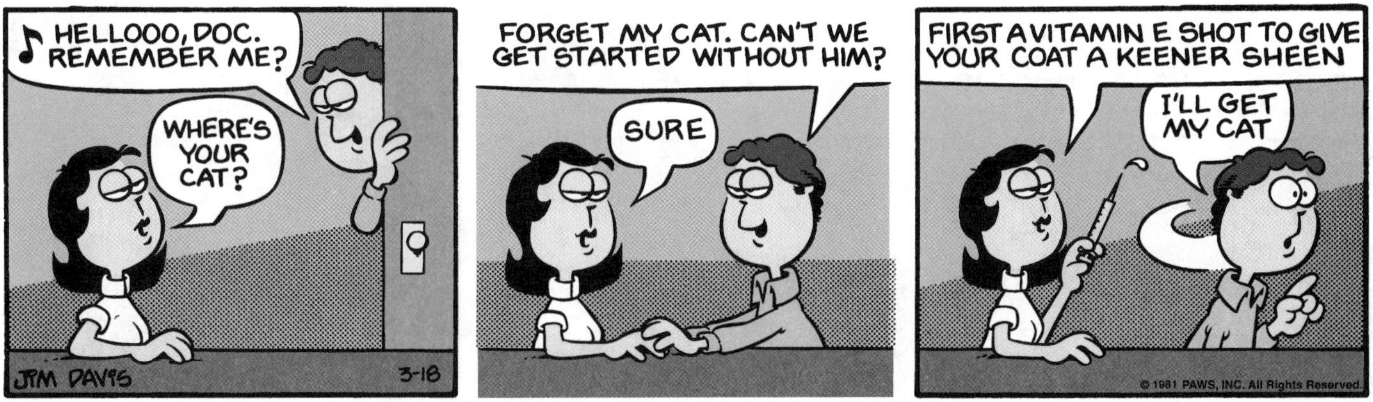
♪ HELLOOO, DOC. REMEMBER ME?
WHERE'S YOUR CAT?
JIM DAVIS
3-18
FORGET MY CAT. CAN'T WE GET STARTED WITHOUT HIM?
SURE
FIRST A VITAMIN E SHOT TO GIVE YOUR COAT A KEENER SHEEN
I'LL GET MY CAT
© 1981 PAWS, INC. All Rights Reserved.

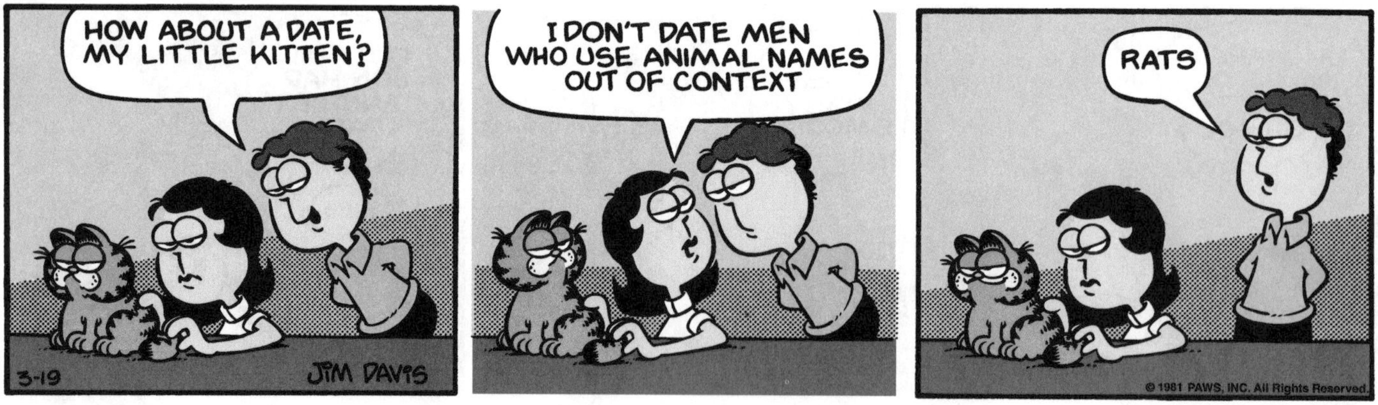
HOW ABOUT A DATE, MY LITTLE KITTEN?
I DON'T DATE MEN WHO USE ANIMAL NAMES OUT OF CONTEXT
RATS
3-19
JIM DAVIS
© 1981 PAWS, INC. All Rights Reserved.

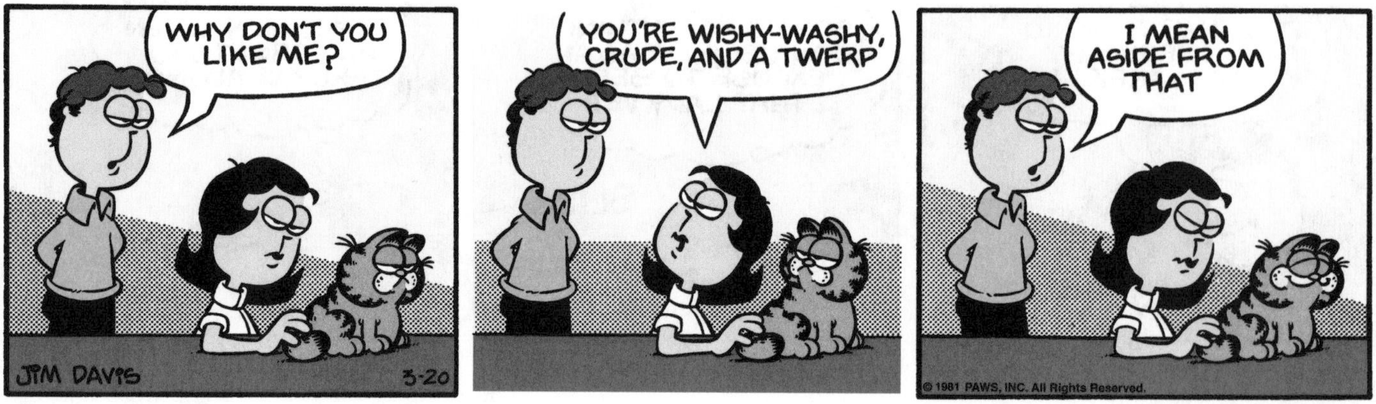
WHY DON'T YOU LIKE ME?
YOU'RE WISHY-WASHY, CRUDE, AND A TWERP
I MEAN ASIDE FROM THAT
JIM DAVIS
3-20
© 1981 PAWS, INC. All Rights Reserved.

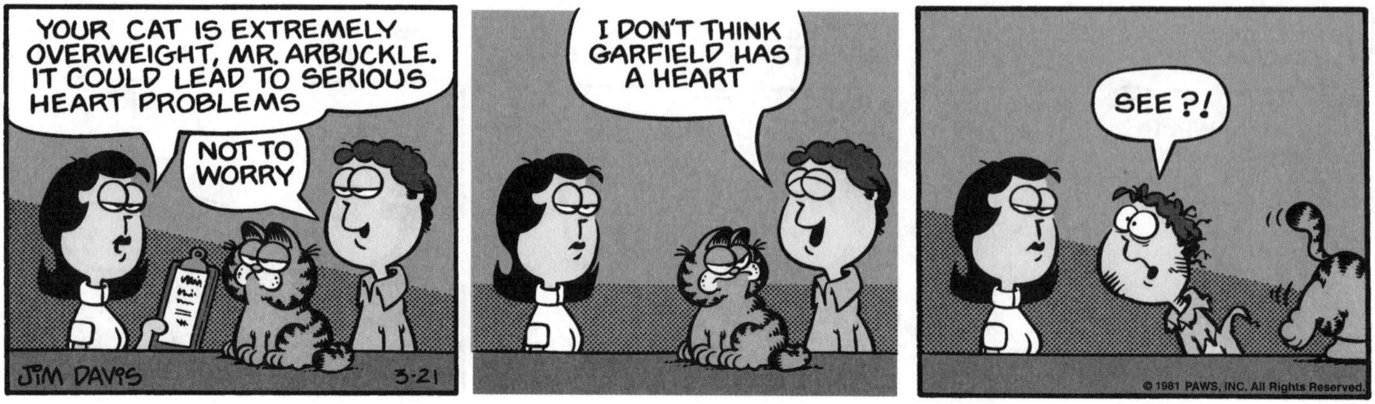
YOUR CAT IS EXTREMELY OVERWEIGHT, MR. ARBUCKLE. IT COULD LEAD TO SERIOUS HEART PROBLEMS
NOT TO WORRY
I DON'T THINK GARFIELD HAS A HEART
SEE ?!
JIM DAVIS
3-21
© 1981 PAWS, INC. All Rights Reserved.

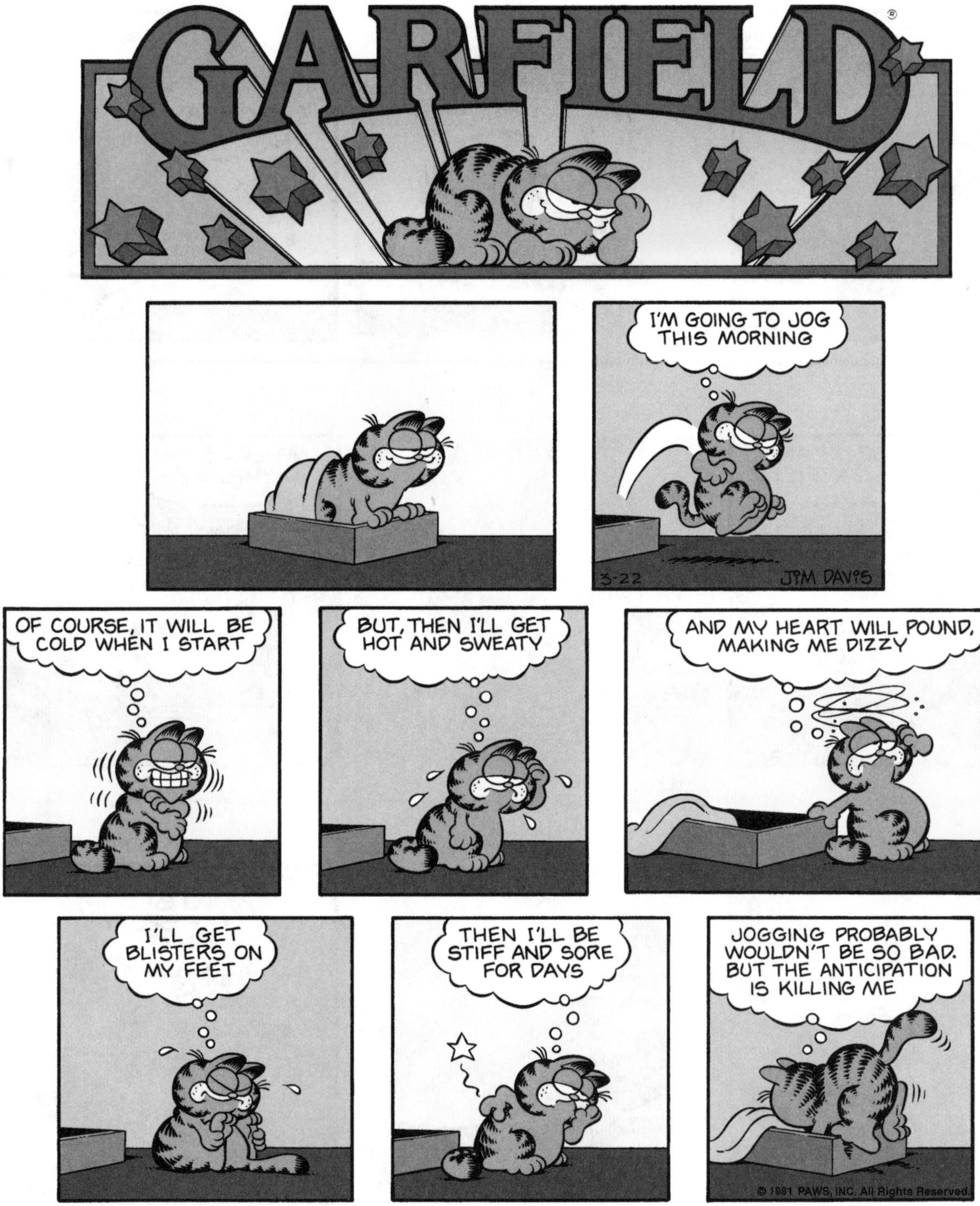

GARFIELD®
I'M GOING TO JOG THIS MORNING
3-22
JIM DAVIS
OF COURSE, IT WILL BE COLD WHEN I START
BUT, THEN I'LL GET HOT AND SWEATY
AND MY HEART WILL POUND, MAKING ME DIZZY
I'LL GET BLISTERS ON MY FEET
THEN I'LL BE STIFF AND SORE FOR DAYS
JOGGING PROBABLY WOULDN'T BE SO BAD. BUT THE ANTICIPATION IS KILLING ME
© 1981 PAWS, INC. All Rights Reserved.

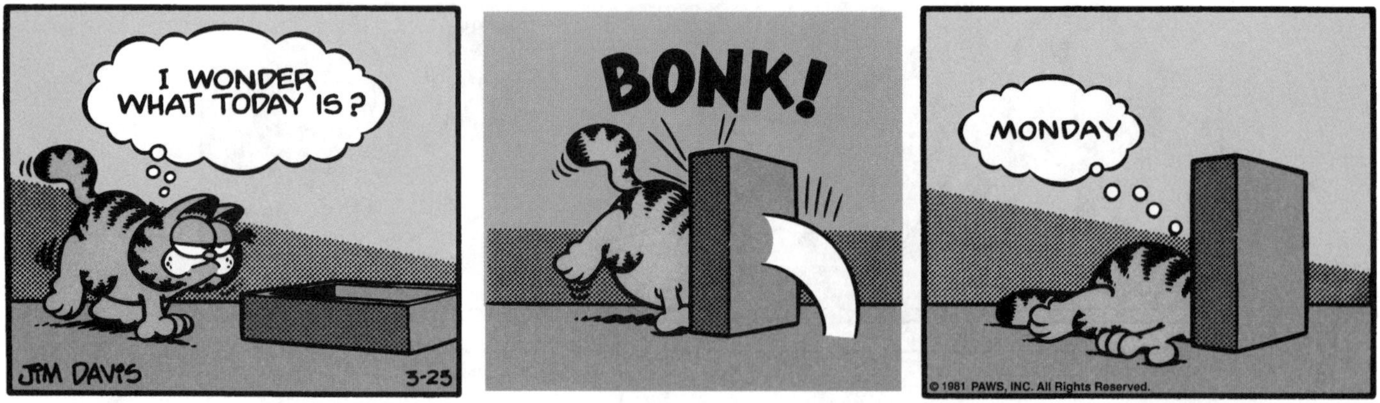
I WONDER WHAT TODAY IS?
JIM DAVIS
3-23
BONK!
MONDAY
© 1981 PAWS, INC. All Rights Reserved.

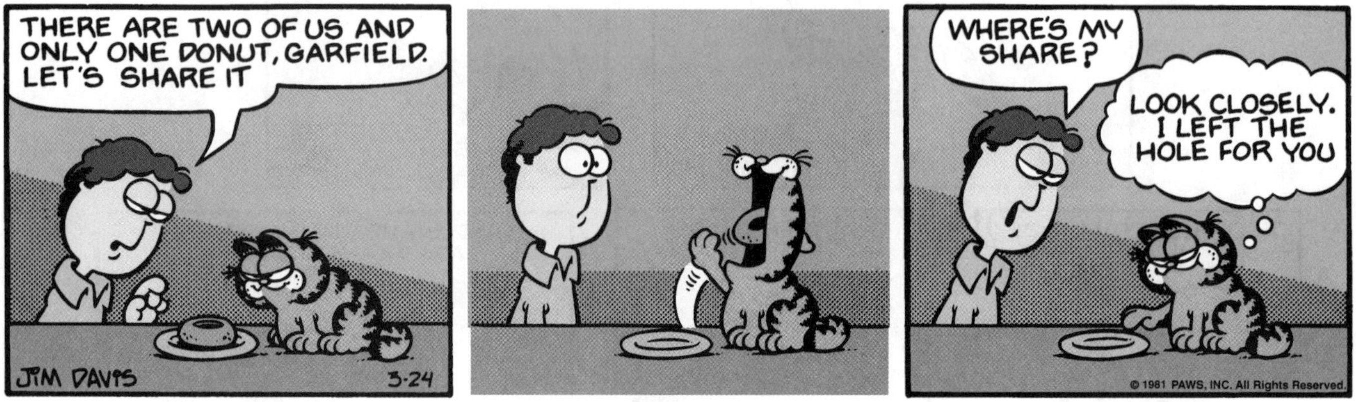
THERE ARE TWO OF US AND ONLY ONE DONUT, GARFIELD. LET'S SHARE IT
JIM DAVIS
3-24
WHERE'S MY SHARE?
LOOK CLOSELY. I LEFT THE HOLE FOR YOU
© 1981 PAWS, INC. All Rights Reserved.

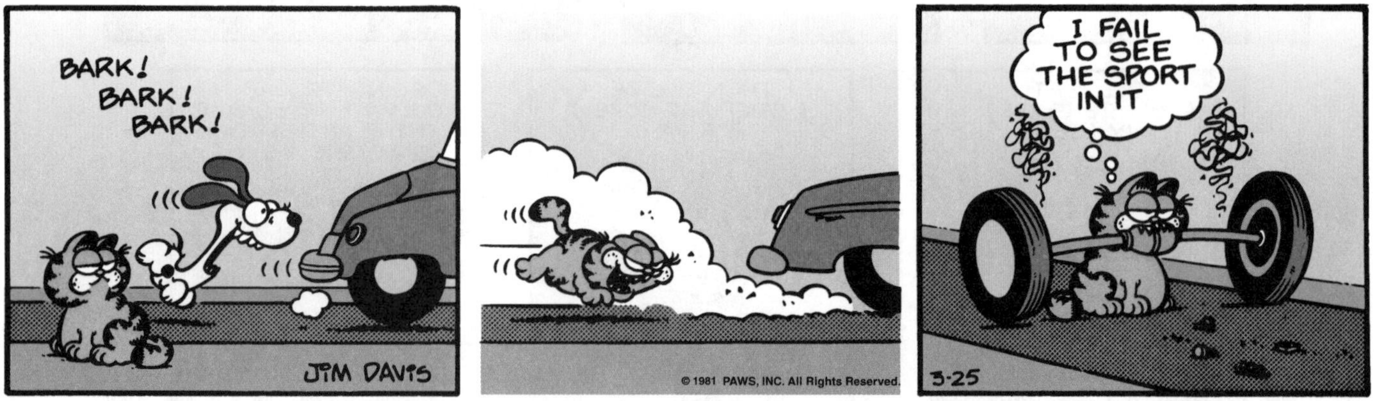
BARK! BARK! BARK!
JIM DAVIS
© 1981 PAWS, INC. All Rights Reserved.
I FAIL TO SEE THE SPORT IN IT
3-25

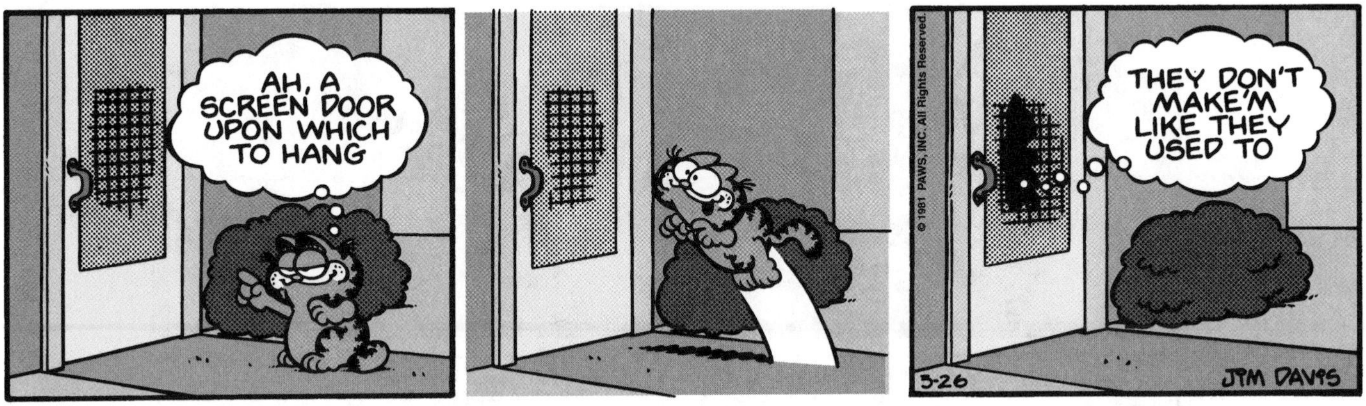
AH, A SCREEN DOOR UPON WHICH TO HANG
THEY DON'T MAKE'M LIKE THEY USED TO
© 1981 PAWS, INC. All Rights Reserved.
3-26
JIM DAVIS

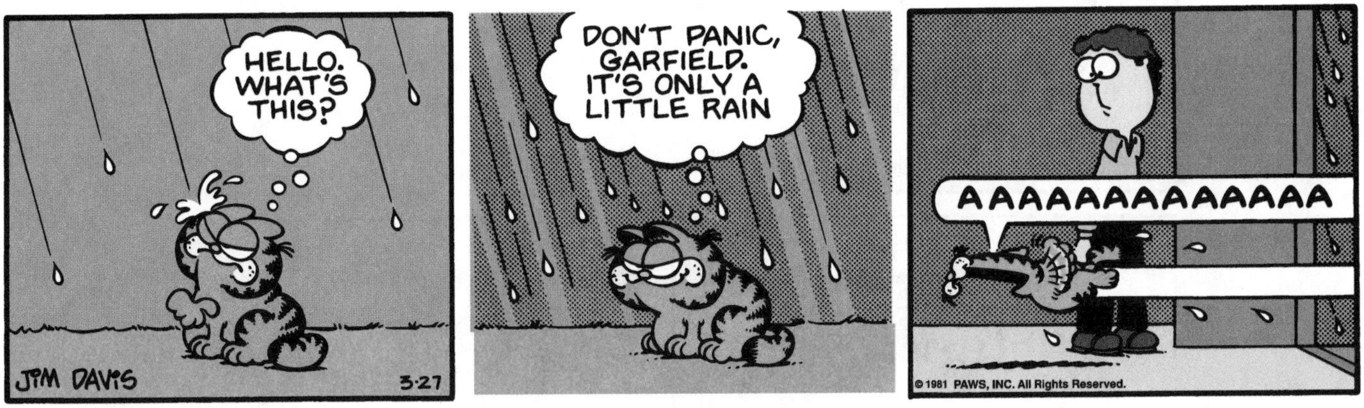
HELLO. WHAT'S THIS?
JIM DAVIS
3-27
DON'T PANIC, GARFIELD. IT'S ONLY A LITTLE RAIN
AAAAAAAAAAAAAA
© 1981 PAWS, INC. All Rights Reserved.

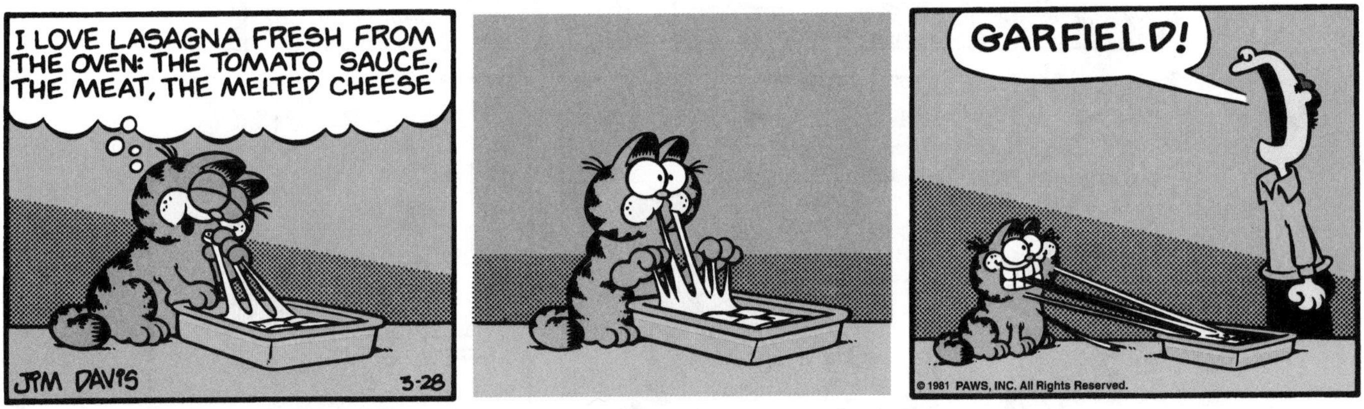
I LOVE LASAGNA FRESH FROM THE OVEN: THE TOMATO SAUCE, THE MEAT, THE MELTED CHEESE
JIM DAVIS
3-28
GARFIELD!
© 1981 PAWS, INC. All Rights Reserved.

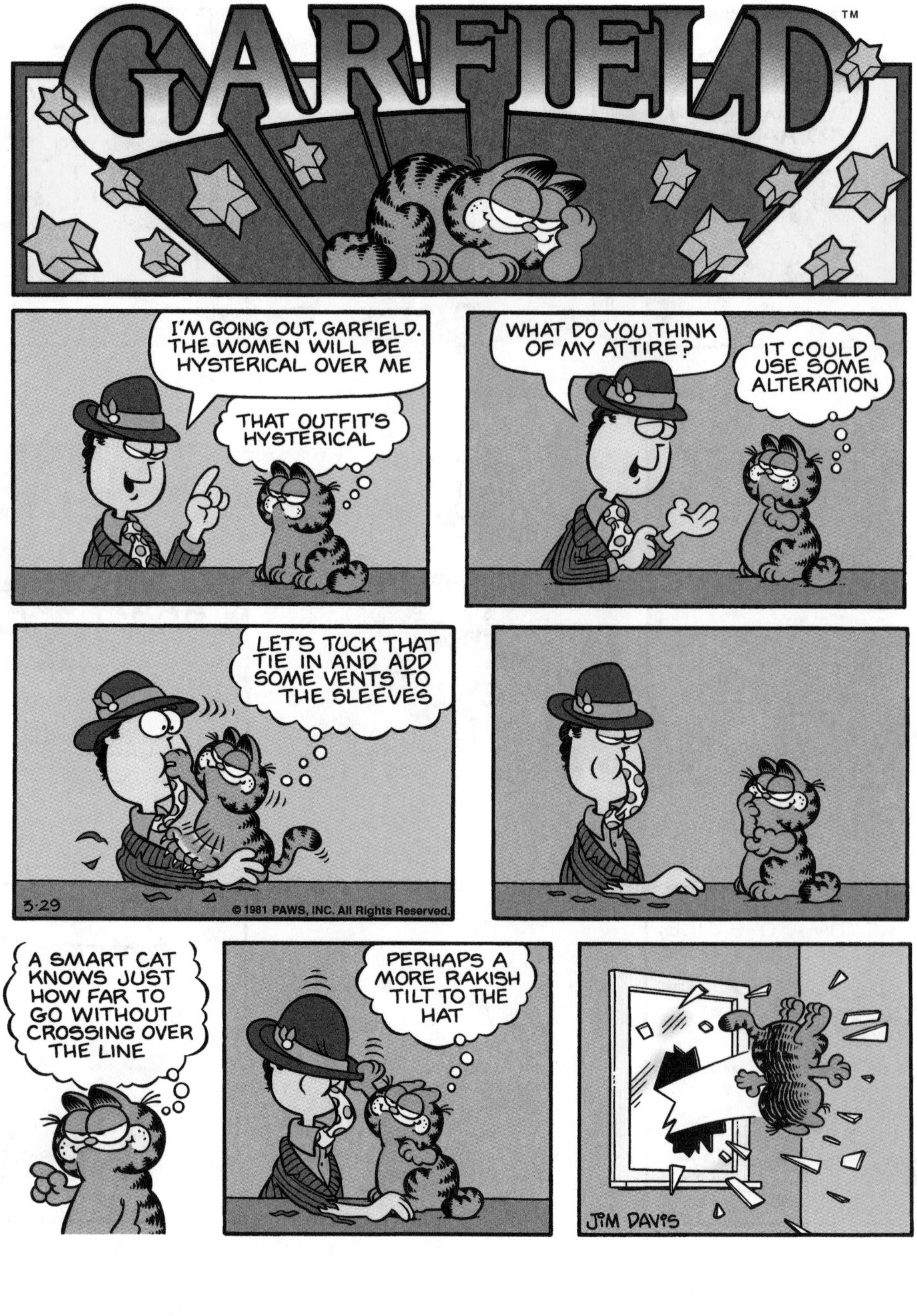
GARFIELD
I'M GOING OUT, GARFIELD. THE WOMEN WILL BE HYSTERICAL OVER ME
THAT OUTFIT'S HYSTERICAL
WHAT DO YOU THINK OF MY ATTIRE?
IT COULD USE SOME ALTERATION
LET'S TUCK THAT TIE IN AND ADD SOME VENTS TO THE SLEEVES
3-29
© 1981 PAWS, INC. All Rights Reserved.
A SMART CAT KNOWS JUST HOW FAR TO GO WITHOUT CROSSING OVER THE LINE
PERHAPS A MORE RAKISH TILT TO THE HAT
JIM DAVIS

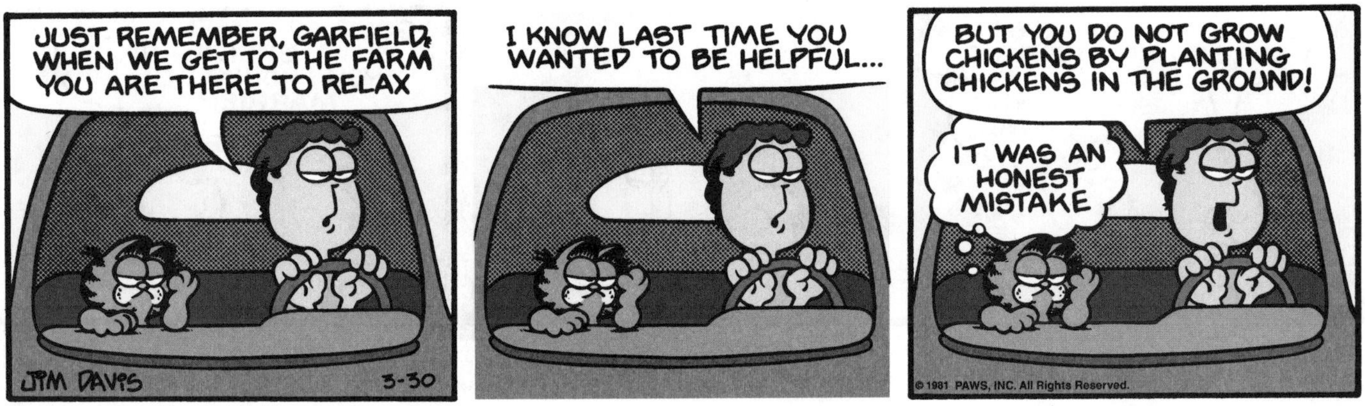
JUST REMEMBER, GARFIELD, WHEN WE GET TO THE FARM YOU ARE THERE TO RELAX
I KNOW LAST TIME YOU WANTED TO BE HELPFUL...
BUT YOU DO NOT GROW CHICKENS BY PLANTING CHICKENS IN THE GROUND!
IT WAS AN HONEST MISTAKE
JIM DAVIS
3-30
© 1981 PAWS, INC. All Rights Reserved.

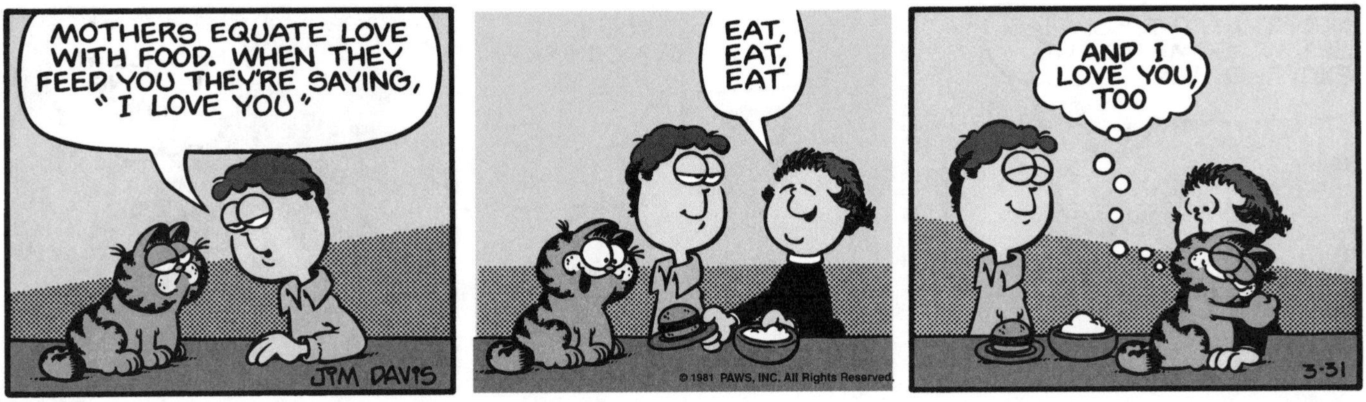
MOTHERS EQUATE LOVE WITH FOOD. WHEN THEY FEED YOU THEY'RE SAYING, "I LOVE YOU"
JIM DAVIS
EAT, EAT, EAT
© 1981 PAWS, INC. All Rights Reserved.
AND I LOVE YOU, TOO
3-31

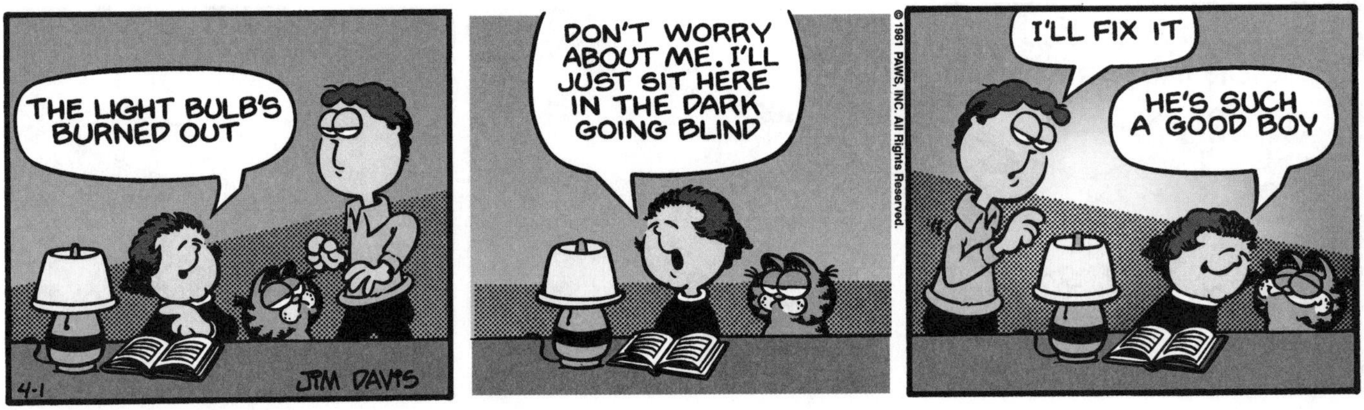
THE LIGHT BULB'S BURNED OUT
4-1
JIM DAVIS
DON'T WORRY ABOUT ME. I'LL JUST SIT HERE IN THE DARK GOING BLIND
© 1981 PAWS, INC. All Rights Reserved.
I'LL FIX IT
HE'S SUCH A GOOD BOY

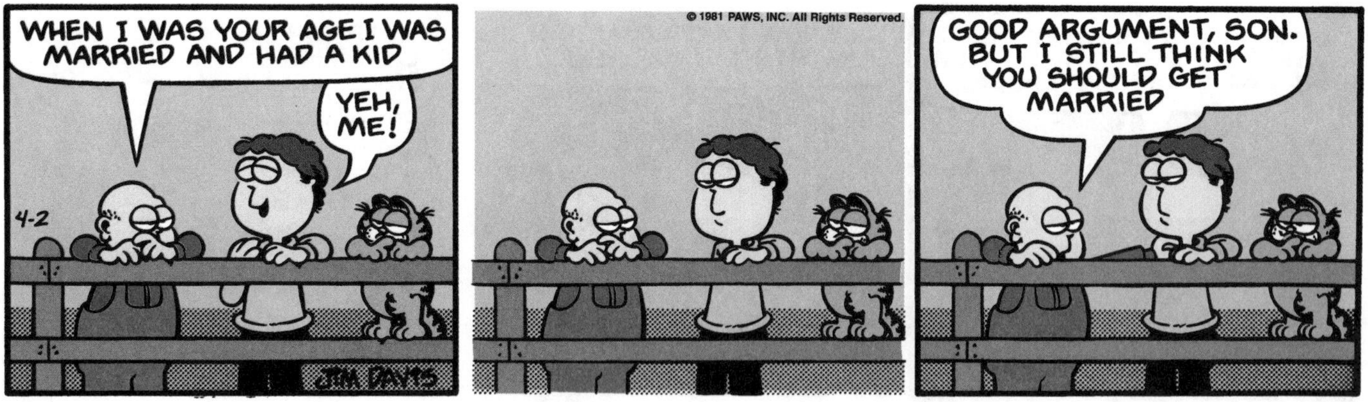
WHEN I WAS YOUR AGE I WAS MARRIED AND HAD A KID
YEH, ME!
4-2
JIM DAVIS
© 1981 PAWS, INC. All Rights Reserved.
GOOD ARGUMENT, SON. BUT I STILL THINK YOU SHOULD GET MARRIED

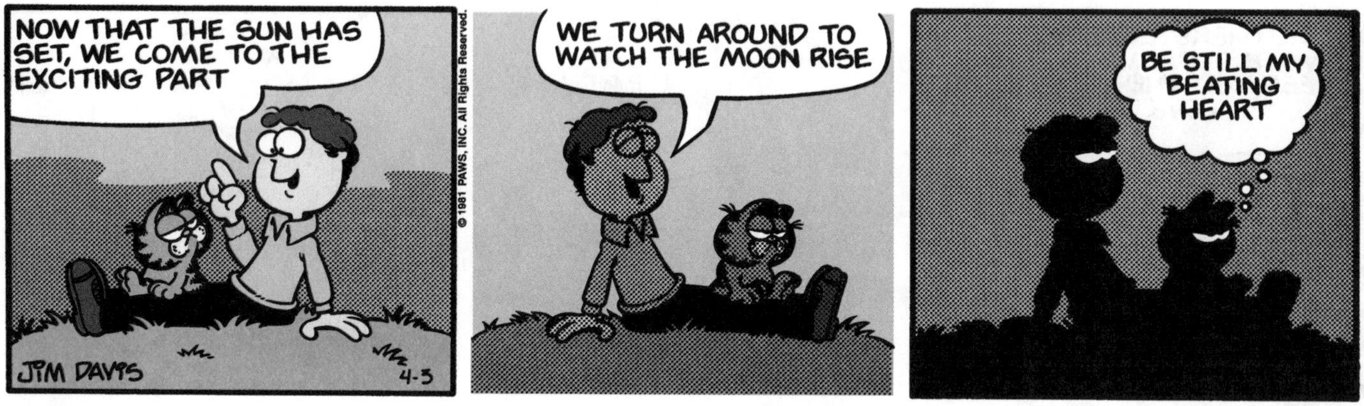
NOW THAT THE SUN HAS SET, WE COME TO THE EXCITING PART
JIM DAVIS
4-3
© 1981 PAWS, INC. All Rights Reserved.
WE TURN AROUND TO WATCH THE MOON RISE
BE STILL MY BEATING HEART

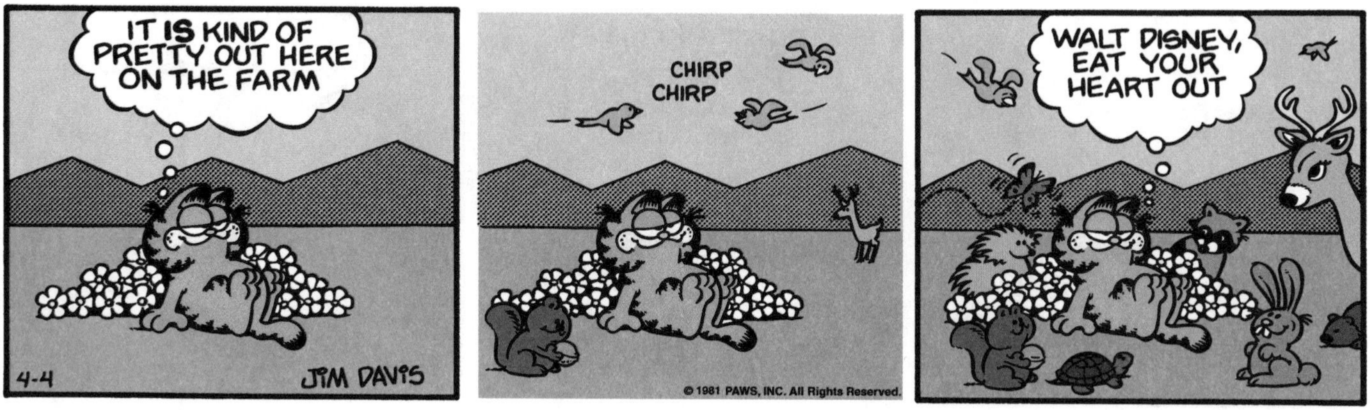
IT IS KIND OF PRETTY OUT HERE ON THE FARM
4-4
JIM DAVIS
CHIRP
CHIRP
© 1981 PAWS, INC. All Rights Reserved.
WALT DISNEY, EAT YOUR HEART OUT

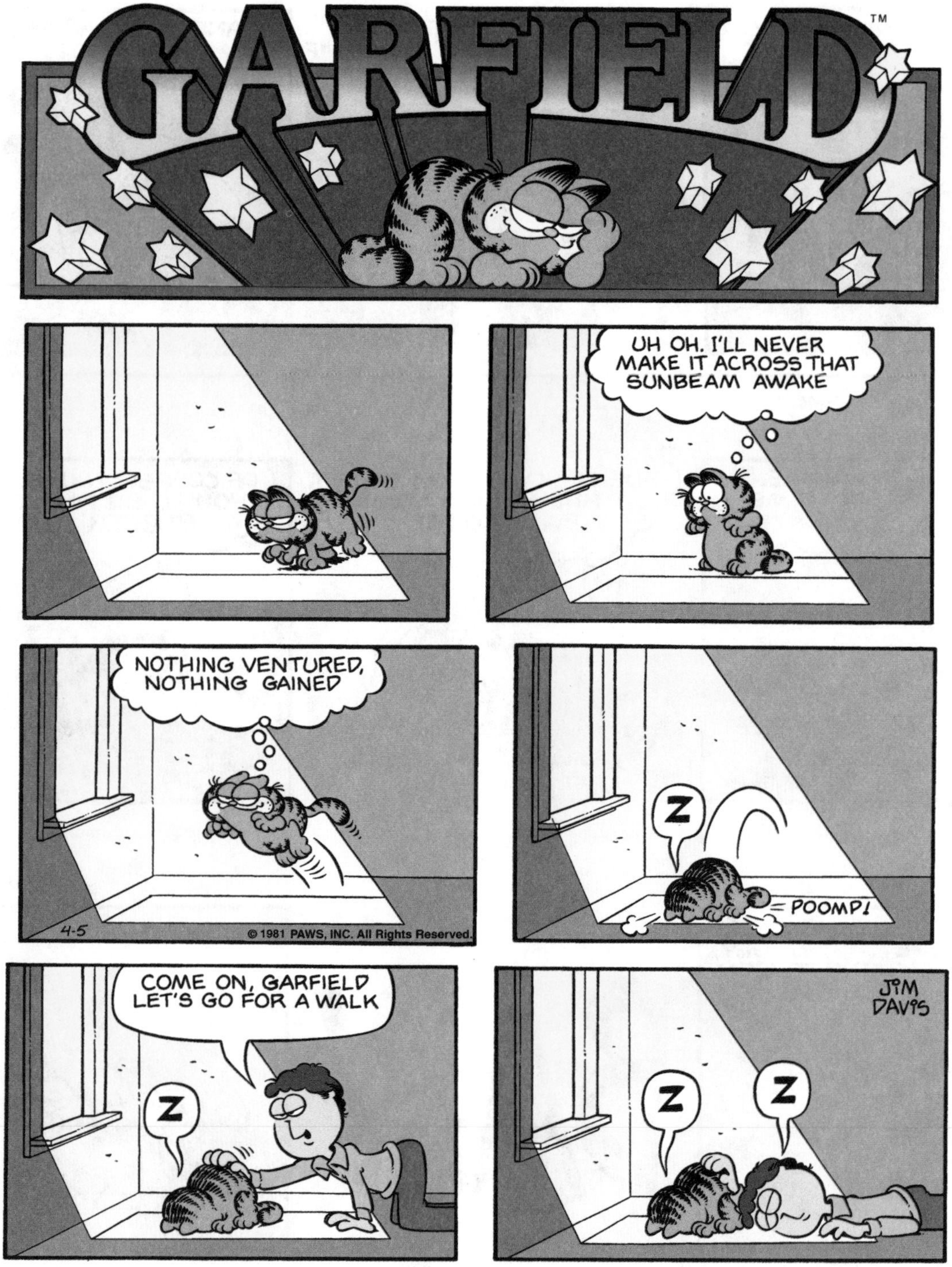
GARFIELD™
UH OH. I'LL NEVER MAKE IT ACROSS THAT SUNBEAM AWAKE
NOTHING VENTURED, NOTHING GAINED
4-5
© 1981 PAWS, INC. All Rights Reserved.
Z
POOMP!
COME ON, GARFIELD LET'S GO FOR A WALK
Z
JIM DAVIS
Z
Z

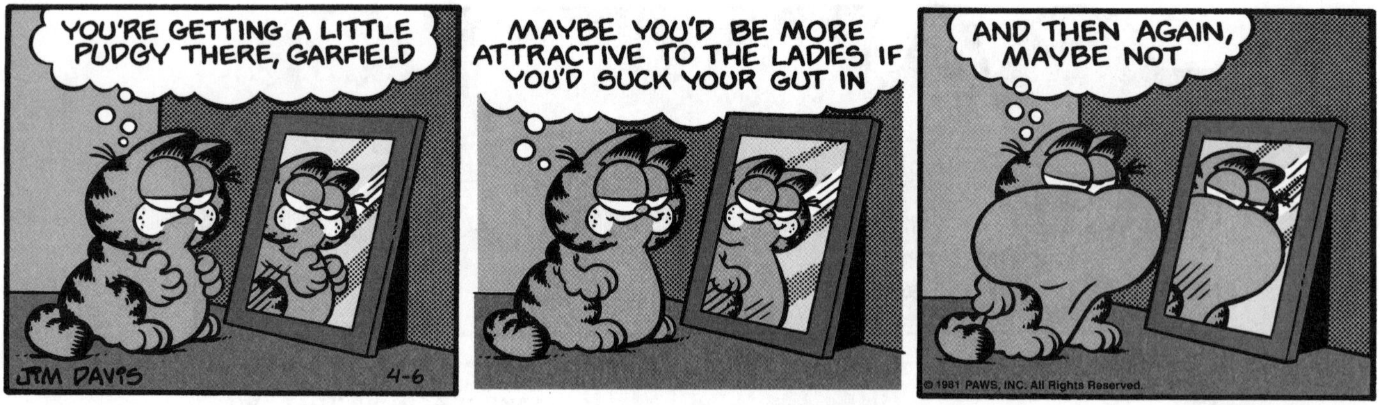
YOU'RE GETTING A LITTLE PUDGY THERE, GARFIELD
JIM DAVIS
4-6
MAYBE YOU'D BE MORE ATTRACTIVE TO THE LADIES IF YOU'D SUCK YOUR GUT IN
AND THEN AGAIN, MAYBE NOT
© 1981 PAWS, INC. All Rights Reserved.

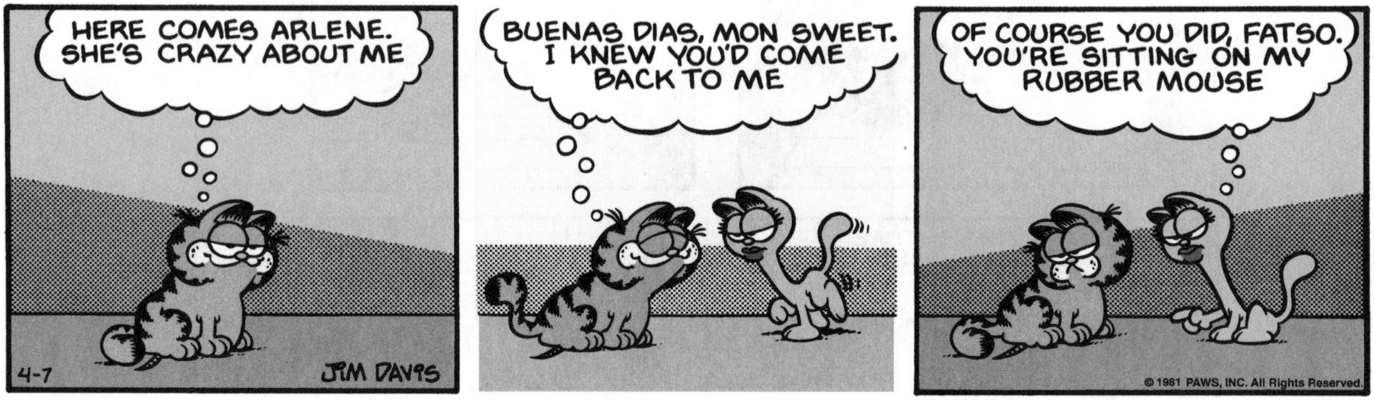
HERE COMES ARLENE. SHE'S CRAZY ABOUT ME
4-7
JIM DAVIS
BUENAS DIAS, MON SWEET. I KNEW YOU'D COME BACK TO ME
OF COURSE YOU DID, FATSO. YOU'RE SITTING ON MY RUBBER MOUSE
© 1981 PAWS, INC. All Rights Reserved.

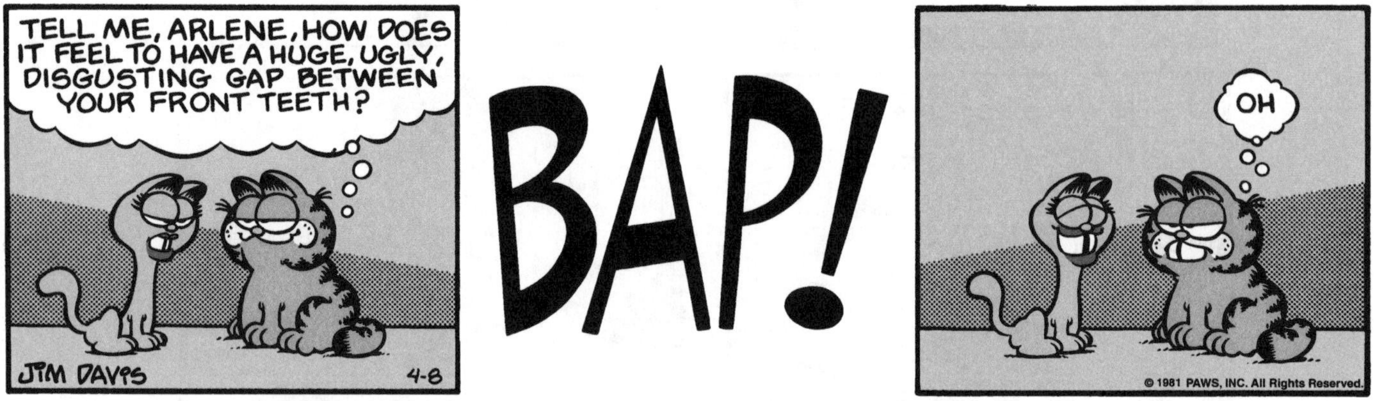
TELL ME, ARLENE, HOW DOES IT FEEL TO HAVE A HUGE, UGLY, DISGUSTING GAP BETWEEN YOUR FRONT TEETH?
JIM DAVIS
4-8
BAP!
OH
© 1981 PAWS, INC. All Rights Reserved.

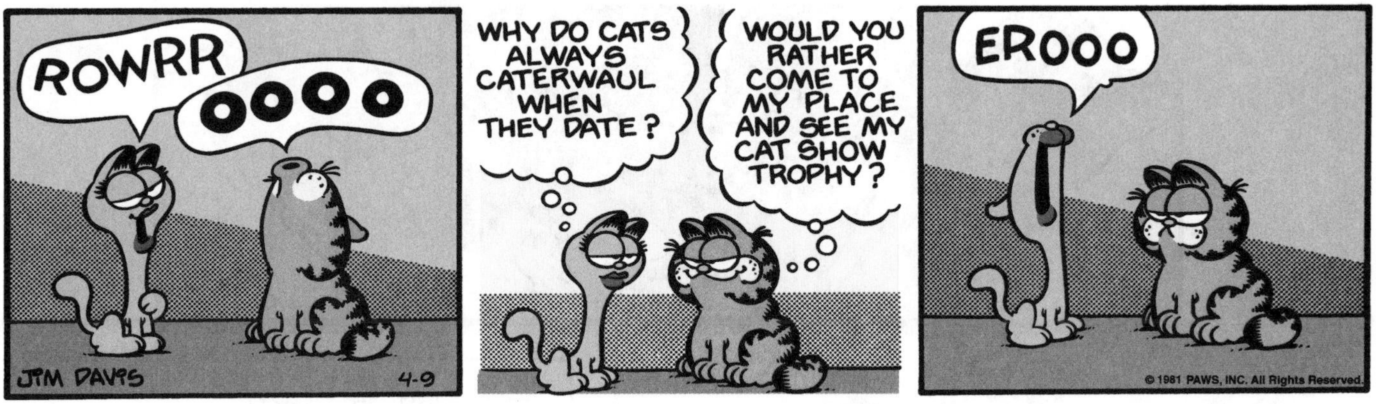
ROWRR
OOOO
JIM DAVIS
4-9
WHY DO CATS ALWAYS CATERWAUL WHEN THEY DATE?
WOULD YOU RATHER COME TO MY PLACE AND SEE MY CAT SHOW TROPHY?
EROOO
© 1981 PAWS, INC. All Rights Reserved.

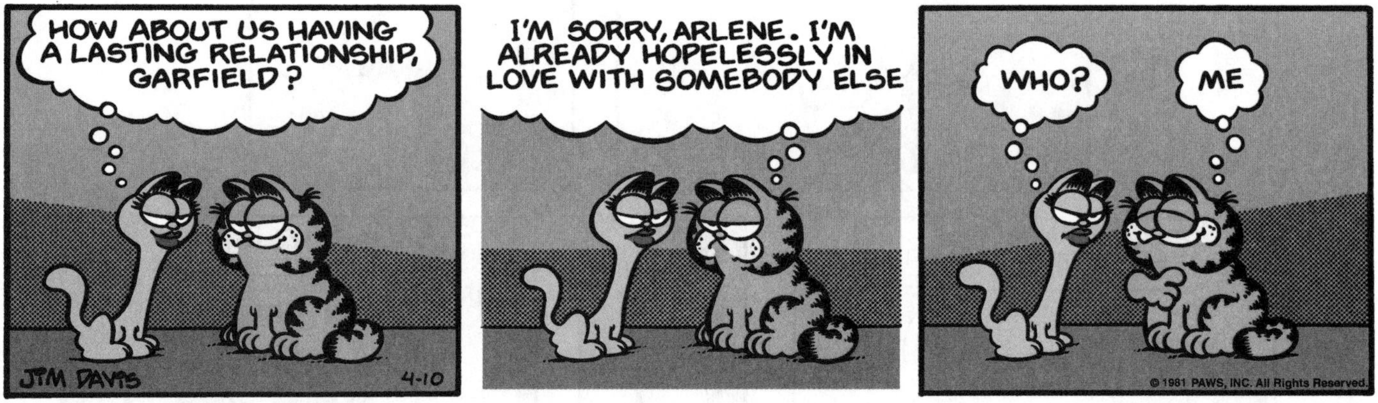
HOW ABOUT US HAVING A LASTING RELATIONSHIP, GARFIELD?
JIM DAVIS
4-10
I'M SORRY, ARLENE. I'M ALREADY HOPELESSLY IN LOVE WITH SOMEBODY ELSE
WHO?
ME
© 1981 PAWS, INC. All Rights Reserved.

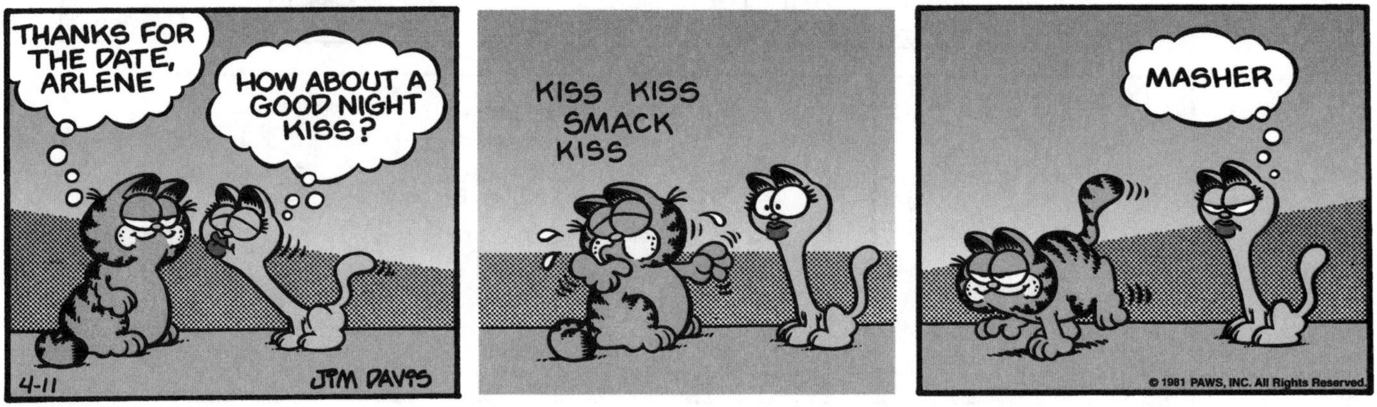
THANKS FOR THE DATE, ARLENE
HOW ABOUT A GOOD NIGHT KISS?
4-11
JIM DAVIS
KISS KISS
SMACK
KISS
MASHER
© 1981 PAWS, INC. All Rights Reserved.

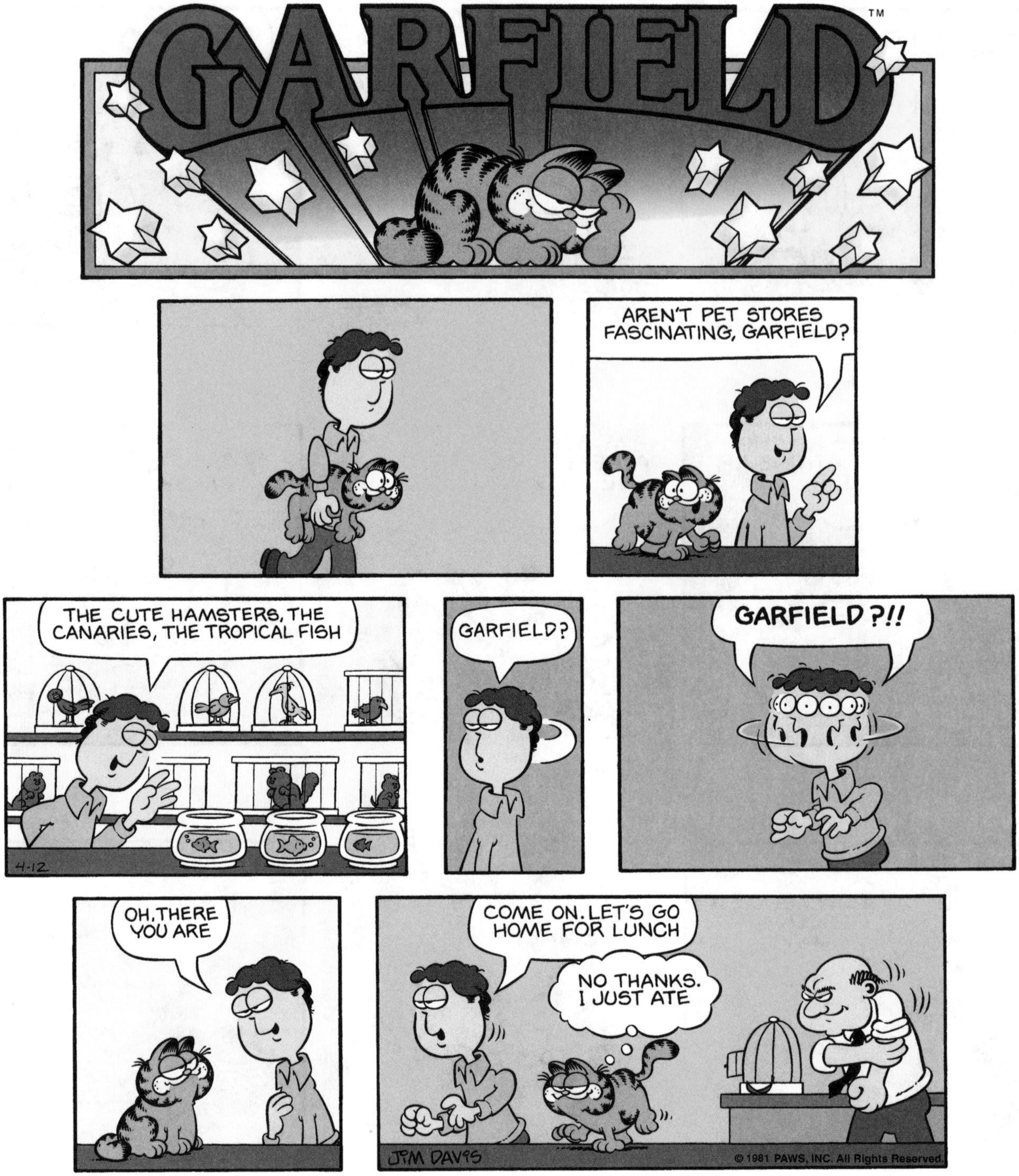
GARFIELD
AREN'T PET STORES FASCINATING, GARFIELD?
THE CUTE HAMSTERS, THE CANARIES, THE TROPICAL FISH
4-12
GARFIELD?
GARFIELD ?!!
OH, THERE YOU ARE
COME ON. LET'S GO HOME FOR LUNCH
NO THANKS. I JUST ATE
JIM DAVIS
© 1981 PAWS, INC. All Rights Reserved.

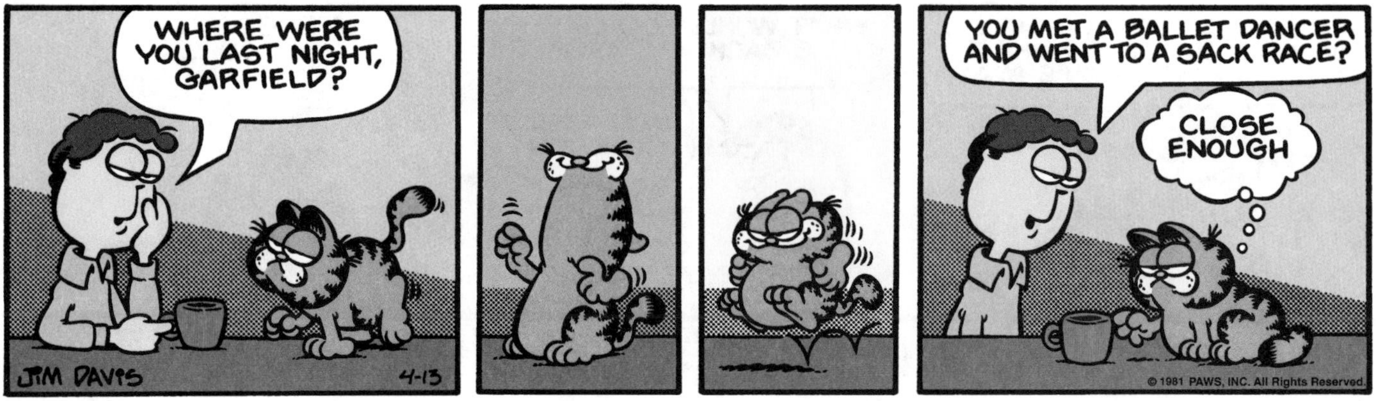
WHERE WERE YOU LAST NIGHT, GARFIELD?
YOU MET A BALLET DANCER AND WENT TO A SACK RACE?
CLOSE ENOUGH
JIM DAVIS
4-13
© 1981 PAWS, INC. All Rights Reserved.

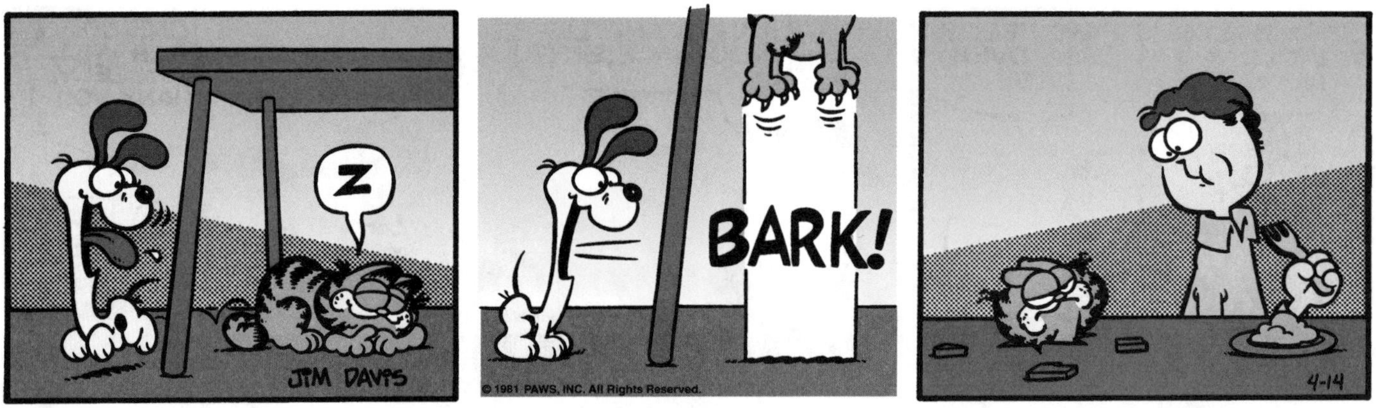
Z
BARK!
JIM DAVIS
© 1981 PAWS, INC. All Rights Reserved.
4-14

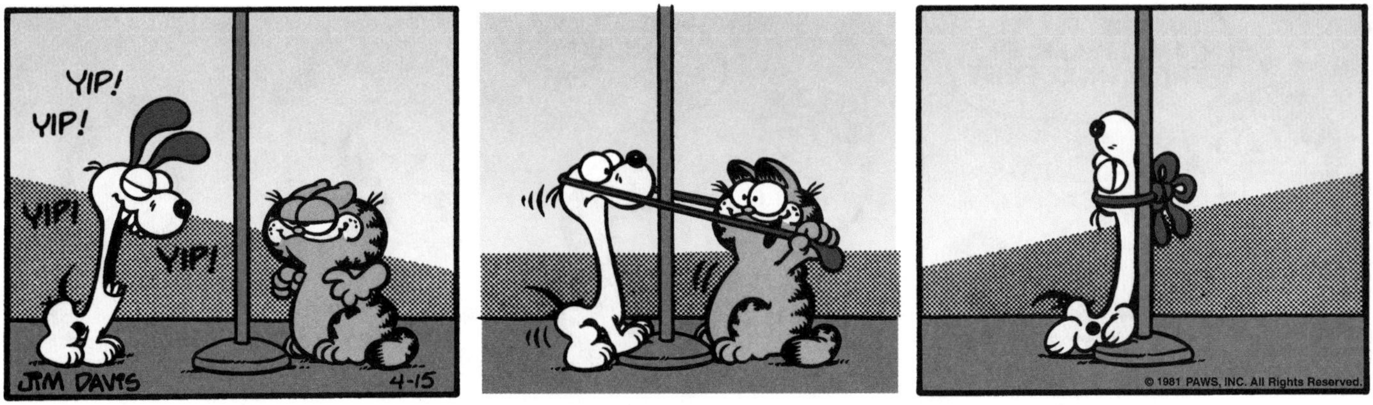
YIP!
YIP!
YIP!
YIP!
JIM DAVIS
4-15
© 1981 PAWS, INC. All Rights Reserved.

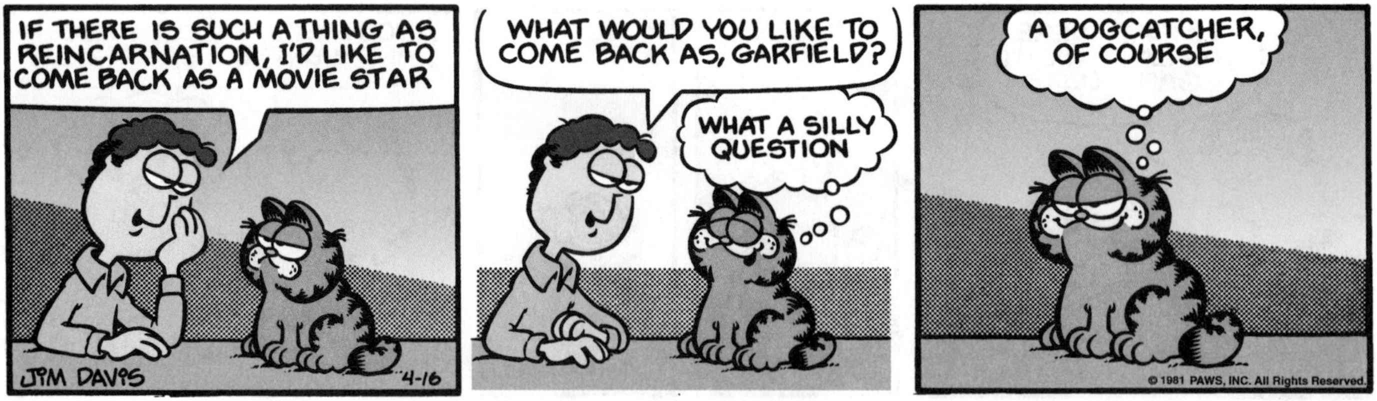
IF THERE IS SUCH A THING AS REINCARNATION, I'D LIKE TO COME BACK AS A MOVIE STAR
JIM DAVIS
4-16
WHAT WOULD YOU LIKE TO COME BACK AS, GARFIELD?
WHAT A SILLY QUESTION
A DOGCATCHER, OF COURSE
© 1981 PAWS, INC. All Rights Reserved.

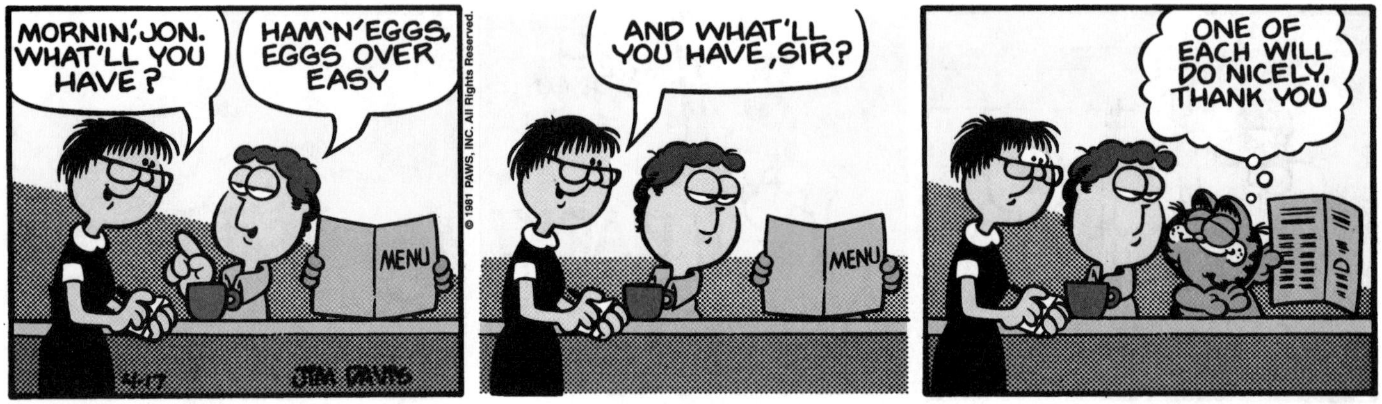
MORNIN', JON. WHAT'LL YOU HAVE?
HAM 'N' EGGS, EGGS OVER EASY
MENU
4-17
JIM DAVIS
© 1981 PAWS, INC. All Rights Reserved.
AND WHAT'LL YOU HAVE, SIR?
MENU
ONE OF EACH WILL DO NICELY, THANK YOU

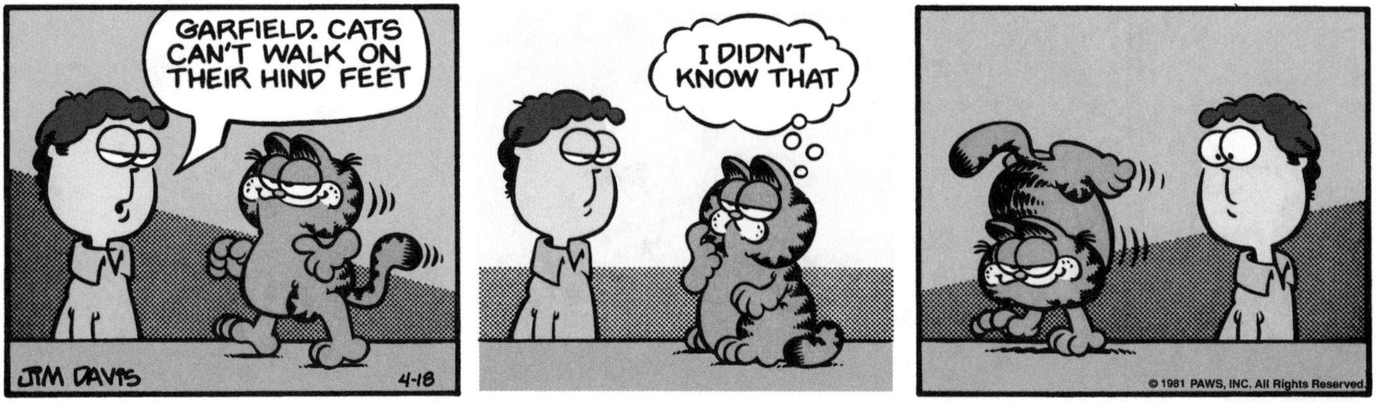
GARFIELD. CATS CAN'T WALK ON THEIR HIND FEET
JIM DAVIS
4-18
I DIDN'T KNOW THAT
© 1981 PAWS, INC. All Rights Reserved.

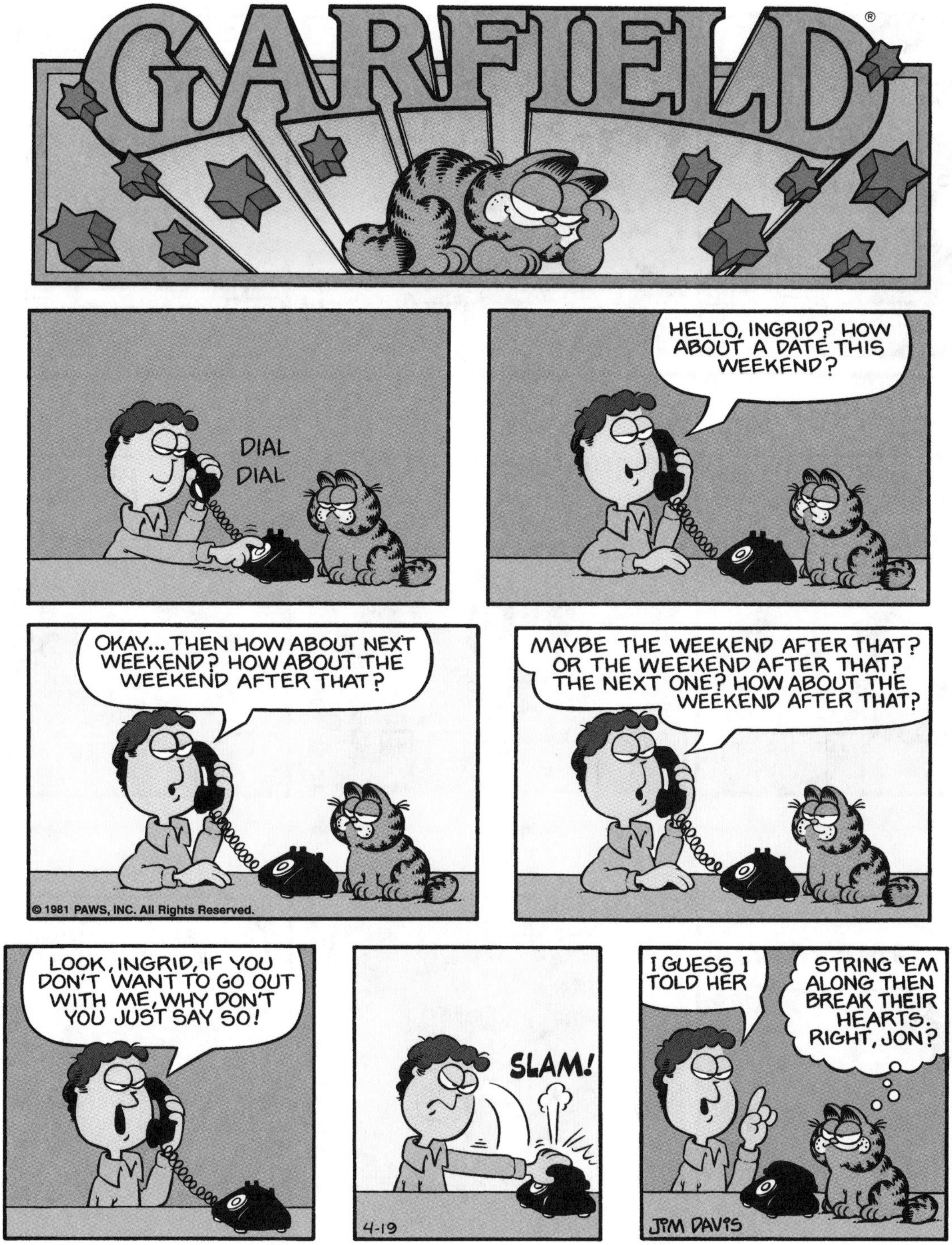
GARFIELD
DIAL
DIAL
HELLO, INGRID? HOW ABOUT A DATE THIS WEEKEND?
OKAY... THEN HOW ABOUT NEXT WEEKEND? HOW ABOUT THE WEEKEND AFTER THAT?
© 1981 PAWS, INC. All Rights Reserved.
MAYBE THE WEEKEND AFTER THAT? OR THE WEEKEND AFTER THAT? THE NEXT ONE? HOW ABOUT THE WEEKEND AFTER THAT?
LOOK, INGRID, IF YOU DON'T WANT TO GO OUT WITH ME, WHY DON'T YOU JUST SAY SO!
SLAM!
4-19
I GUESS I TOLD HER
STRING 'EM ALONG THEN BREAK THEIR HEARTS. RIGHT, JON?
JIM DAVIS

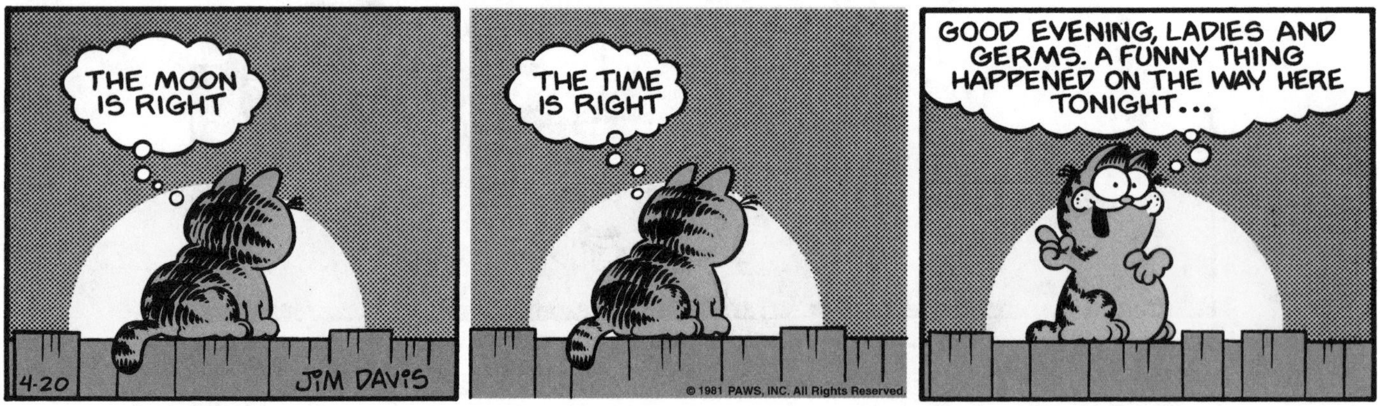
THE MOON IS RIGHT
THE TIME IS RIGHT
GOOD EVENING, LADIES AND GERMS. A FUNNY THING HAPPENED ON THE WAY HERE TONIGHT...
4-20
JIM DAVIS
© 1981 PAWS, INC. All Rights Reserved.

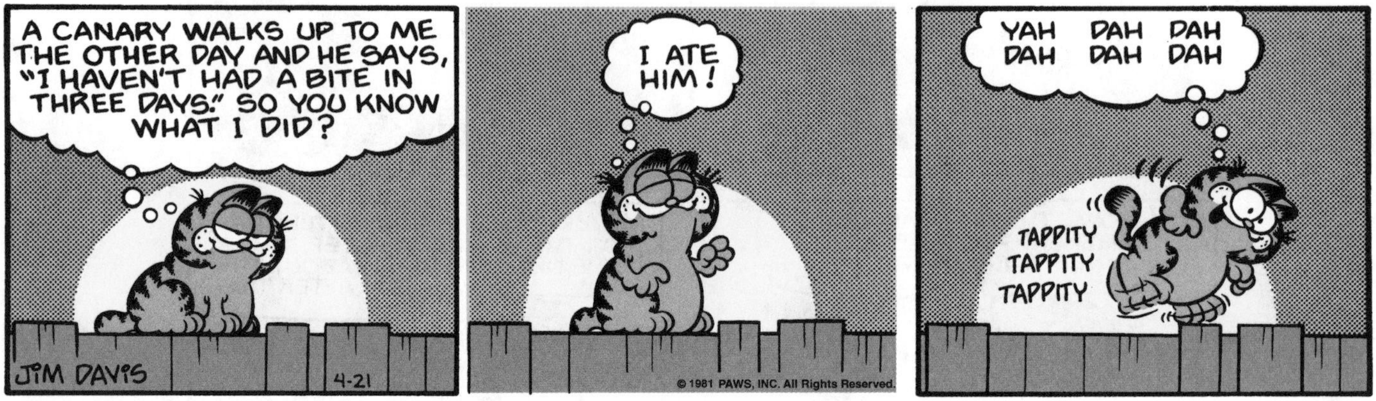
A CANARY WALKS UP TO ME THE OTHER DAY AND HE SAYS, "I HAVEN'T HAD A BITE IN THREE DAYS." SO YOU KNOW WHAT I DID?
JIM DAVIS
4-21
I ATE HIM!
© 1981 PAWS, INC. All Rights Reserved.
YAH DAH DAH DAH DAH DAH
TAPPITY TAPPITY TAPPITY

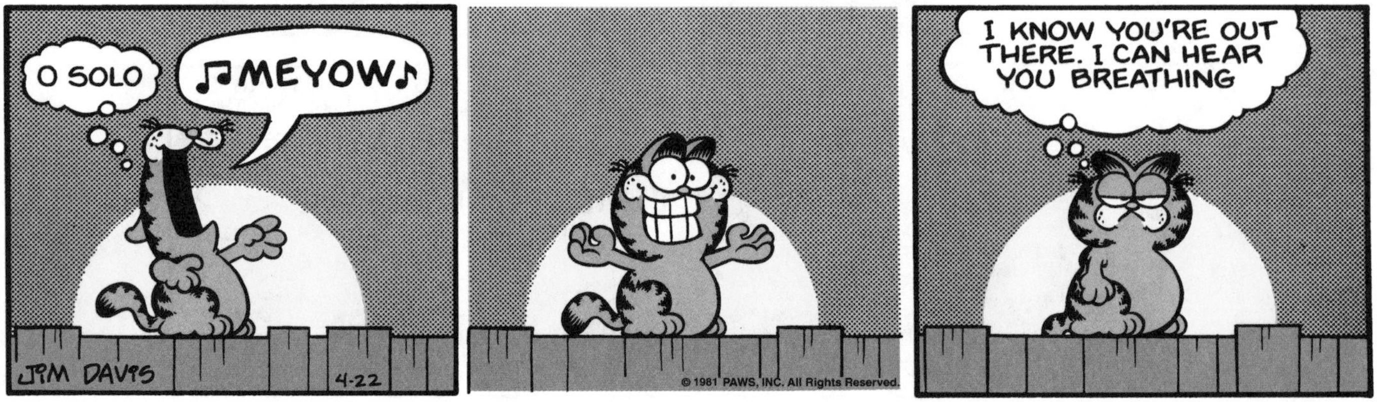
O SOLO
♫MEYOW♪
JIM DAVIS
4-22
© 1981 PAWS, INC. All Rights Reserved.
I KNOW YOU'RE OUT THERE. I CAN HEAR YOU BREATHING

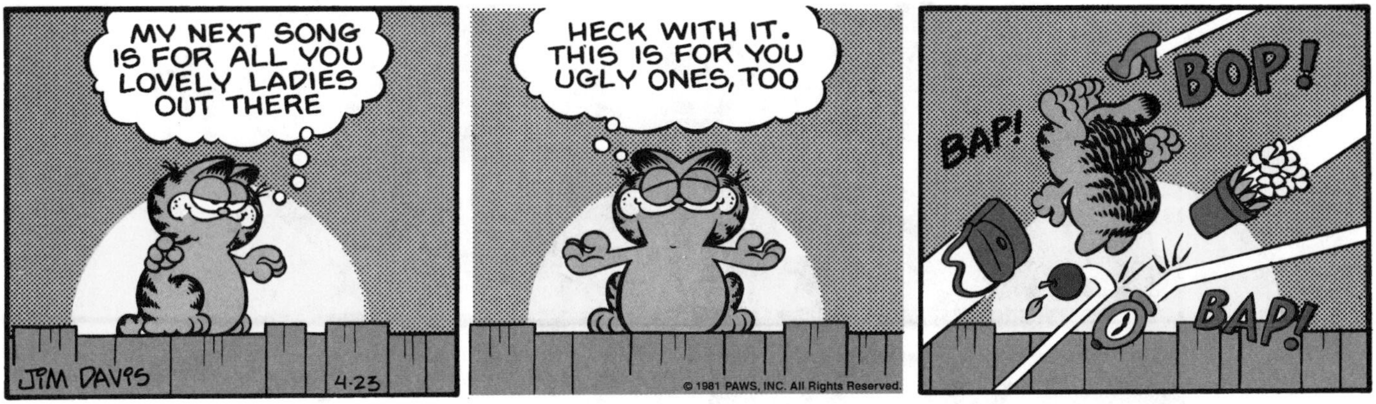
MY NEXT SONG IS FOR ALL YOU LOVELY LADIES OUT THERE
JIM DAVIS
4-23
HECK WITH IT. THIS IS FOR YOU UGLY ONES, TOO
© 1981 PAWS, INC. All Rights Reserved.
BAP!
BOP!
BAP!

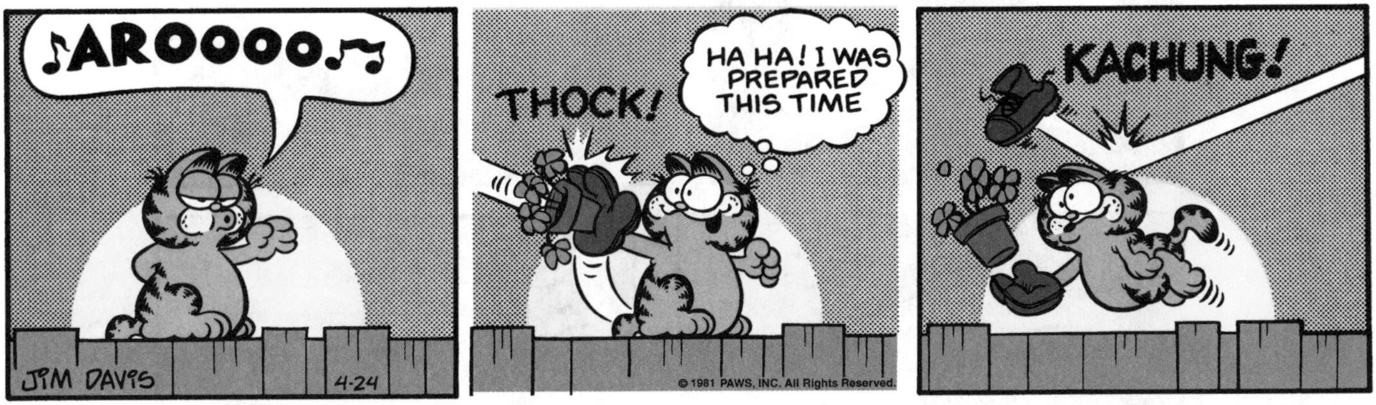
♪AROOOO.♫
JIM DAVIS
4-24
THOCK!
HA HA! I WAS PREPARED THIS TIME
© 1981 PAWS, INC. All Rights Reserved.
KACHUNG!

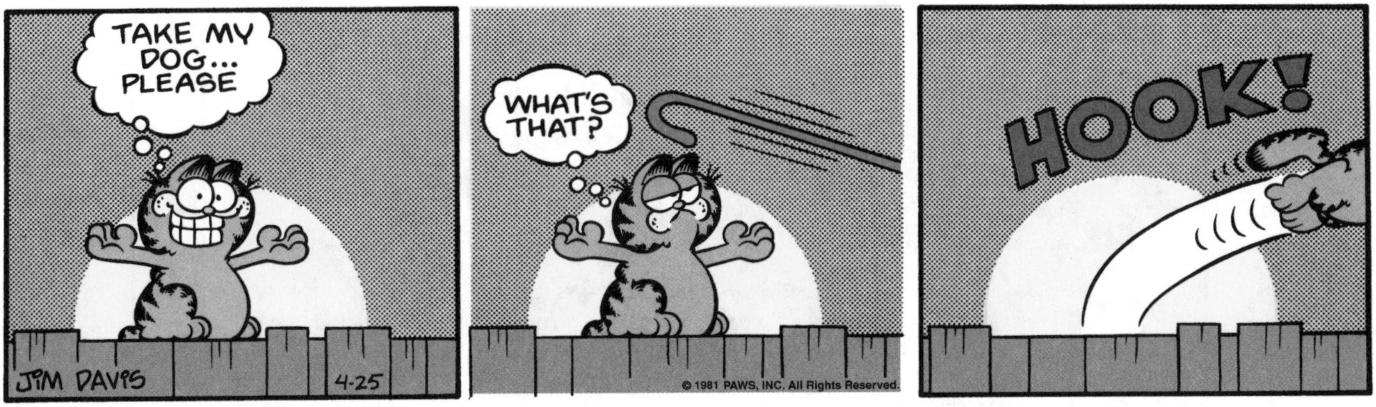
TAKE MY DOG... PLEASE
JIM DAVIS
4-25
WHAT'S THAT?
© 1981 PAWS, INC. All Rights Reserved.
HOOK!

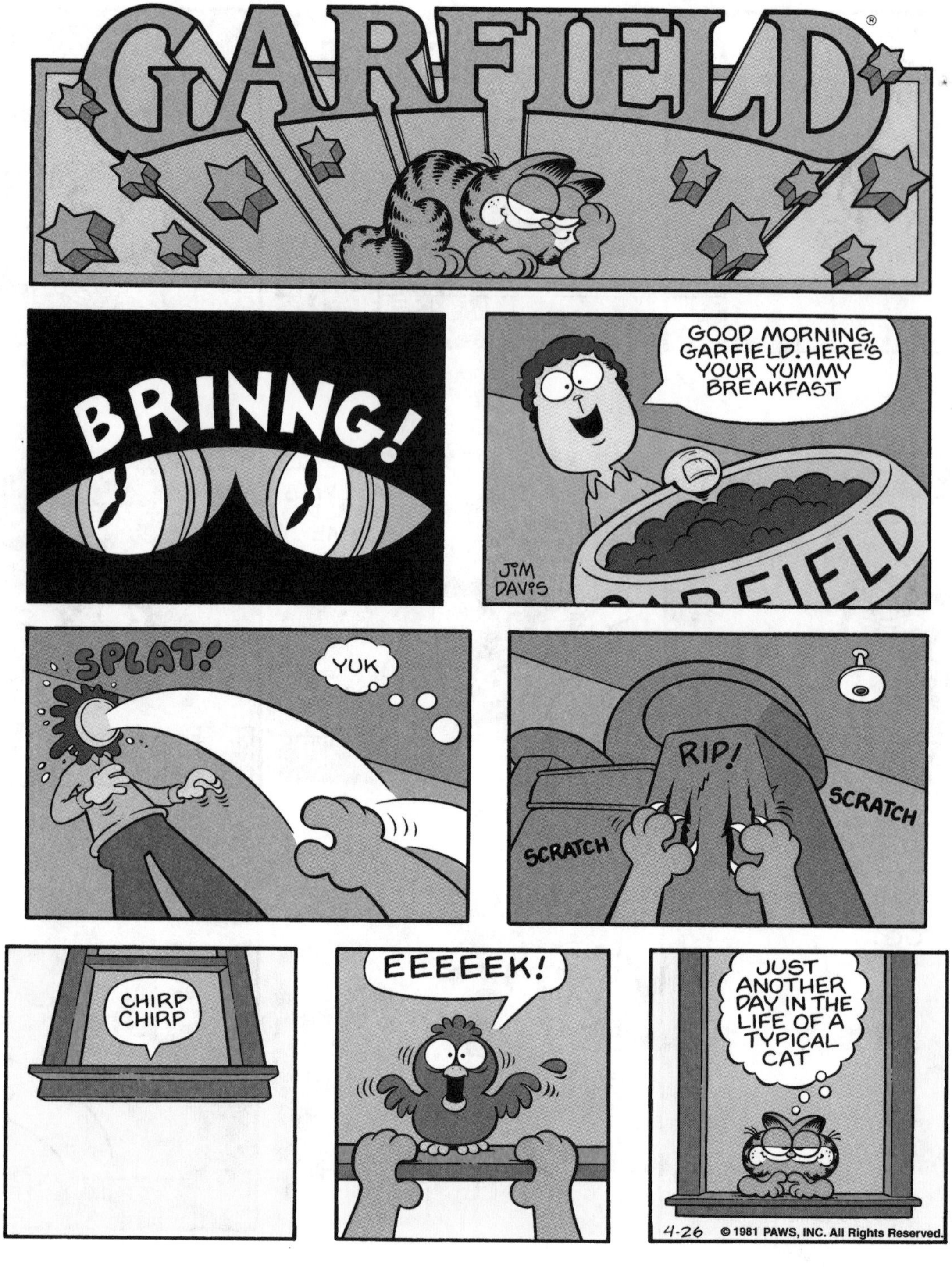
GARFIELD®
BRINNG!
GOOD MORNING, GARFIELD. HERE'S YOUR YUMMY BREAKFAST
GARFIELD
JIM DAVIS
SPLAT!
YUK
RIP!
SCRATCH
SCRATCH
CHIRP CHIRP
EEEEEK!
JUST ANOTHER DAY IN THE LIFE OF A TYPICAL CAT
4-26
© 1981 PAWS, INC. All Rights Reserved.

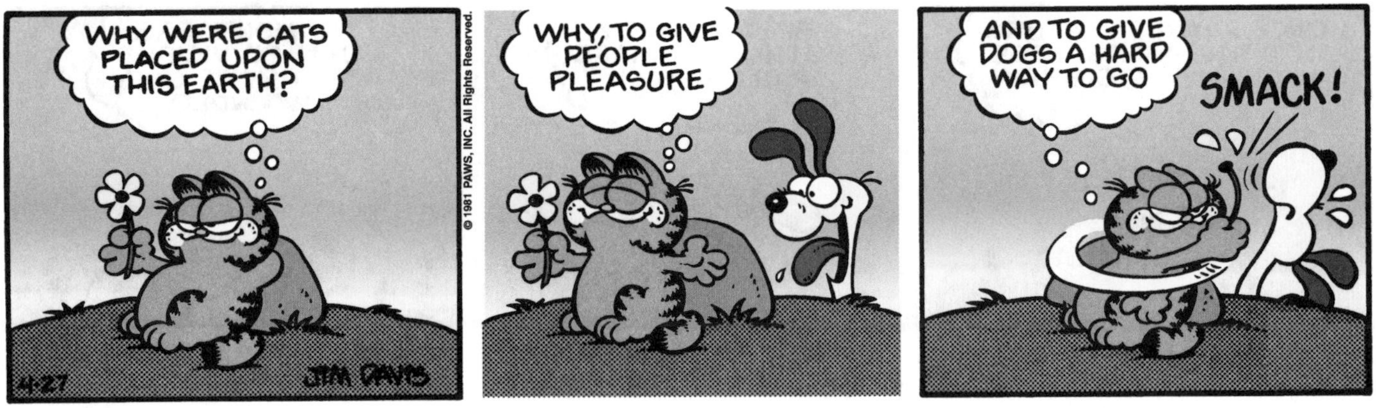
WHY WERE CATS PLACED UPON THIS EARTH?
4-27
JIM DAVIS
© 1981 PAWS, INC. All Rights Reserved.
WHY, TO GIVE PEOPLE PLEASURE
AND TO GIVE DOGS A HARD WAY TO GO
SMACK!

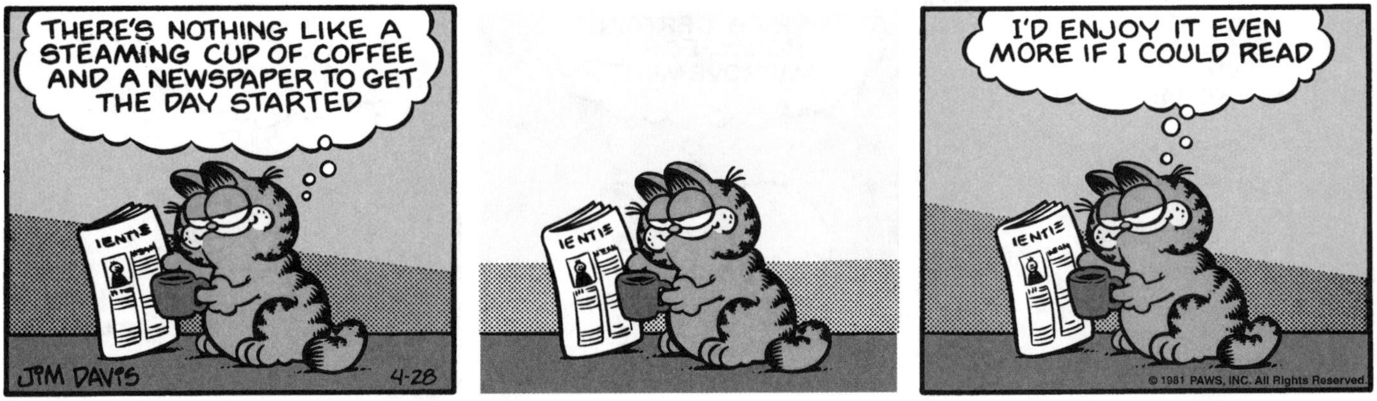
THERE'S NOTHING LIKE A STEAMING CUP OF COFFEE AND A NEWSPAPER TO GET THE DAY STARTED
JIM DAVIS
4-28
I'D ENJOY IT EVEN MORE IF I COULD READ
© 1981 PAWS, INC. All Rights Reserved.

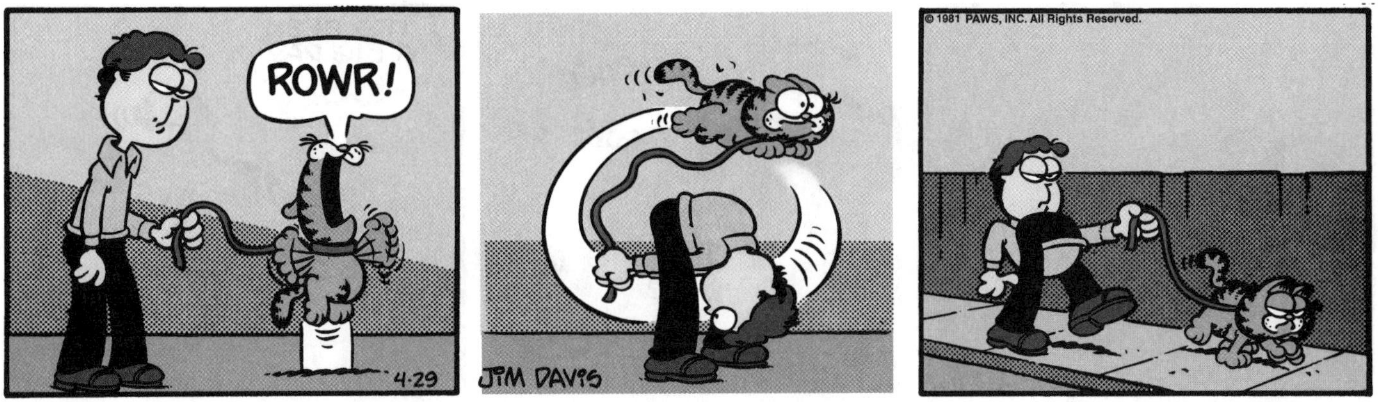
ROWR!
4-29
JIM DAVIS
© 1981 PAWS, INC. All Rights Reserved.

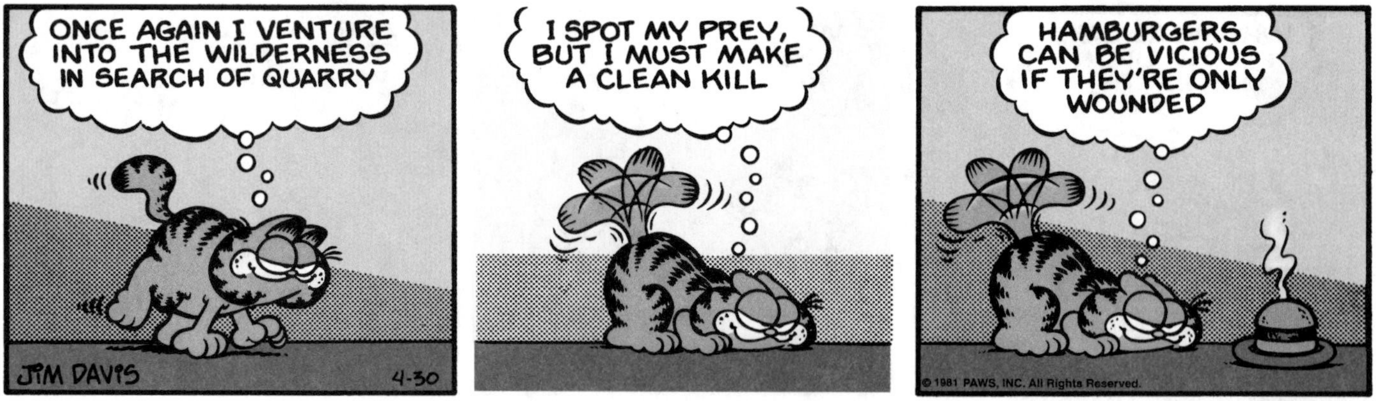
ONCE AGAIN I VENTURE INTO THE WILDERNESS IN SEARCH OF QUARRY
JIM DAVIS
4-30
I SPOT MY PREY, BUT I MUST MAKE A CLEAN KILL
HAMBURGERS CAN BE VICIOUS IF THEY'RE ONLY WOUNDED
© 1981 PAWS, INC. All Rights Reserved.

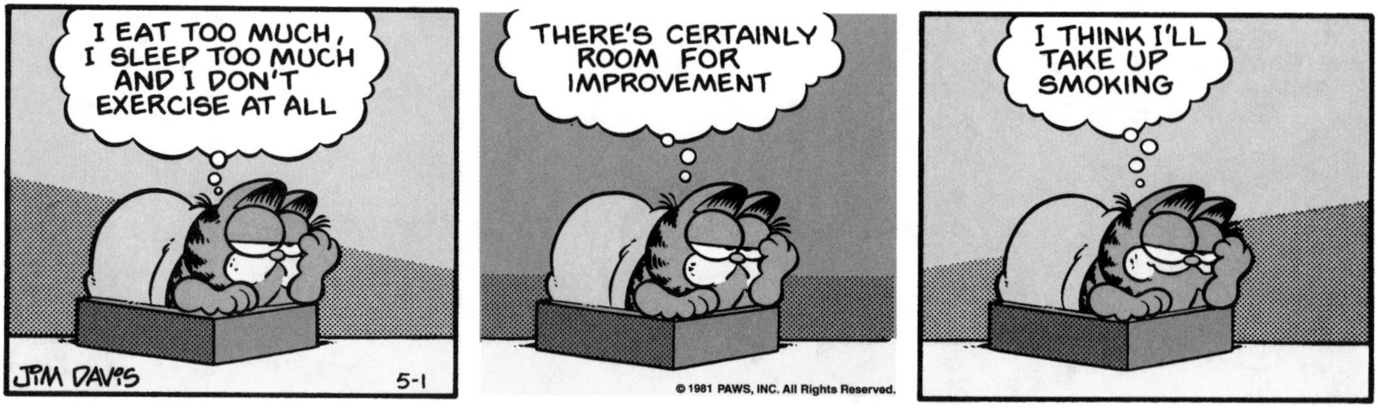
I EAT TOO MUCH, I SLEEP TOO MUCH AND I DON'T EXERCISE AT ALL
JIM DAVIS
5-1
THERE'S CERTAINLY ROOM FOR IMPROVEMENT
© 1981 PAWS, INC. All Rights Reserved.
I THINK I'LL TAKE UP SMOKING

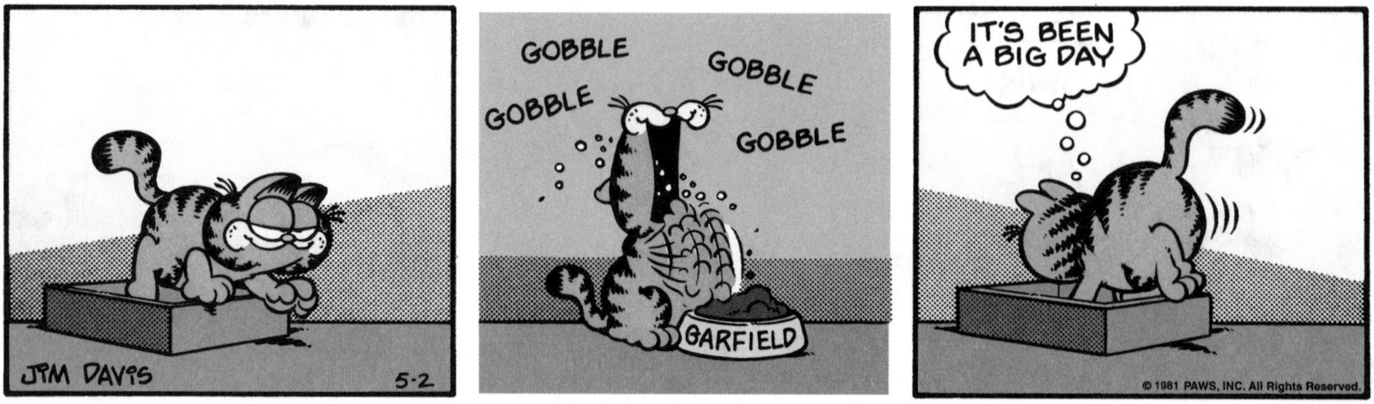
JIM DAVIS
5-2
GOBBLE
GOBBLE
GOBBLE
GOBBLE
GARFIELD
IT'S BEEN A BIG DAY
© 1981 PAWS, INC. All Rights Reserved.

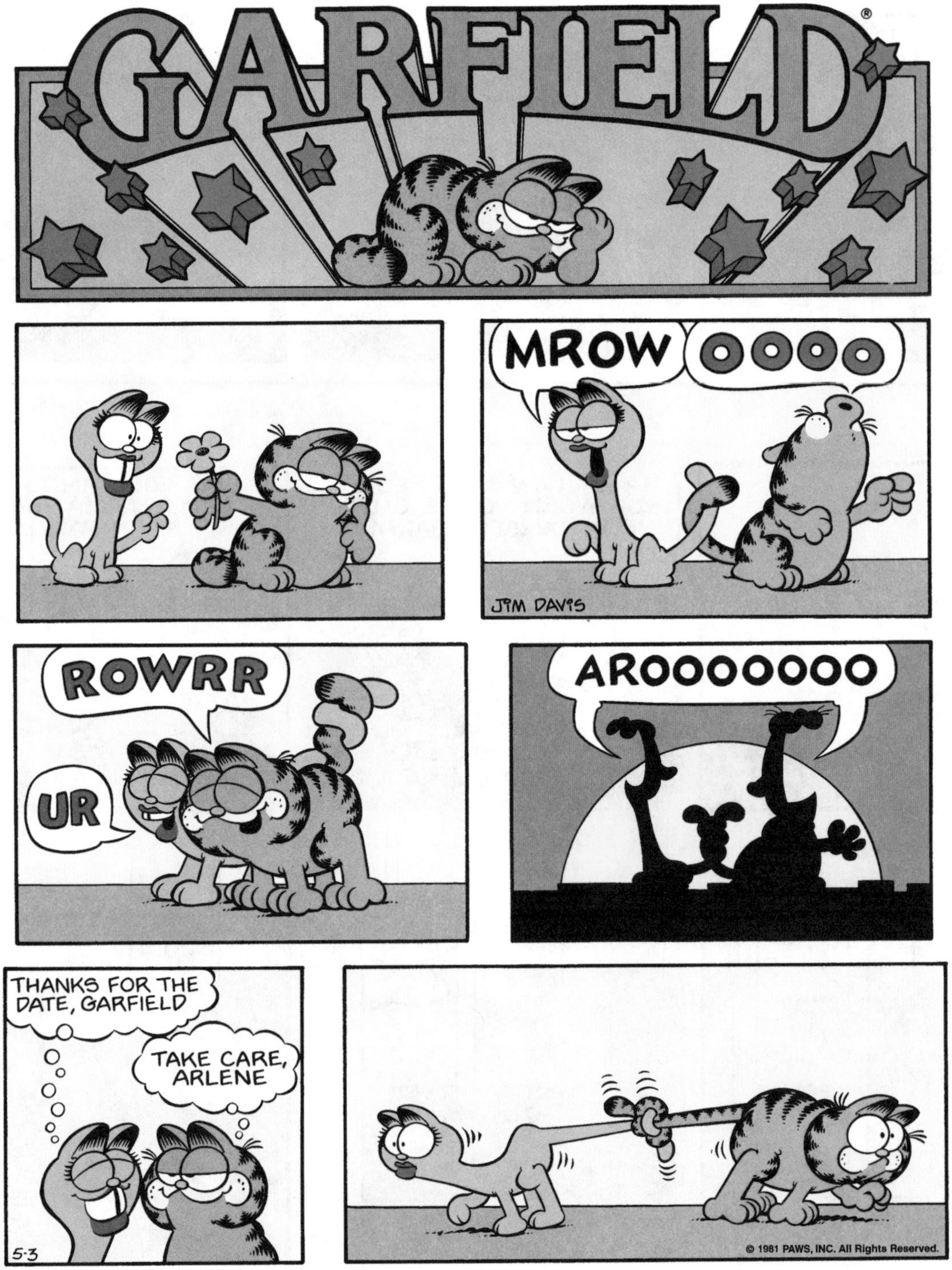
GARFIELD
MROW
OOOO
JIM DAVIS
ROWRR
UR
AROOOOOOO
THANKS FOR THE DATE, GARFIELD
TAKE CARE, ARLENE
5-3
© 1981 PAWS, INC. All Rights Reserved.

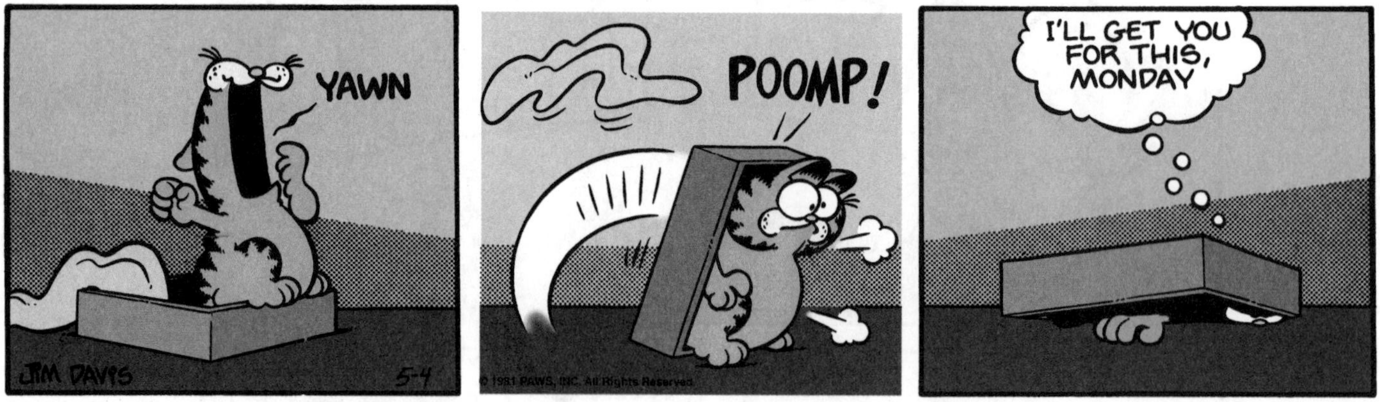
YAWN
JIM DAVIS
5-4
POOMP!
© 1981 PAWS, INC. All Rights Reserved.
I'LL GET YOU FOR THIS, MONDAY

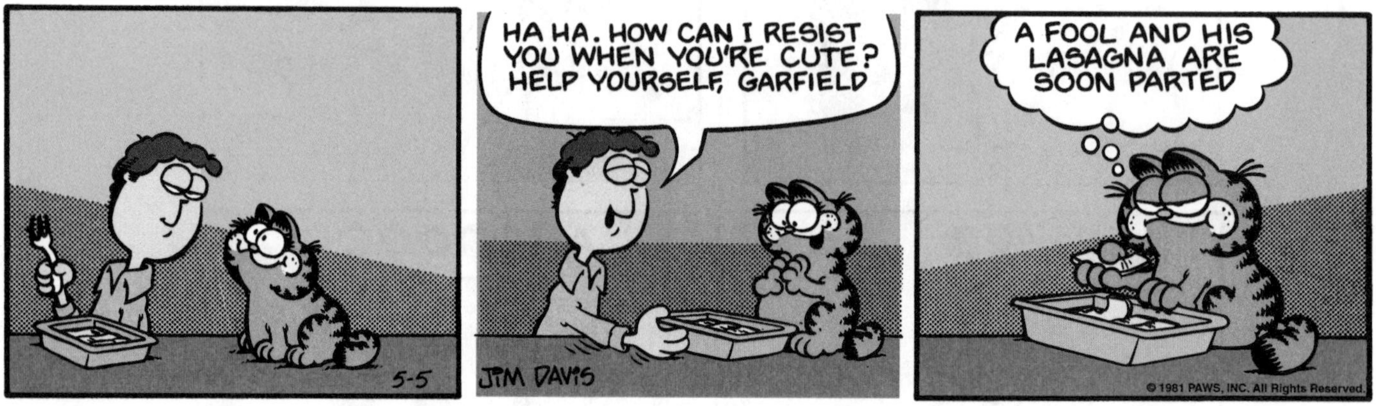
5-5
HA HA. HOW CAN I RESIST YOU WHEN YOU'RE CUTE? HELP YOURSELF, GARFIELD
JIM DAVIS
A FOOL AND HIS LASAGNA ARE SOON PARTED
© 1981 PAWS, INC. All Rights Reserved.

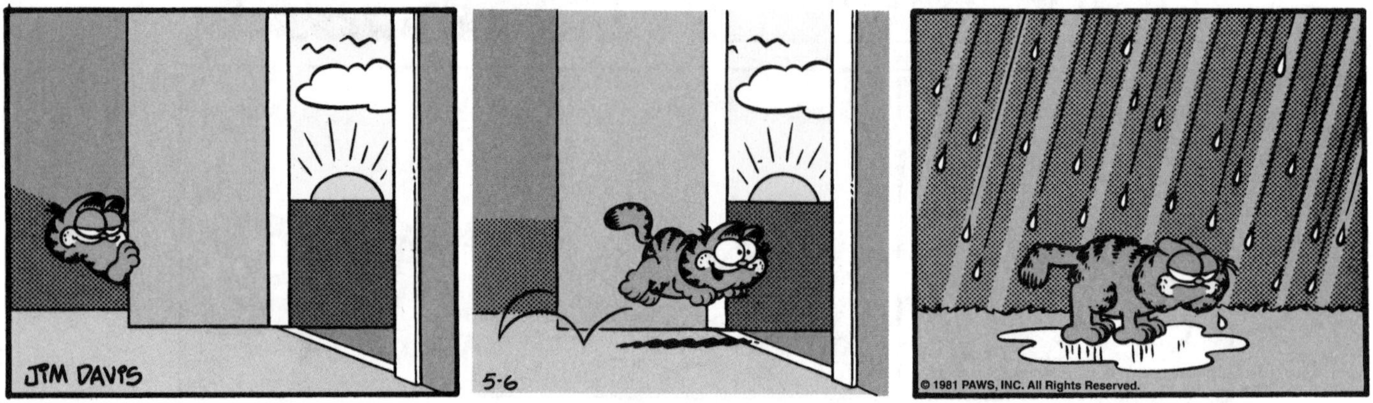
JIM DAVIS
5-6
© 1981 PAWS, INC. All Rights Reserved.

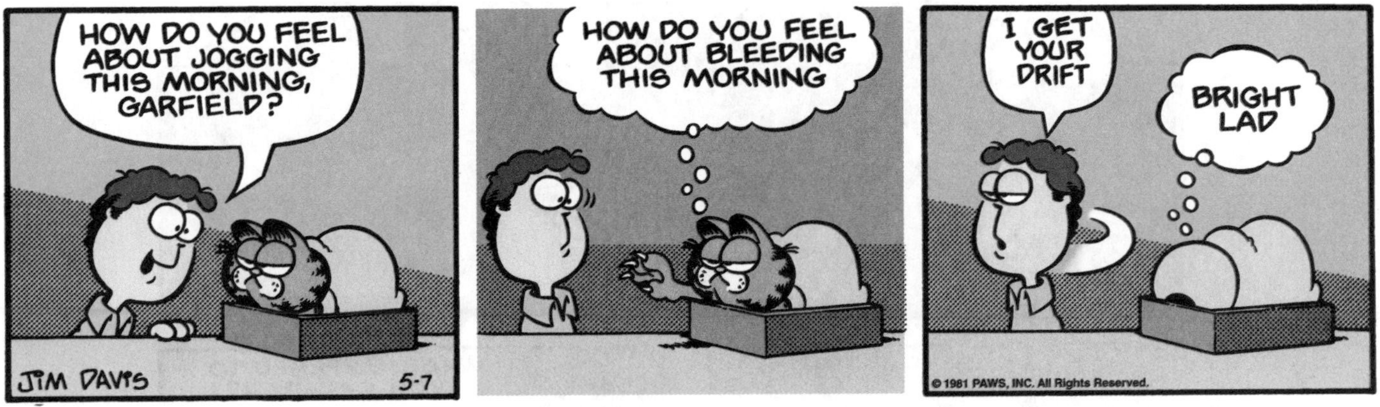
HOW DO YOU FEEL ABOUT JOGGING THIS MORNING, GARFIELD?
JIM DAVIS
5-7
HOW DO YOU FEEL ABOUT BLEEDING THIS MORNING
I GET YOUR DRIFT
BRIGHT LAD
© 1981 PAWS, INC. All Rights Reserved.

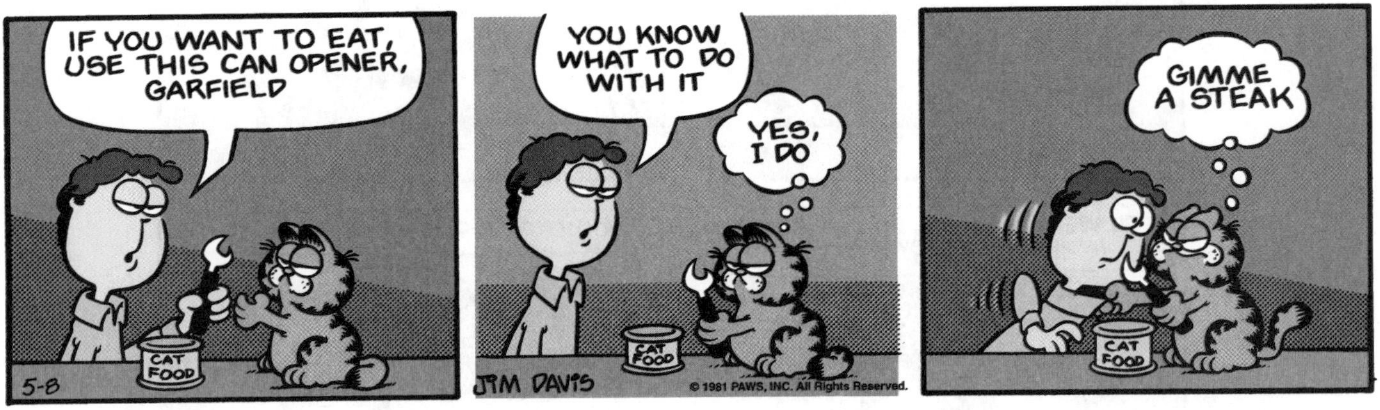
IF YOU WANT TO EAT, USE THIS CAN OPENER, GARFIELD
CAT FOOD
5-8
YOU KNOW WHAT TO DO WITH IT
YES, I DO
CAT FOOD
JIM DAVIS
© 1981 PAWS, INC. All Rights Reserved.
GIMME A STEAK
CAT FOOD

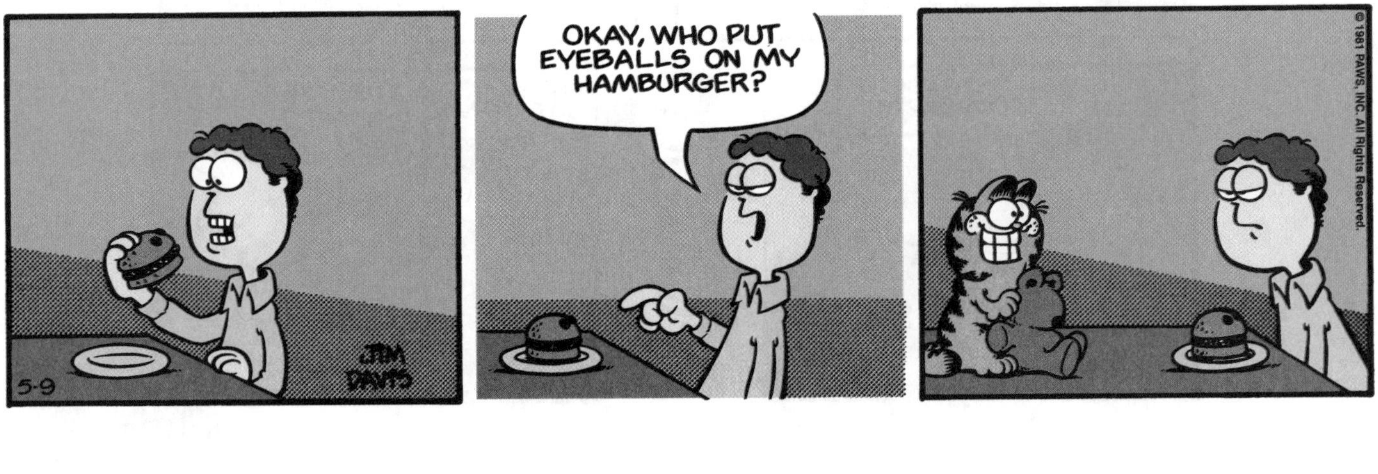
5-9
JIM DAVIS
OKAY, WHO PUT EYEBALLS ON MY HAMBURGER?
© 1981 PAWS, INC. All Rights Reserved.

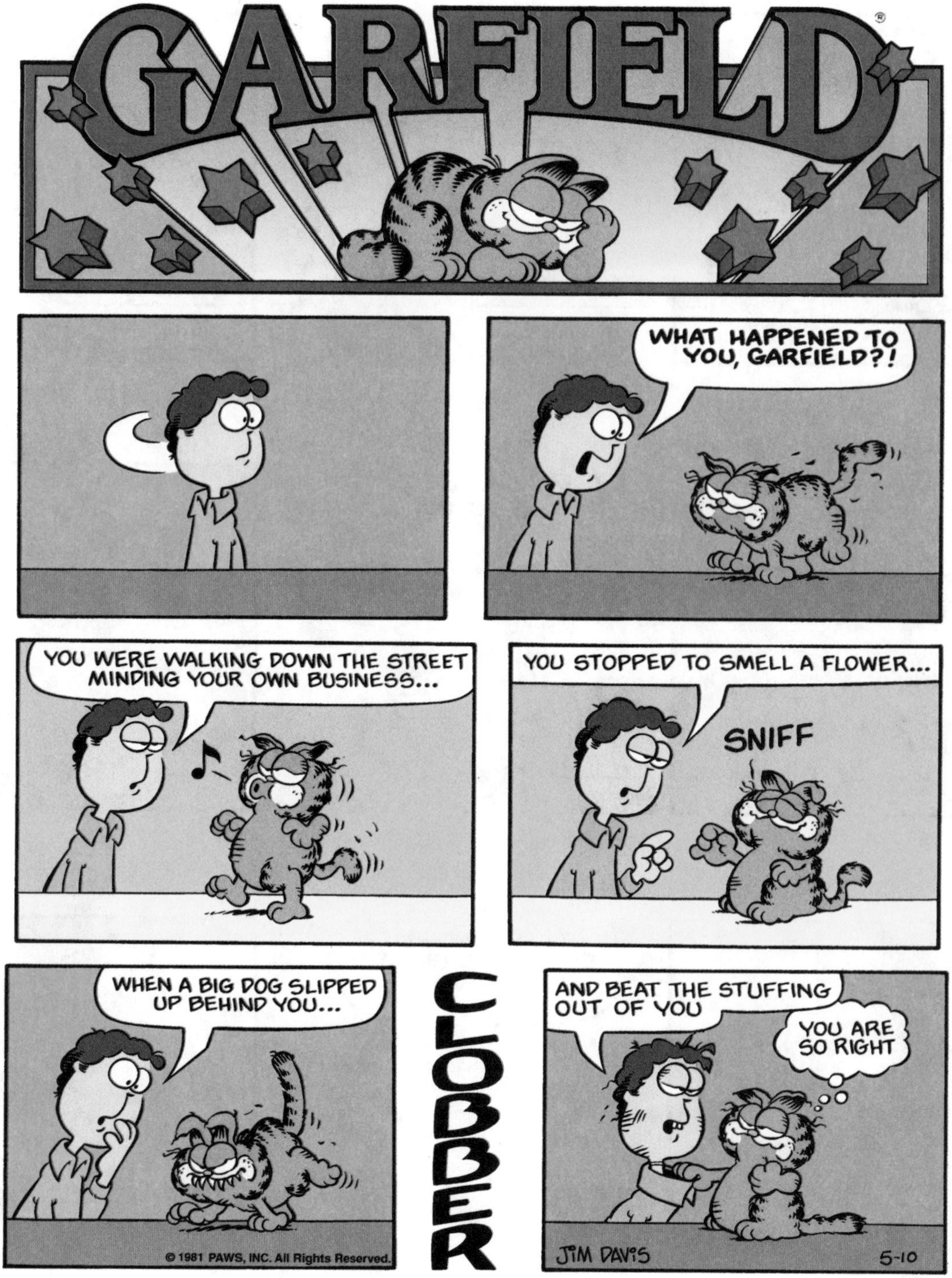
GARFIELD
WHAT HAPPENED TO YOU, GARFIELD?!
YOU WERE WALKING DOWN THE STREET MINDING YOUR OWN BUSINESS...
YOU STOPPED TO SMELL A FLOWER...
SNIFF
WHEN A BIG DOG SLIPPED UP BEHIND YOU...
CLOBBER
AND BEAT THE STUFFING OUT OF YOU
YOU ARE SO RIGHT
© 1981 PAWS, INC. All Rights Reserved.
JIM DAVIS
5-10

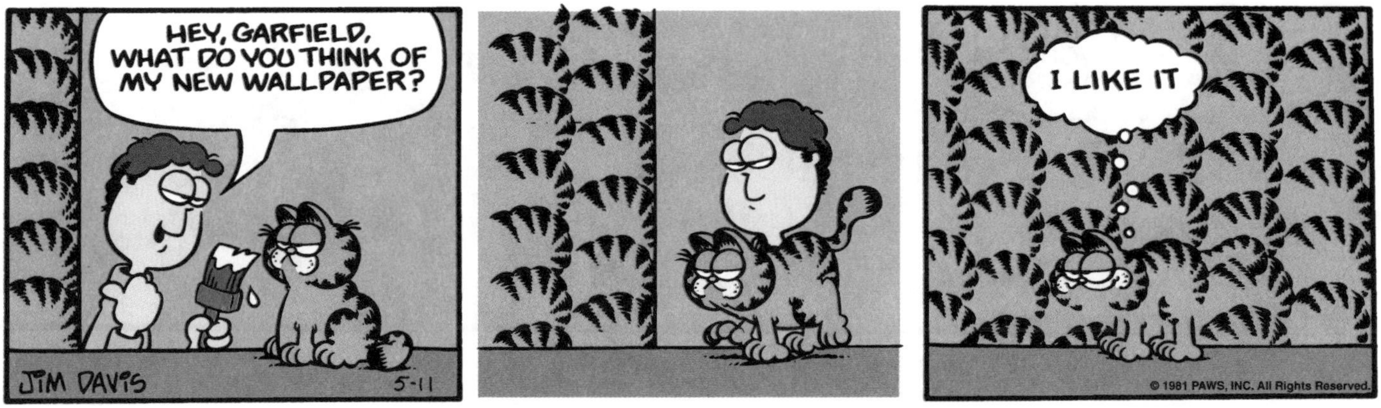
HEY, GARFIELD, WHAT DO YOU THINK OF MY NEW WALLPAPER?
JIM DAVIS
5-11
I LIKE IT
© 1981 PAWS, INC. All Rights Reserved.

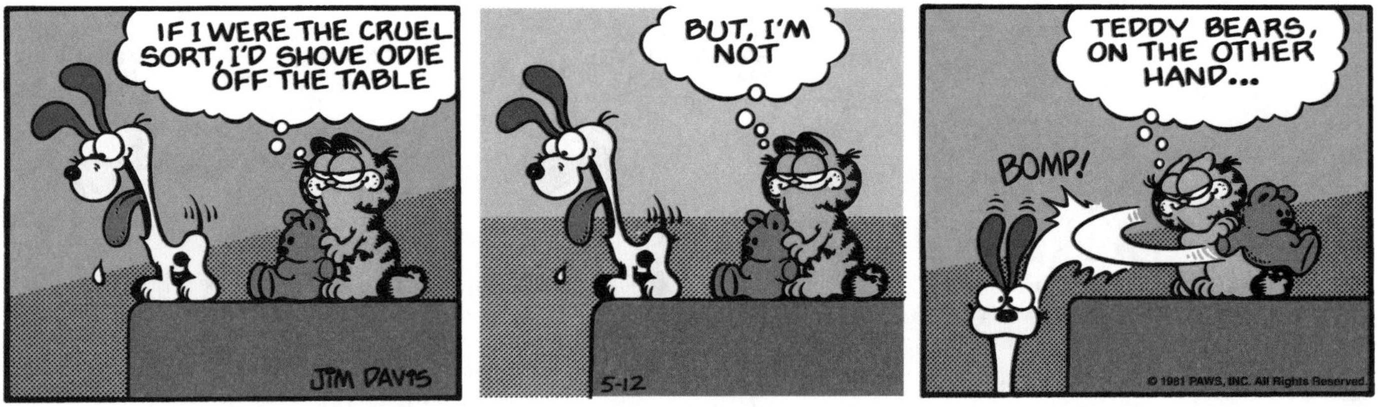
IF I WERE THE CRUEL SORT, I'D SHOVE ODIE OFF THE TABLE
JIM DAVIS
BUT, I'M NOT
5-12
TEDDY BEARS, ON THE OTHER HAND...
BOMP!
© 1981 PAWS, INC. All Rights Reserved.

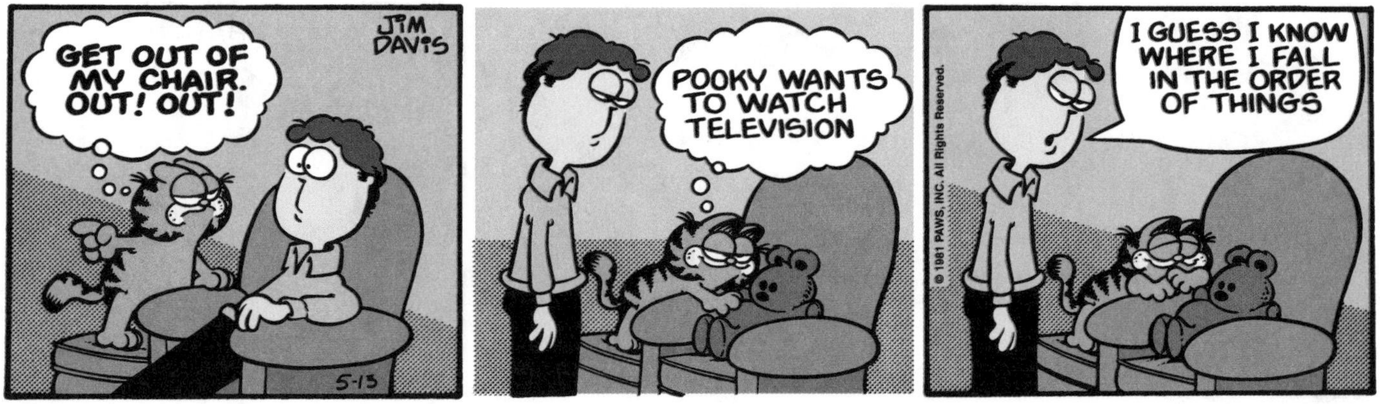
JIM DAVIS
GET OUT OF MY CHAIR. OUT! OUT!
5-13
POOKY WANTS TO WATCH TELEVISION
© 1981 PAWS, INC. All Rights Reserved.
I GUESS I KNOW WHERE I FALL IN THE ORDER OF THINGS

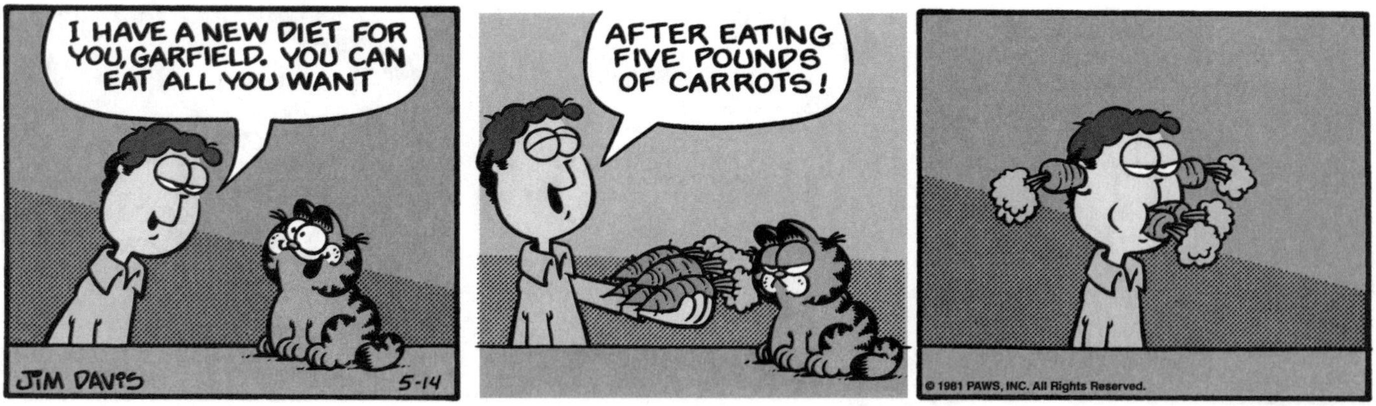
I HAVE A NEW DIET FOR YOU, GARFIELD. YOU CAN EAT ALL YOU WANT
JIM DAVIS
5-14
AFTER EATING FIVE POUNDS OF CARROTS!
© 1981 PAWS, INC. All Rights Reserved.

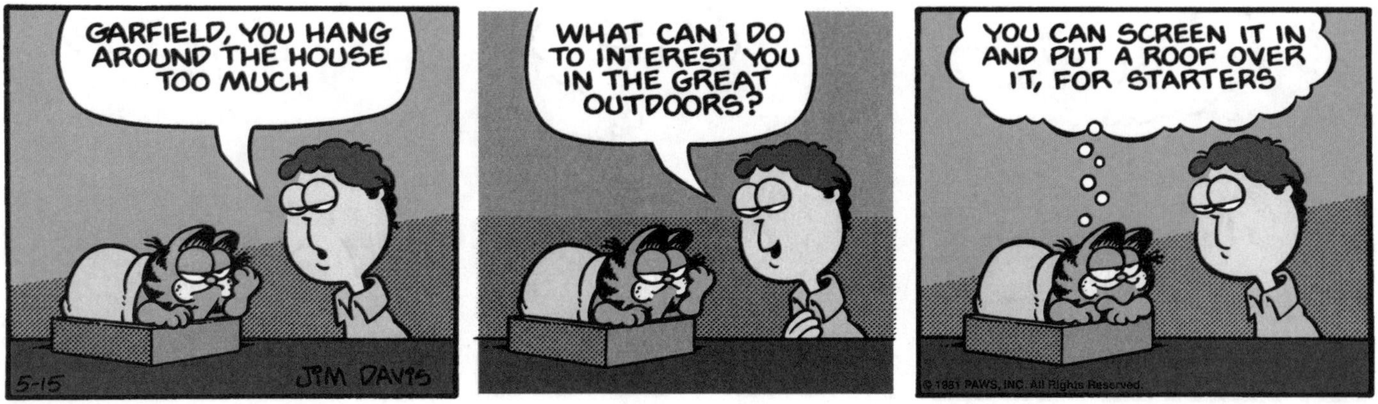
GARFIELD, YOU HANG AROUND THE HOUSE TOO MUCH
5-15
JIM DAVIS
WHAT CAN I DO TO INTEREST YOU IN THE GREAT OUTDOORS?
YOU CAN SCREEN IT IN AND PUT A ROOF OVER IT, FOR STARTERS
© 1981 PAWS, INC. All Rights Reserved.

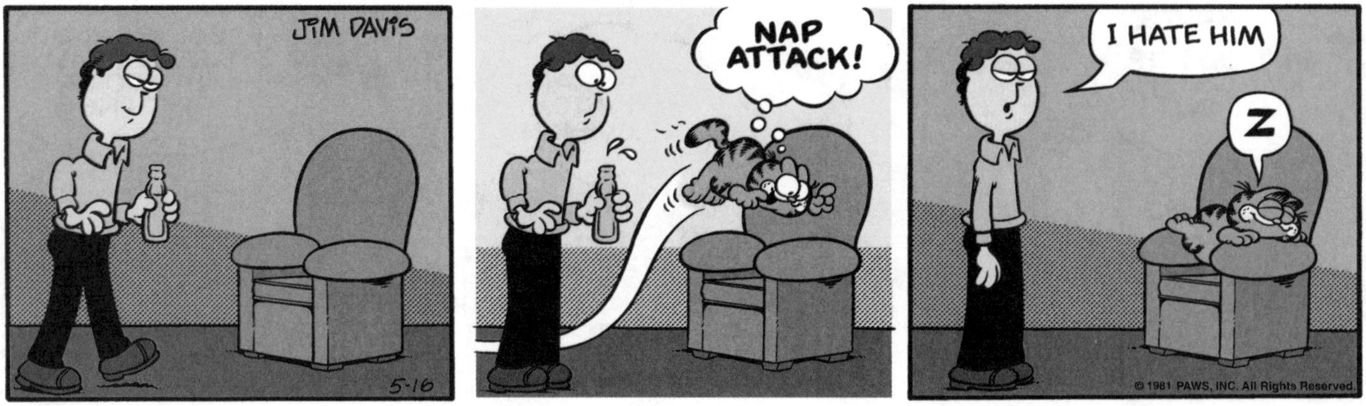
JIM DAVIS
5-16
NAP ATTACK!
I HATE HIM
Z
© 1981 PAWS, INC. All Rights Reserved.

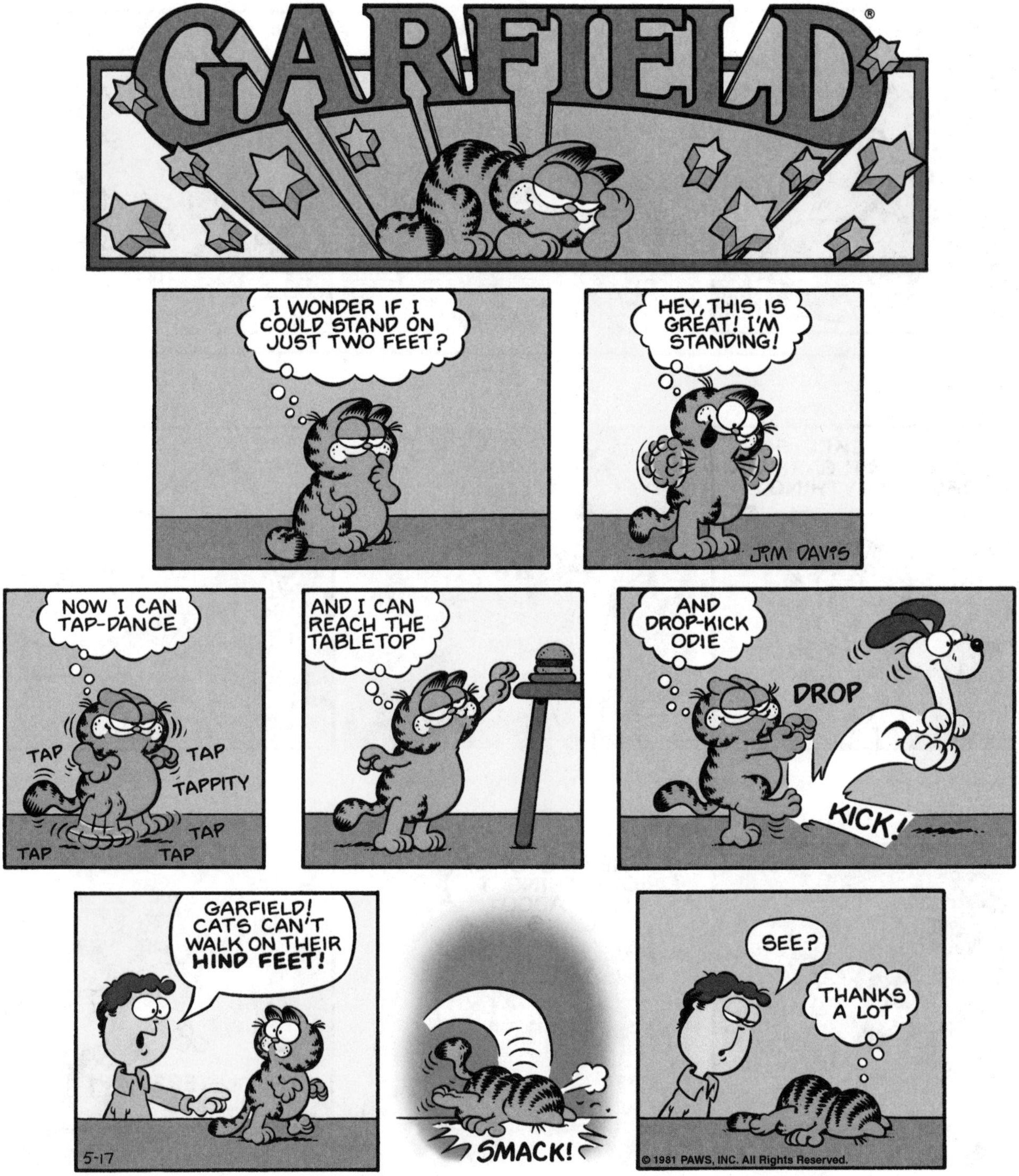
GARFIELD®
I WONDER IF I COULD STAND ON JUST TWO FEET?
HEY, THIS IS GREAT! I'M STANDING!
JIM DAVIS
NOW I CAN TAP-DANCE
TAP
TAP
TAPPITY
TAP
TAP
TAP
AND I CAN REACH THE TABLETOP
AND DROP-KICK ODIE
DROP
KICK!
GARFIELD! CATS CAN'T WALK ON THEIR HIND FEET!
5-17
SMACK!
SEE?
THANKS A LOT
© 1981 PAWS, INC. All Rights Reserved.

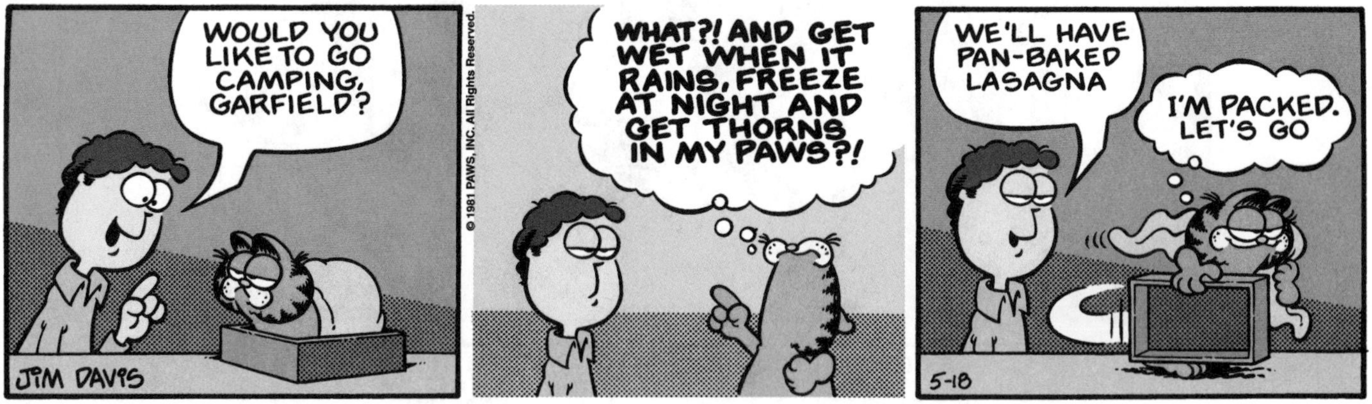
WOULD YOU LIKE TO GO CAMPING, GARFIELD?
JIM DAVIS
© 1981 PAWS, INC. All Rights Reserved.
WHAT?! AND GET WET WHEN IT RAINS, FREEZE AT NIGHT AND GET THORNS IN MY PAWS?!
WE'LL HAVE PAN-BAKED LASAGNA
I'M PACKED. LET'S GO
5-18

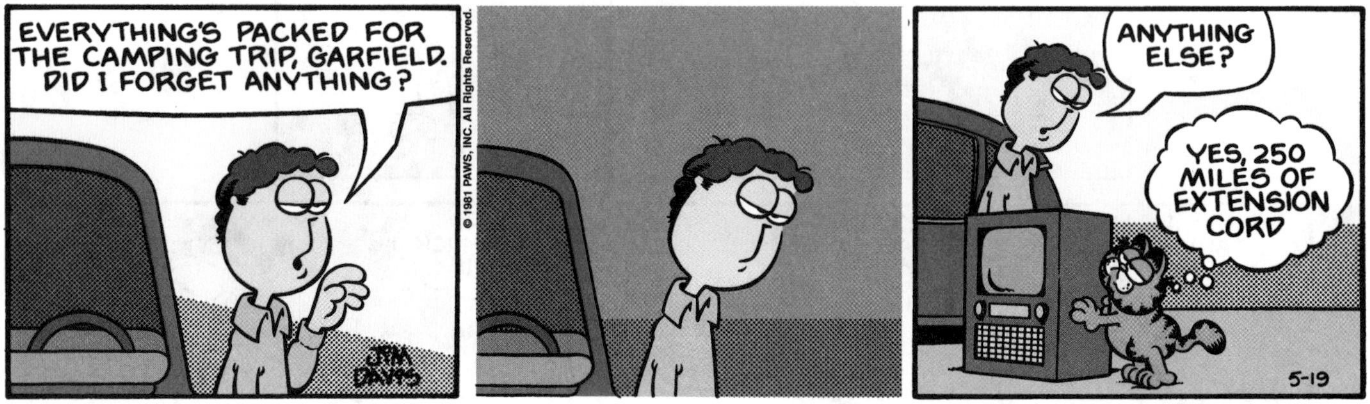
EVERYTHING'S PACKED FOR THE CAMPING TRIP, GARFIELD. DID I FORGET ANYTHING?
JIM DAVIS
© 1981 PAWS, INC. All Rights Reserved.
ANYTHING ELSE?
YES, 250 MILES OF EXTENSION CORD
5-19

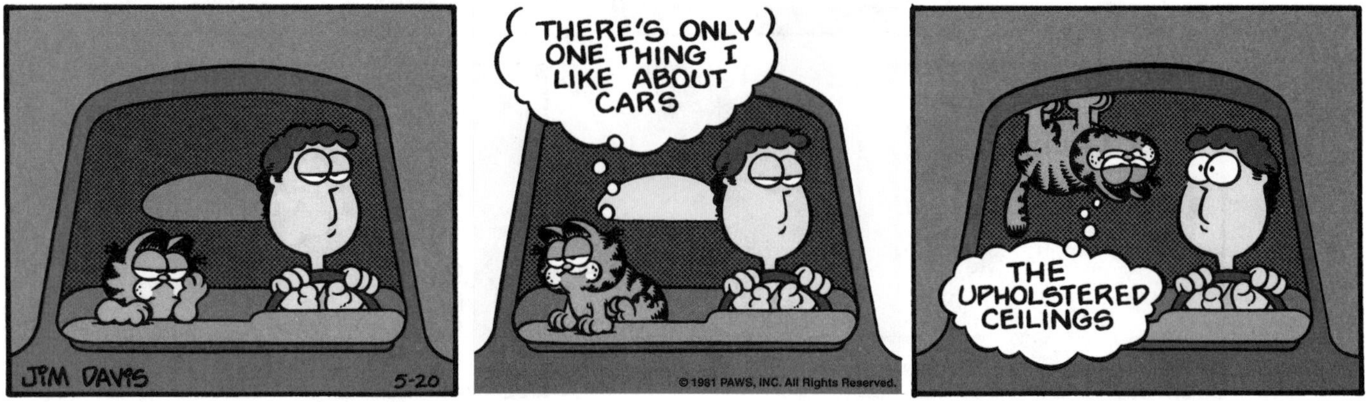
JIM DAVIS
5-20
THERE'S ONLY ONE THING I LIKE ABOUT CARS
© 1981 PAWS, INC. All Rights Reserved.
THE UPHOLSTERED CEILINGS

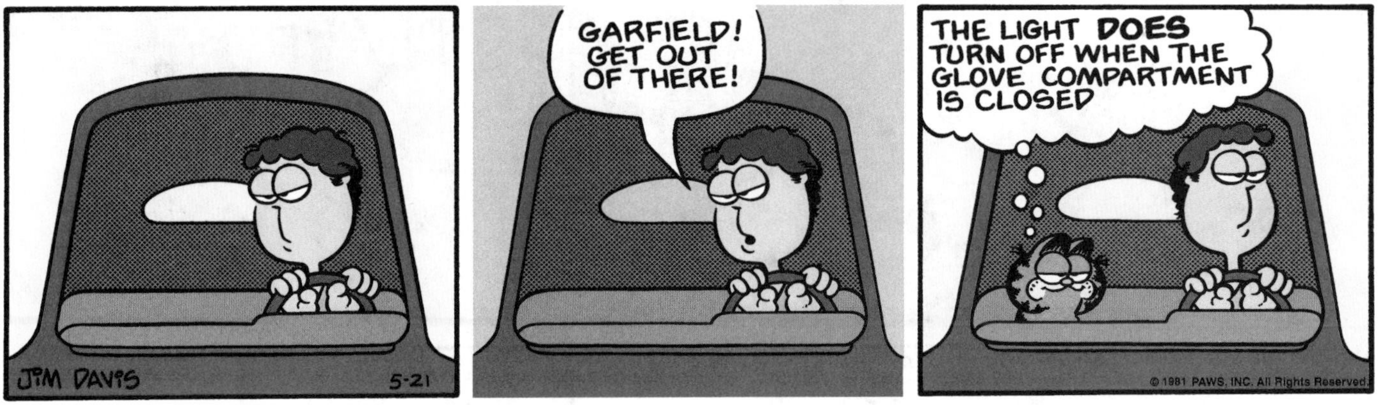

JIM DAVIS
5-21
GARFIELD! GET OUT OF THERE!
THE LIGHT **DOES** TURN OFF WHEN THE GLOVE COMPARTMENT IS CLOSED
© 1981 PAWS, INC. All Rights Reserved.

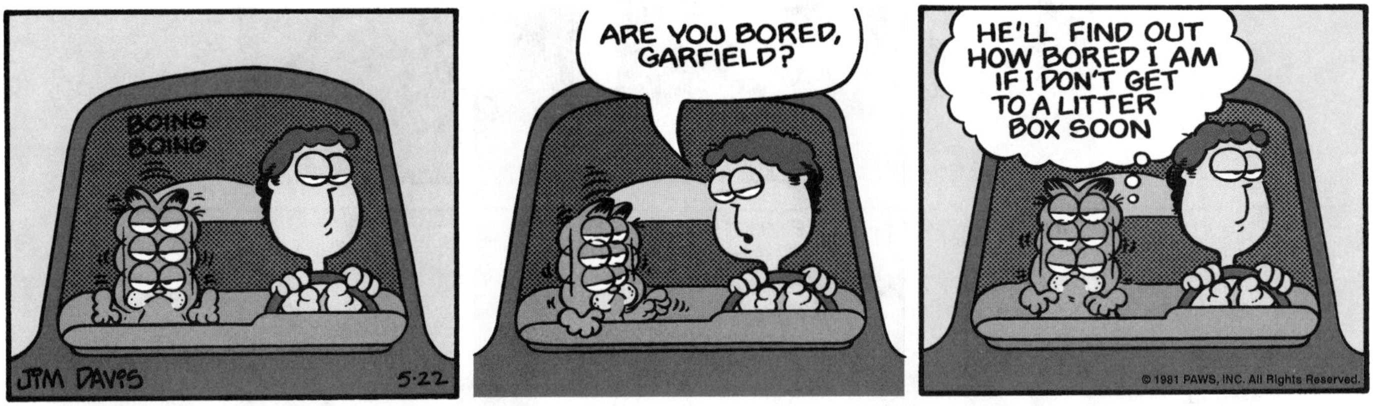

BOING BOING
JIM DAVIS
5-22
ARE YOU BORED, GARFIELD?
HE'LL FIND OUT HOW BORED I AM IF I DON'T GET TO A LITTER BOX SOON
© 1981 PAWS, INC. All Rights Reserved.

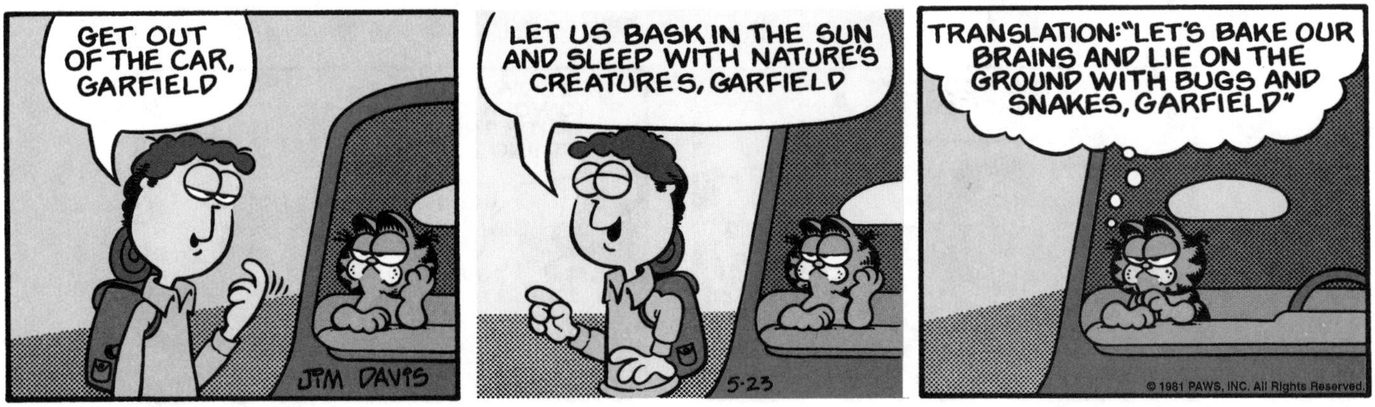

GET OUT OF THE CAR, GARFIELD
JIM DAVIS
LET US BASK IN THE SUN AND SLEEP WITH NATURE'S CREATURES, GARFIELD
5-23
TRANSLATION: "LET'S BAKE OUR BRAINS AND LIE ON THE GROUND WITH BUGS AND SNAKES, GARFIELD"
© 1981 PAWS, INC. All Rights Reserved.

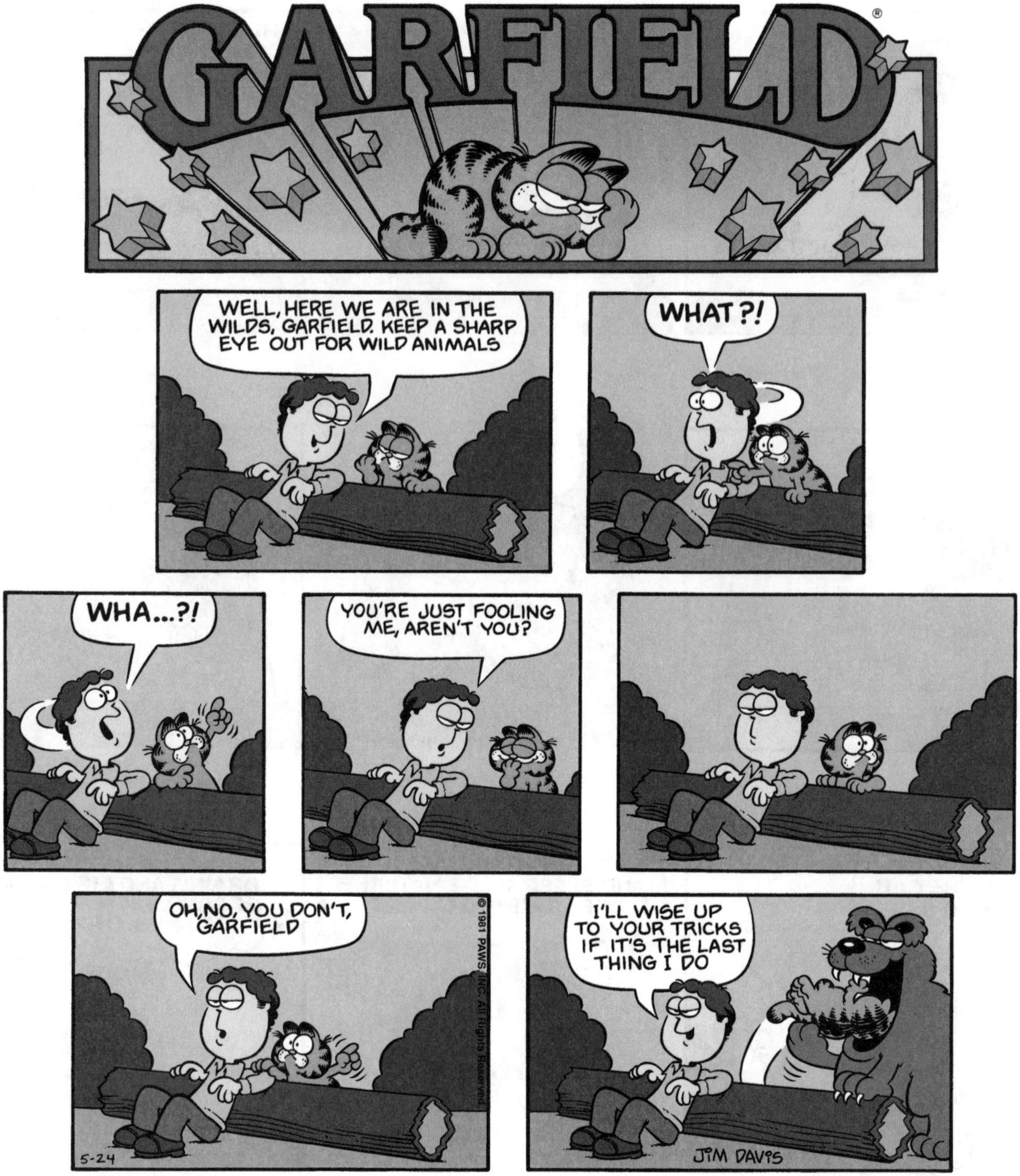
GARFIELD®
WELL, HERE WE ARE IN THE WILDS, GARFIELD. KEEP A SHARP EYE OUT FOR WILD ANIMALS
WHAT?!
WHA...?!
YOU'RE JUST FOOLING ME, AREN'T YOU?
OH, NO, YOU DON'T, GARFIELD
I'LL WISE UP TO YOUR TRICKS IF IT'S THE LAST THING I DO
5-24
JIM DAVIS
© 1981 PAWS, INC. All Rights Reserved.

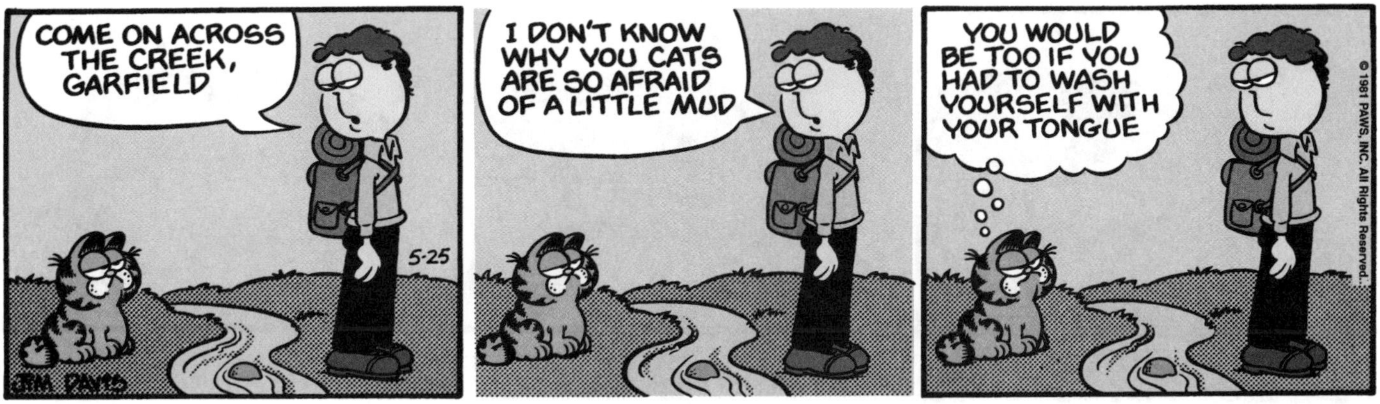
COME ON ACROSS THE CREEK, GARFIELD
JIM DAVIS
5-25
I DON'T KNOW WHY YOU CATS ARE SO AFRAID OF A LITTLE MUD
YOU WOULD BE TOO IF YOU HAD TO WASH YOURSELF WITH YOUR TONGUE
© 1981 PAWS, INC. All Rights Reserved.

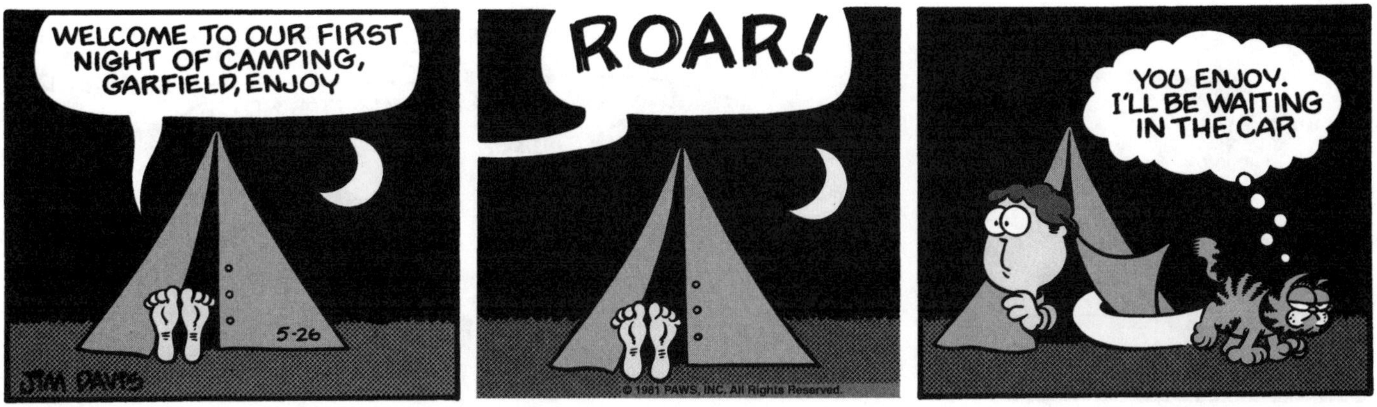
WELCOME TO OUR FIRST NIGHT OF CAMPING, GARFIELD, ENJOY
JIM DAVIS
5-26
ROAR!
© 1981 PAWS, INC. All Rights Reserved.
YOU ENJOY. I'LL BE WAITING IN THE CAR

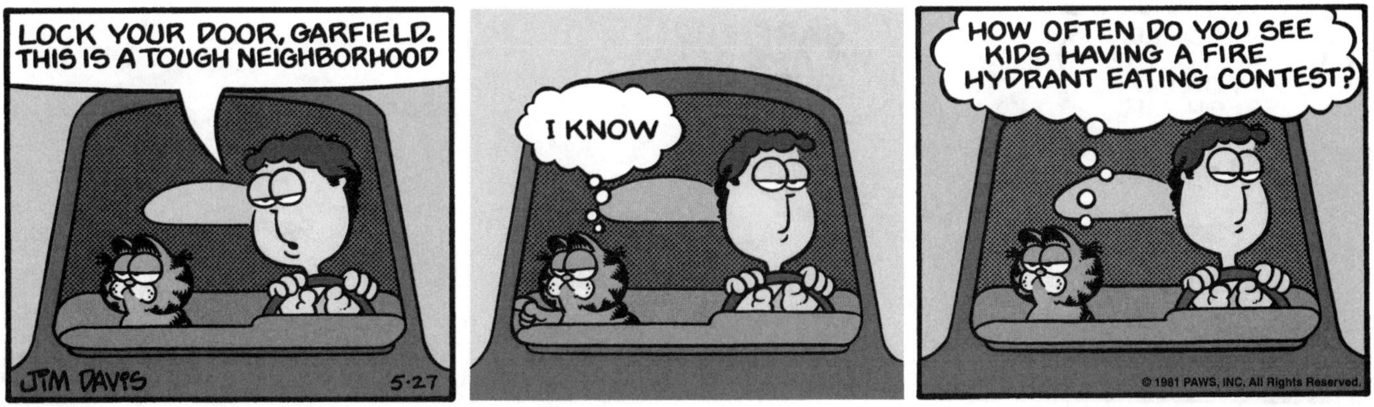
LOCK YOUR DOOR, GARFIELD. THIS IS A TOUGH NEIGHBORHOOD
JIM DAVIS
5-27
I KNOW
HOW OFTEN DO YOU SEE KIDS HAVING A FIRE HYDRANT EATING CONTEST?
© 1981 PAWS, INC. All Rights Reserved.

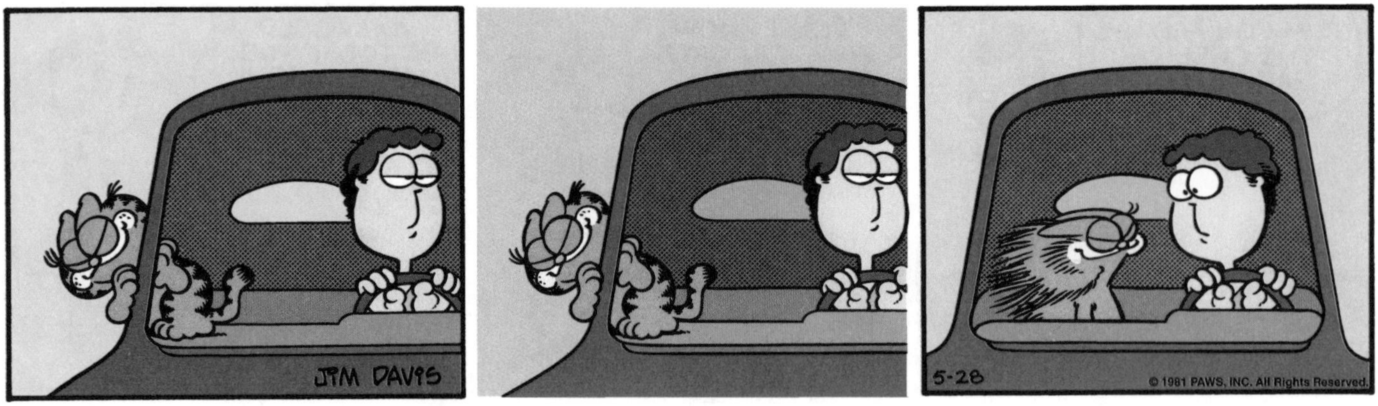
JIM DAVIS
5-28
© 1981 PAWS, INC. All Rights Reserved.

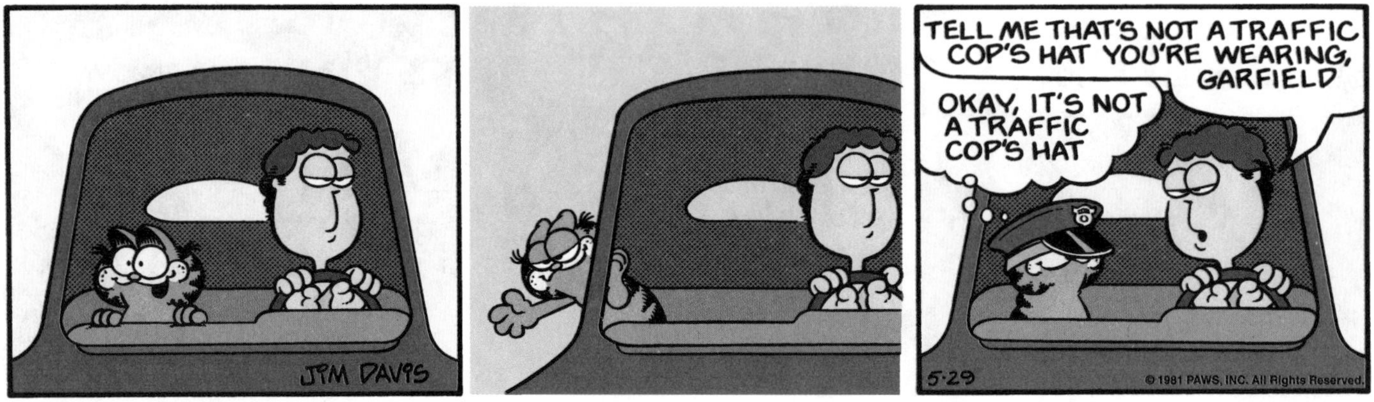
JIM DAVIS
TELL ME THAT'S NOT A TRAFFIC COP'S HAT YOU'RE WEARING, GARFIELD
OKAY, IT'S NOT A TRAFFIC COP'S HAT
5·29
© 1981 PAWS, INC. All Rights Reserved.

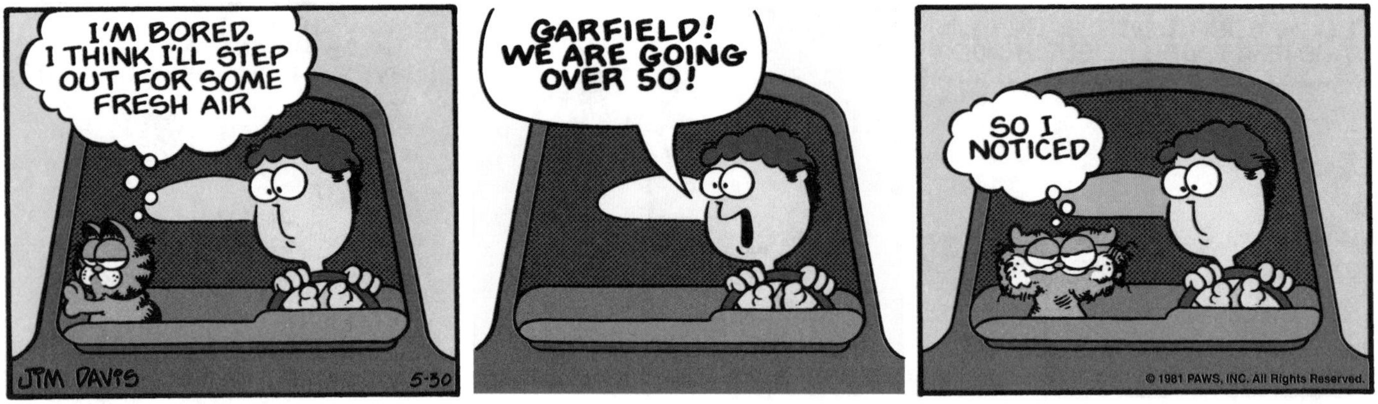
I'M BORED. I THINK I'LL STEP OUT FOR SOME FRESH AIR
JIM DAVIS
5-30
GARFIELD! WE ARE GOING OVER 50!
SO I NOTICED
© 1981 PAWS, INC. All Rights Reserved.

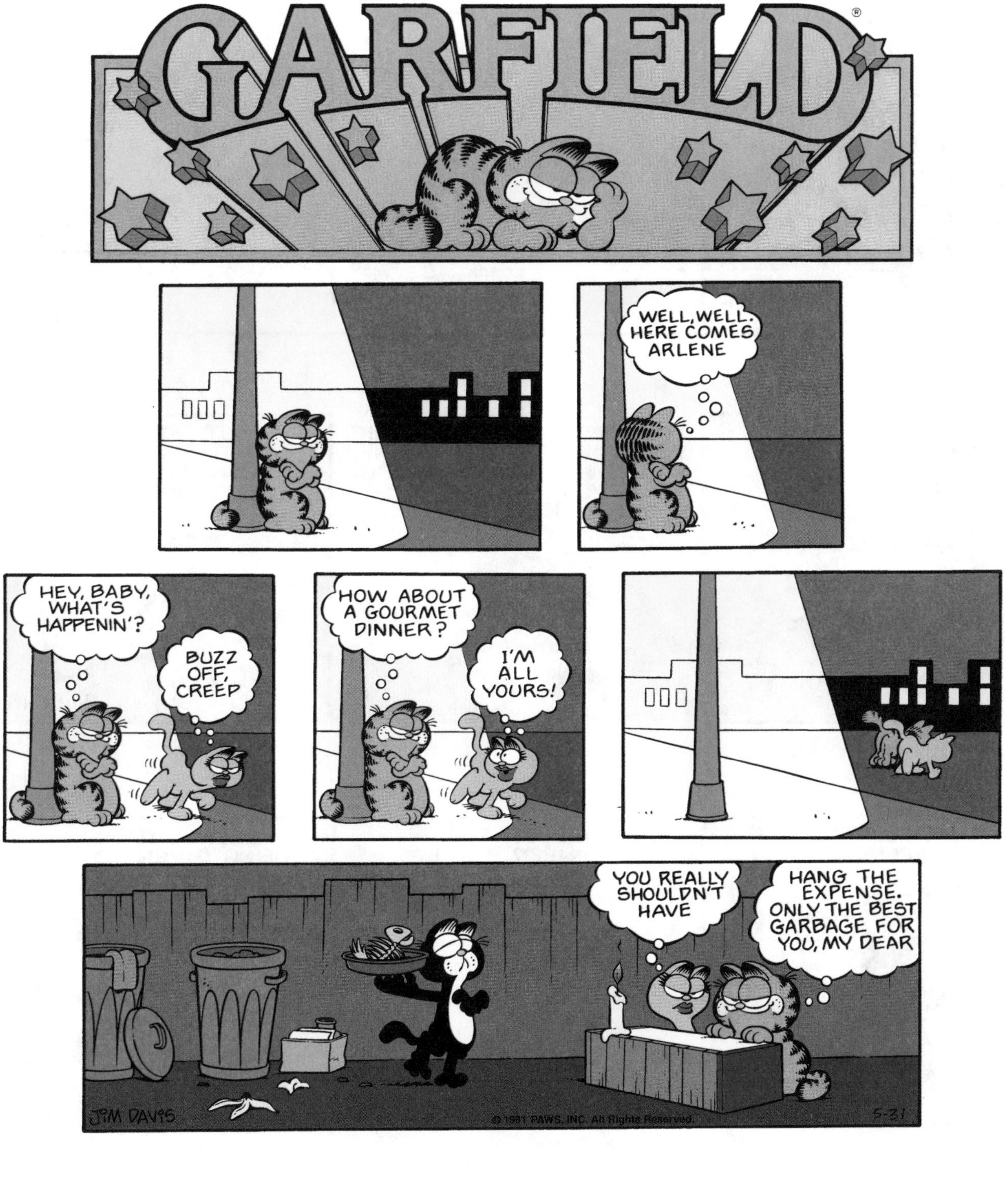
GARFIELD
WELL, WELL. HERE COMES ARLENE
HEY, BABY, WHAT'S HAPPENIN'?
BUZZ OFF, CREEP
HOW ABOUT A GOURMET DINNER?
I'M ALL YOURS!
YOU REALLY SHOULDN'T HAVE
HANG THE EXPENSE. ONLY THE BEST GARBAGE FOR YOU, MY DEAR
JIM DAVIS
© 1981 PAWS, INC. All Rights Reserved.
5-31

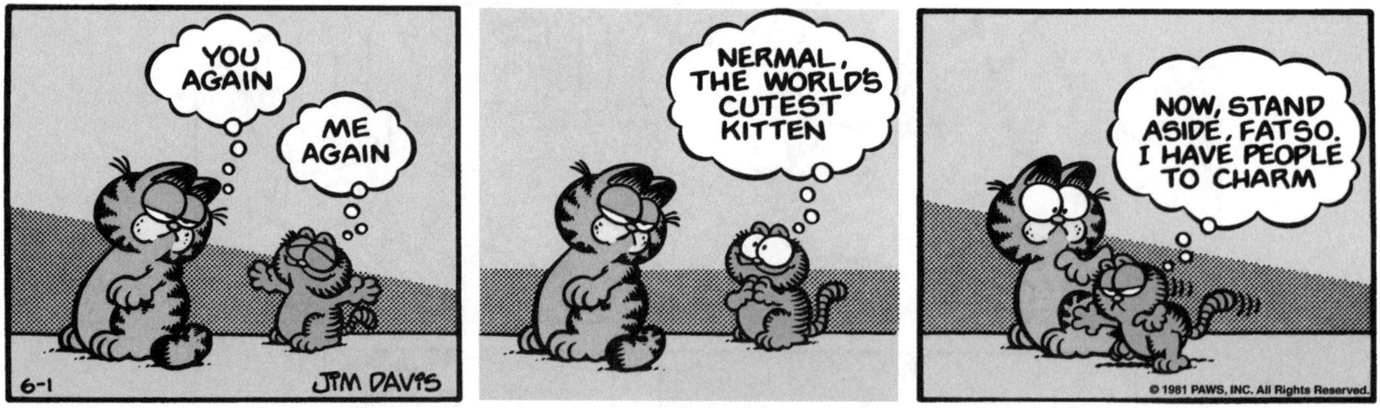
YOU AGAIN
ME AGAIN
NERMAL, THE WORLD'S CUTEST KITTEN
NOW, STAND ASIDE, FATSO. I HAVE PEOPLE TO CHARM
6-1
JIM DAVIS
© 1981 PAWS, INC. All Rights Reserved.

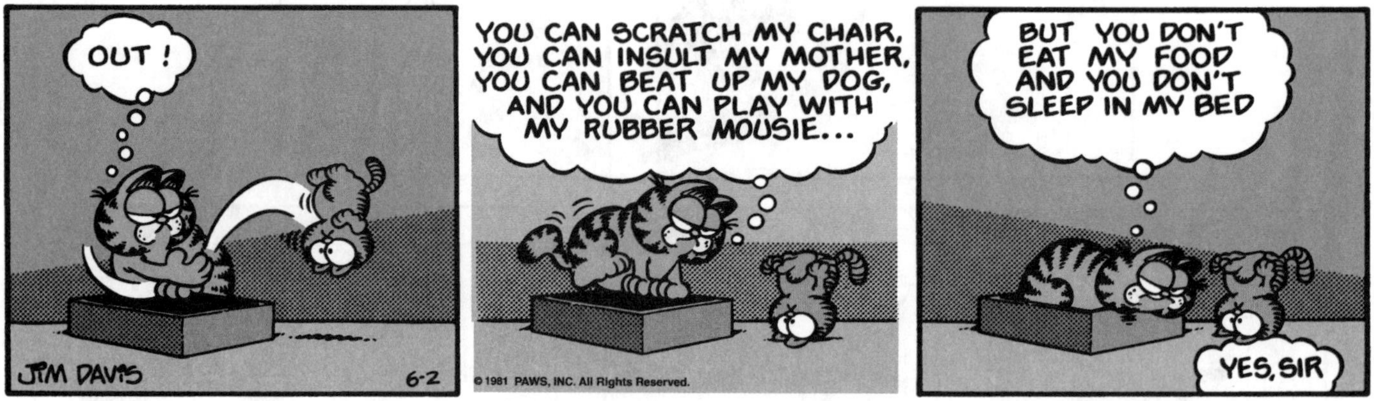
OUT!
YOU CAN SCRATCH MY CHAIR, YOU CAN INSULT MY MOTHER, YOU CAN BEAT UP MY DOG, AND YOU CAN PLAY WITH MY RUBBER MOUSIE...
BUT YOU DON'T EAT MY FOOD AND YOU DON'T SLEEP IN MY BED
YES, SIR
JIM DAVIS
6-2
© 1981 PAWS, INC. All Rights Reserved.

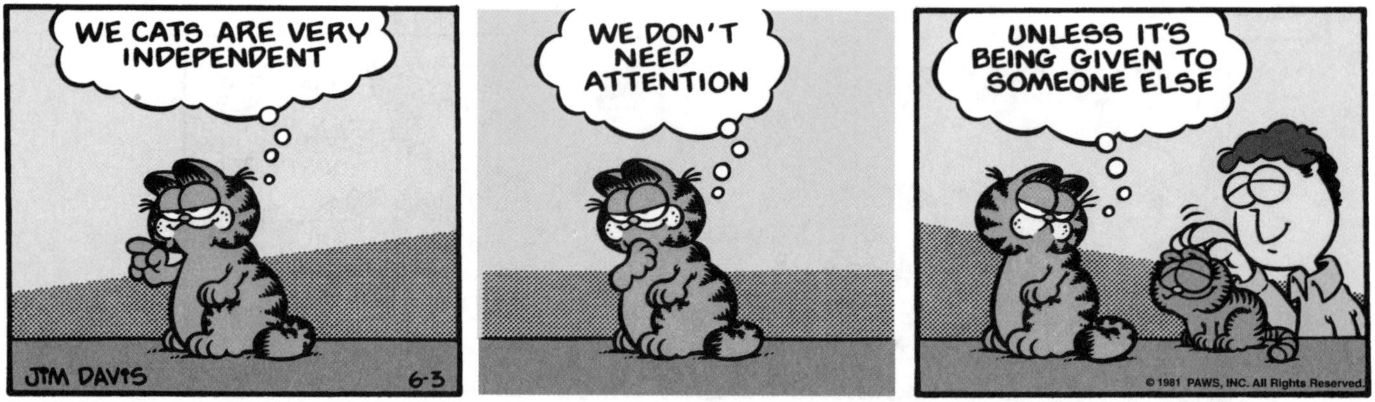
WE CATS ARE VERY INDEPENDENT
WE DON'T NEED ATTENTION
UNLESS IT'S BEING GIVEN TO SOMEONE ELSE
JIM DAVIS
6-3
© 1981 PAWS, INC. All Rights Reserved.

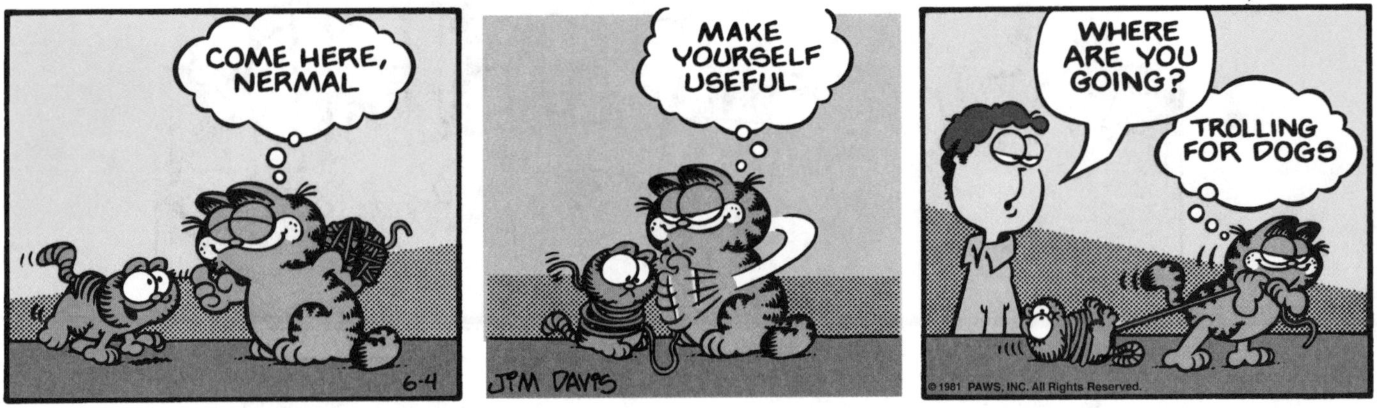
COME HERE, NERMAL
6-4
MAKE YOURSELF USEFUL
JIM DAVIS
WHERE ARE YOU GOING?
TROLLING FOR DOGS
© 1981 PAWS, INC. All Rights Reserved.

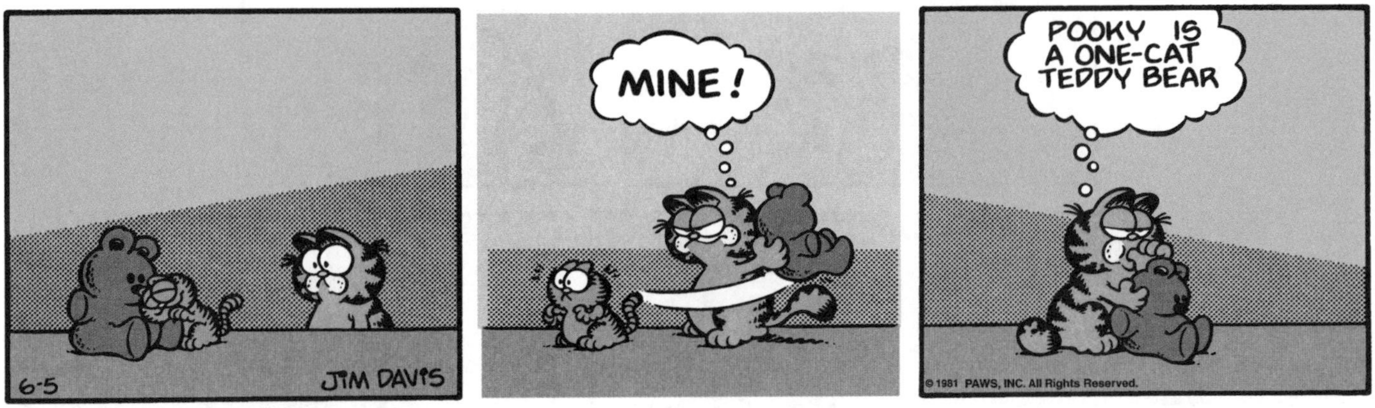
6-5
JIM DAVIS
MINE!
POOKY IS A ONE-CAT TEDDY BEAR
© 1981 PAWS, INC. All Rights Reserved.

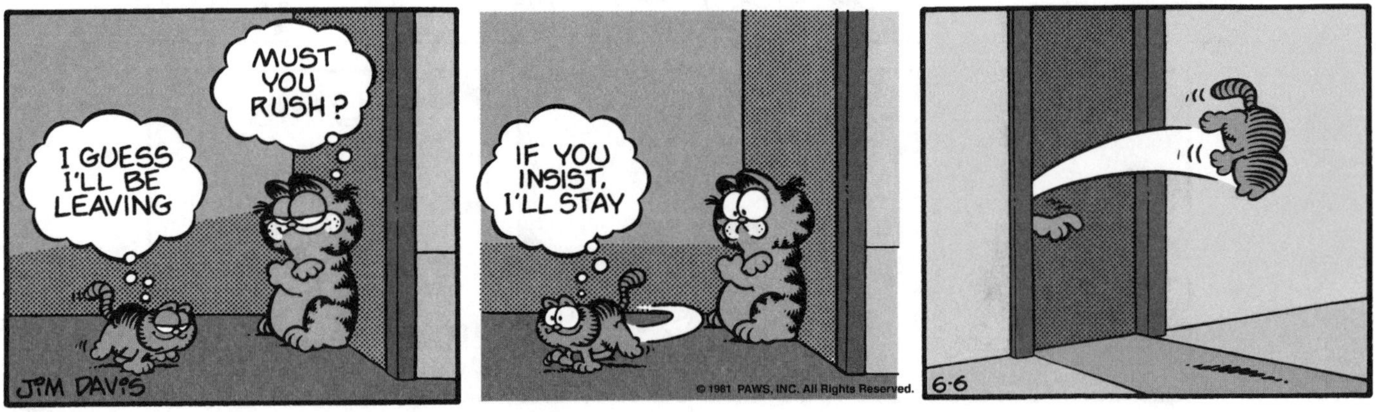
I GUESS I'LL BE LEAVING
MUST YOU RUSH?
JIM DAVIS
IF YOU INSIST, I'LL STAY
© 1981 PAWS, INC. All Rights Reserved.
6-6

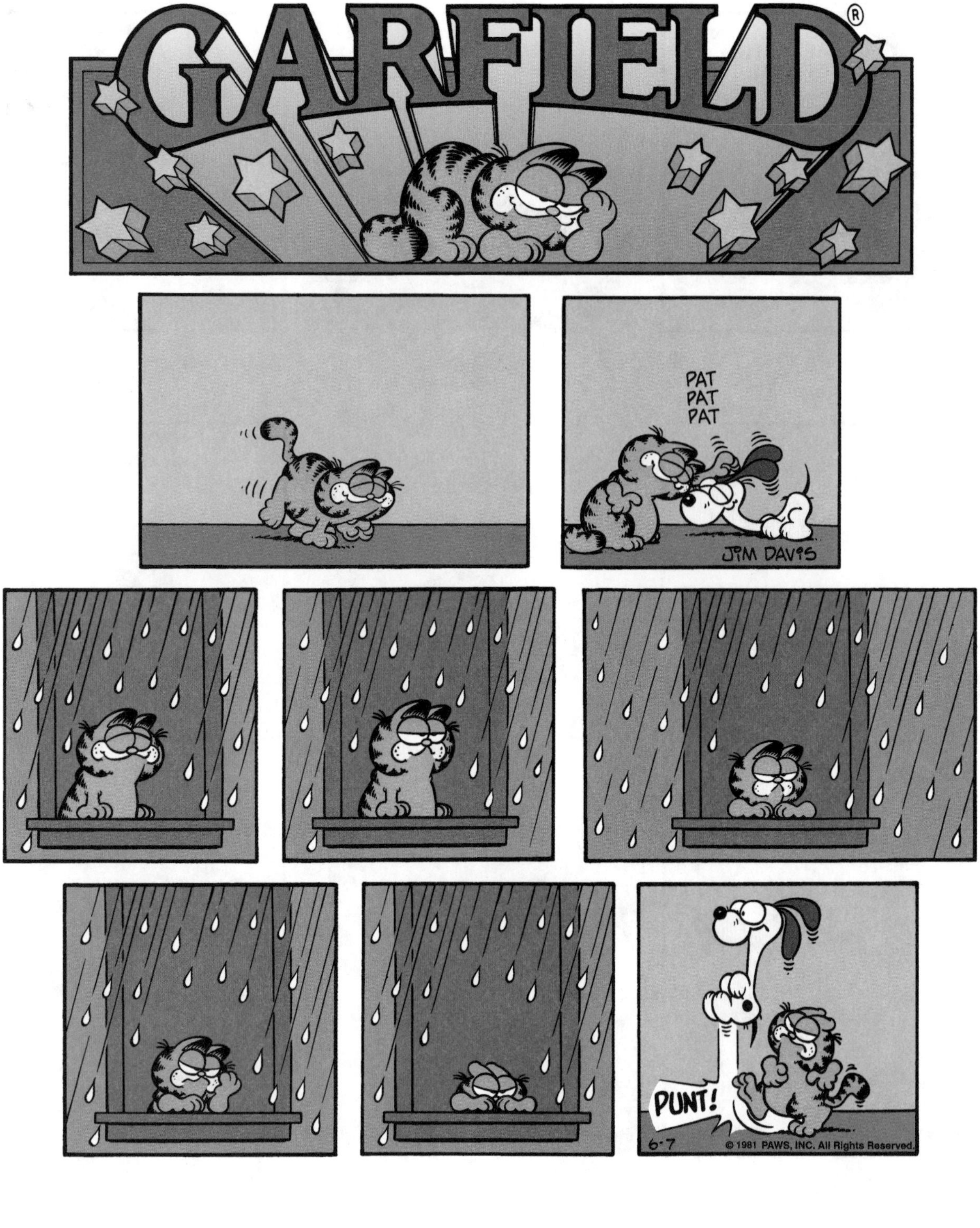
GARFIELD®
PAT
PAT
PAT
JIM DAVIS
PUNT!
6-7
© 1981 PAWS, INC. All Rights Reserved.